T0270675

THE GAS AND FLAME MEN

The Gas and Flame Men

Baseball and the Chemical Warfare
Service during World War I

JIM LEEKE

Potomac Books
An imprint of the University of Nebraska Press

All rights reserved. Potomac Books is an imprint of the
University of Nebraska Press.
Manufactured in the United States of America. ⊗

Library of Congress Cataloging-in-Publication Data
Names: Leeke, Jim, 1949– author.
Title: The gas and flame men: baseball and the Chemical
Warfare Service during World War I / Jim Leeke.
Other titles: Baseball and the Chemical Warfare Service
during World War I
Description: Lincoln: Potomac Books, an imprint of
the University of Nebraska Press, [2024] | Includes
bibliographical references and index.
Identifiers: LCCN 2023027643
ISBN 9781640126053 (hardback)
ISBN 9781640126114 (epub)
ISBN 9781640126121 (pdf)
Subjects: LCSH: United States. Army. Gas Regiment,
1st—Biography. | United States. Army. Engineer
Regiment, 30th (Gas and Flame)—Biography. | United
States. Army. Chemical Warfare Service—History. |
Cobb, Ty, 1886–1961. | Sisler, George, 1893–1973. | Rixey,
Eppa, Jr., 1891–1963. | Mathewson, Christy, 1880–1925.
| Street, Gabby, 1882–1951 | Baseball—United States—
History—20th century. | Baseball players—United
States—Biography. | World War, 1914–1918—Chemical
warfare—France. | BISAC: HISTORY / Wars & Conflicts
/ World War I | SPORTS & RECREATION / Baseball /
History
Classification: LCC D570.345 1st L44 2024 | DDC—dc23/
eng/20230824
LC record available at https://lccn.loc.gov/2023027643

Set in Lyon Text by K. Andresen.

To the memory of John Toffey,
teacher, coach, author

I think war is all that Sherman said it was
and a little bit worse.

—Capt. Christopher Mathewson

God, how I hate the Twentieth Century.

—George C. Scott, *Patton*

Contents

	List of Illustrations	xi
1.	Nashville	1
2.	Gabby	5
3.	Frightfulness	14
4.	Winter	30
5.	Good Scout	45
6.	CWS	54
7.	France	63
8.	Summer	73
9.	Final Innings	89
10.	Shipping Out	101
11.	Autumn	112
12.	Choignes	122
13.	Homecomings	130
14.	Saranac Lake	146
15.	Cooperstown	159
	Acknowledgments	167
	List of Abbreviations	169
	Notes	171
	Bibliography	199
	Index	207

Illustrations

Following page 72

1. Charles "Gabby" Street
2. Sgt. Gabby Street
3. Eppa Rixey
4. Lt. Joe Hanlon
5. Branch Rickey
6. Christy Mathewson
7. "We Want Matty"
8. Ty Cobb
9. Percy D. Haughton
10. Maj. Gen. William Sibert
11. Brig. Gen. Amos Fries
12. Maj. Gen. Charles Richardson
13. Chemical Warfare Service poster for troops
14. Soldiers playing ball in masks
15. Gas troops preparing Livens projectors
16. Company C, First Gas Regiment
17. Doughboys entering gas chamber
18. Pfc. Gabby Street
19. Maj. Branch Rickey's AEF identity card
20. Capt. Christy Mathewson on board SS *Rotterdam*
21. Capt. Ty Cobb
22. "Soft bombproof places"
23. Lt. George Sisler
24. Lt. Eppa Rixey at First Army HQ
25. Authorized CWS insignia

1

....

Nashville

Charles "Gabby" Street stepped out of a cold spring downpour into a downtown Nashville hotel. Ballplayers from the American League Washington Senators sat around inside playing pinochle and reading newspapers, their late-March exhibition game with the Nashville Volunteers washed out.

The news was as gloomy as the weather, front pages rumbling about the European war and America's long slide toward involvement. "President [Woodrow] Wilson took steps today to place the nation on a war footing," one article began.[1] A few players cast their papers aside and headed out for nearby motion picture theaters.

One or two perhaps recognized the big fellow stepping into the lobby. Gabby looked exactly like what he was: an aging catcher and former Senator, who played now for the local team that fans called the Vols. He took life at the gallop, on the field and off.

"Gabby was no angel in younger days, nor was he frugal. Admits he liked to play around with one foot on brass rail," *Sporting News* later recalled.[2] Bad habits had hampered his career early on, "and he lacked only the development of a little common sense to land among the majors," a Washington newspaper once said. "This streak of light dawned on him when he married [in 1907] and decided to settle down."[3]

Thirty-four years old now, with a wife but no children, Gabby had been up to the Major Leagues and back down again. Fourteen professional seasons behind the plate had left him with bouts of rheumatism and a "collection of knitty fingers," all but one of which he had broken, some two or three times.[4] He'd once caught eight doubleheaders in nine days, "an experience that would have put nine catchers out of ten in the hospital for keeps."[5] An inch under six feet tall and weighing 185 pounds, Gabby was tough and determined and not about to give up the national pastime.

He gazed about the lobby, looking for the Kansas farm boy he'd helped shape into a pitching star in the nation's capital. Walter Johnson was five years younger than the catcher. Fans called him "Barney," after racecar driver Barney Oldfield, and also "the Big Train." Both nicknames derived from the tremendous speed of his fastball. Johnson credited Gabby with helping him learn how to pitch in the big leagues after his call-up to Washington nearly a decade ago.

"When 'Gabby' Street was in his prime," the hurler had written, "he was the best catcher I ever saw, I think. Perhaps old-timers can recall back-stops who surpassed him, but to me he was the ideal man behind the bat." Gabby kept pitchers at ease by chattering like a magpie behind the plate. "'Ease up on this fellow, Walter; he has a wife and two children,' he would call jokingly when some batter was hugging the plate and getting a 'toe-hold' for a crack at one of my fast ones," Johnson wrote. "'This fellow hasn't made a hit off you since you joined the League,' would probably be his next remark. And so on throughout the game."[6]

Johnson clasped his one-time mentor's hand here in Nashville, a clutch of sportswriters looking on with pencils poised. "The meeting of the smoke king and famous Gabby yesterday was the first reunion these athletes have had since Gabby dropped out of the big show five years ago," the *Washington Herald* said.[7] To no one's surprise, it was the backstop who spoke first.

"Barney, you're looking great," Gabby said, his Alabama upbringing evident in his drawl. "So are you," Johnson replied, lying only a little. "It was a touching sight," Louis A. Dougher wrote for the *Washington Times*, "to see these old pals of many wonderful mound battles in the American League shake hands in the lobby of the Hermitage Hotel."[8]

The friends settled in and began catching up. Johnson was starting his eleventh season in Washington, while Gabby had long since fallen into the Southern Association, a Class A circuit two rungs below the American League. "The star of the king of pitchers still is all a glitter," the *Washington Star's* Denman Thompson wrote. "That of Street lacks the luster of the majors, though in Dixie Gabby still is rated with the wisest."[9]

The gap in their status didn't affect the reunion. "Walter Johnson, the noblest pitching Roman of them all, sat in the Hermitage lobby practically all afternoon chinning with Gabby Street," sportswriter Bob Pigue wrote in the *Nashville Banner*, "or rather getting chinned by Gabby, as it takes a peach of a bird to get in a word edgewise when this Mr. Charles Gabby Street is anywhere close."[10]

"I guess I'm getting old," the catcher said, as time flowed past like rainwater outside, "but I'm good for a couple of more years down here where the sun shines in the summer. My wing is still delivering the goods, my legs are quitting me though, and I do lose some good hits because I can't get down to first, but they'll have to come out with a sheriff and his deputies to take me off the diamond. I'm going to stick till they come for me with the hearse."[11]

The hurler said he was slowing, too, but his former battery mate wasn't having it. Johnson could lose two thirds of his good stuff, Gabby said, and still be a wonder. "He not only is a wonderful pitcher, but a fine gentleman," the catcher added after their chinning session. "It was good to see him again, mighty good."

Vols manager Roy Ellam sent automobiles for the Senators the following day, as the cold and damp weather continued. The players toured Nashville and the surrounding countryside and even visited the state prison sixteen miles away. Back in town cameramen got Gabby and Johnson to shake hands again for the newsreels.

Years from now, when their playing days were done, the Big Train would include Gabby Street on his personal list of all-time Major Leaguers, ranking him with Babe Ruth, Ty Cobb, Joe Jackson, and other horsehide luminaries. "Since Gabby left the major leagues there has never been a catcher in his class," he told scribes in Tennessee. Then the pitcher added:

"He had the best throwing arm in the big show, and whenever a runner would start to steal, Gabby's peg was on a line and would cut him down. I've seen many catchers in the big leagues since Gabby left, but I've yet to discover one who can show the stuff that Gabby did in his prime.

"I'm mighty glad to see Gabby doing so well in Nashville, for he's a great fellow all the way, and deserves all the success in the world."[12]

The weather never cooperated for the two old pals, and the Senators left town without playing their exhibition with the Volunteers. But other events were vastly more important.

Nearly two years earlier, a German U-boat had sunk the passenger liner *Lusitania* and begun a ruinous decline in relations between Berlin and Washington. On April 6, 1917, ten days after the Big Train departed Nashville, the United States declared war on Germany. America entered the European conflict on the side of Great Britain, France, and Belgium.

Ballplayers throughout the Southern Association and in other leagues around the country started their year amid uncertainty and worry. "The fast gathering war clouds threaten the most prosperous season in outlook in the history of Dixie's major [league]," the *Nashville Tennessean* said, "but unless the pressure of the United States being involved in the world conflict produces unexpected happenings, the season will pass off as successfully as anticipated."[13]

Nashville's veteran catcher took the war bulletins stoically. "Gabby Street galloped around the running track some three miles yesterday," sportswriter Claude "Blinkey" Horn wrote in the *Tennessean*, "but will never again repeat the long-distance racing, since the scales showed he had sloughed off some four pounds, somewhere on his lengthy journey." Horn added that Gabby "is already down to fighting trim, and wailed long and loud over the loss of the poundage."[14]

Staying trim wasn't all that occupied the veteran backstop's mind as the Vols prepared for their season opener. Gabby likely was already thinking about a greater and grimmer contest, one he wouldn't fight with bat and ball in the safety of a grassy park.

2

....

Gabby

Charles Evard Street was born in Huntsville, Alabama, on September 30, 1882, the second of five children in a farming family. He was a soldier before he was a ballplayer, following an uncle into the First Alabama Volunteer Infantry at age fifteen during the Spanish-American War. A sports editor wrote later that "the Streets were just naturally a fighting clan."[1]

Charlie was an unruly soldier who spent much of his enlistment in the guardhouse. His regiment had reached Jacksonville, Florida, when combat ended in Cuba, which the teenager surely regretted. He began his baseball career not long afterward, playing semipro and independent ball after high school in Huntsville.

The tyro attended South Kentucky College in 1901–02 at Hopkinsville, "where he majored in catching for the school's baseball team."[2] He made his professional debut the next year with the Hopkinsville Browns in the Kentucky–Illinois–Tennessee League, a new Class D circuit fans called the Kitty League. Charlie accepted sixty dollars a month to catch for the club, he recalled, because it was "big money," equivalent to about $1,800 today.[3]

Hopkinsville traded him in 1904 to the Terre Haute Hottentots of the Class B Central League, which at the end of the season sold his contract to the Cincinnati Reds. The National League club had room for Charlie as a backup catcher because another late call-up, Branch Rickey of the Texas League, hadn't stayed after catching a pair of exhibition games.

"Joe Kelley managed the club, and he was no choir-boy," the *Brooklyn Eagle* said long afterward. Learning that Rickey (keeping a promise to his mother) didn't play ball on Sundays, Kelley snapped, "You'll catch here tomorrow, kid, or you're through!"[4] Other reasons cited for Rickey's departure were that he simply hadn't impressed the club and that he was committed to teaching and coaching football at a college in Pennsylvania. "Just how many more of the half-baked are to be given autumn try-outs is not now known," *Sporting Life* gibed.[5]

Rickey left town and Charlie Street landed the Reds job. His new teammates called the catcher "Alabam'." Aside from a brief stint on loan to the Boston Beaneaters, he managed to stick with the Reds through 1905, before slipping back to the Minors the following year. He had played eleven games for the San Francisco Seals in the Pacific Coast League (PCL) when the great earthquake of April 1906 hurled him out of bed.

The Seal was living at the Golden Gate Hotel, popular with ballplayers and actors. Charlie scrambled into the street with cast members from *Beauty and the Beast* and *Babes in Toyland*, getting drenched when a roof water tower collapsed. The group huddled that night in Golden Gate Park with the city ablaze around them. The catcher spent two days clearing city streets of bricks and rubble under soldiers' orders before hopping a ferry across the bay to Oakland.

Charlie later said he had been planning to jump the Seals and join the Williamsport, Pennsylvania, club in the independent Tri-State League. The fire that followed the temblor consumed his ticket along with the railway office. He made his way slowly eastward with help from friends and refugee organizations, and he played the rest of the season in the Keystone State with the Williamsport Millionaires.

"Charlie was playing with Frisco when the earthquake came, and he demanded and got his unconditional release, so he had the right to go to the outlaws or anywhere else he pleased," fans in Huntsville read. "He came East with only the clothes on his back, and he was gladly taken up by [manager] Jimmy Sebring for his Williamsport outfit. And now Charlie is not only hitting them out at the rate of two and three bingles daily, but he is the star backstop and base runner of the whole outlaw league."[6]

The Alabaman made Williamsport his winter home for many years. Charlie returned to the PCL in 1907 and married Williamsport native Mabel Grace Hirst in Bakersfield during spring training. The Seals were glad to have him back.

"It is not his faculty for receiving and steadying his pitcher that makes him valuable so much as his ability to make the baserunners hug the cushions," a San Francisco newspaper said. "His wonderful throwing arm is believed by many to be his chief stock in trade."[7]

The catcher enjoyed such a good season that the Senators beat out at least two other Major League clubs to sign him the following winter. A story soon made the rounds, helped along by Charlie, that he had caught a record 179 games during the Seals' lengthy 203-game season. "I could have made it 185 just as easy as not," he told a Cincinnati sportswriter, adding "[I] never did quite so well in my life."[8] A Bay Area paper scoffed, but cited a record that was impressive enough without embellishments.

"Official figures show that Street took part in 159 games last season on the coast, 154 being behind the bat and 5 at first base and in the field," the *San Francisco Examiner* said. "Where he made a coast record of the catchers was the catching of 54 games straight when both his hands were injured. Street was one of the best catchers on the coast for many years, and Washington gets a man that will always be trying and who will deliver the goods."[9]

Washington's manager was Joseph Cantillon, known in baseball circles as "Pongo Joe." He later took credit for anointing the Senators' new backstop "Gabby," although not for what sportswriter Tom Rice called his "conversational proclivities."[10] Cantillon explained that he'd hung the moniker on him because "Street called so many others that."[11] The nickname actually was an artifact from Gabby's upbringing in the Deep South at the turn of the century.

"Down south, if you see a black boy, and want him, and don't know his name, you yell 'Hey Gabby,'" the catcher said years afterward.[12] He later softened the story as race relations began changing within baseball and America. "In Huntsville, he related, he was in the habit of calling everybody he didn't know Gabby. On trains he addressed all porters as Gabby and his team-mates soon transferred the nickname to Street."[13]

The handle unintentionally reflected the catcher's friendly chatter behind the plate, which is how most fans understood it. "Gabby" became a beloved nickname.

Gabby joined veteran catchers Jack Warner and Mike Kahoe on Washington's 1908 roster. Kahoe came to regard the newcomer as the best backstop in the game. "He can't hit much, but he can field and throw,"

Kahoe said after Gabby's first season with the Senators. "I saw him throw out nine men at second base in a double-header at Cleveland one day and then they quit trying for an extra sack. He has the pitchers ducking when he snaps to second. I have been in major circles off and on for many years and his pegging has everything faded I ever saw."[14]

The rookie was best remembered, however, not for catching a historic game or for rapping out a vital home run, but for snaring a baseball dropped from the top of the Washington Monument. The stunt on August 21, 1908, settled a $500 bet between two members of the local Metropolitan Club. They rolled balls down a chute pointed out the windows near the peak of the 555-foot-tall obelisk. Thirteen whizzed by before the catcher corralled the fourteenth.[15] The *Washington Star* broke the story that evening in a front-page exclusive, calling the catch an "unprecedented, though oft-attempted feat."[16]

The *Star* added the next day, "Very few men have had the nerve even to attempt the task. And those few either didn't come within gunshot of the ball or weren't able to hold it when it struck their hands. But Charlie, who really doesn't look strong enough to catch cold, not only got the ball in his mit [*sic*], but held on to it like grim death to an India famine sufferer."[17]

The paper rounded up an expert at the U.S. Navy Ordnance Department who calculated that the ball had been hurtling earthward at 155 feet per second when Gabby nabbed it. The expert said it was equivalent to catching a 117-pound weight dropped one foot.

"When Street made the wonderful catch he was in shirt sleeves and wore the glove that he uses in catching championship games," the *Washington Herald* reported.[18] The *Washington Times* added, "The most dangerous part of the trick was the possibility of Street's arm being stiffly braced in which case the jar would have been sufficient to dislocate the member at the shoulder."[19]

"The ball did not seem to hit the glove any harder than some of those fast ones Walter Johnson serves up," Gabby said. "There was a slight wind at the start and in the first few trials it made the drop of the ball rather uncertain and for that reason I could not get to it. When we went around to the north side [of the monument] I found it easy, and . . . I succeeded in getting under the ball, which looked about as big as a chestnut, but felt as heavy as a ton of coal."[20] After the catch he went to the Washington ballpark and "caught a good game" for Johnson, who five-hit the Detroit Tigers in a 3–1 victory.[21]

Walter Johnson had debuted with Washington as a raw nineteen-year-old hurler in August 1907. Gabby became his primary catcher after his own arrival in 1908, backed by Kahoe and Warner.

Good coaching and managing were fine for a young hurler, the Big Train later wrote, "but pitching in a real game, with a smart catcher handling your delivery, is what brings out the best that is in you. Jack Warner and 'Gabby' Street soon put me wise to most of the tricks of the trade. I followed their instructions and judgment explicitly, and so got the best results."[22]

Johnson won fourteen and lost fourteen games in 1908, with Gabby playing in 131 games and Warner in thirty-one. Late in the season Gabby suffered another in a seemingly endless series of injuries, a foul tip breaking his right little finger.

"The bones were knocked out of joint and broke through the skin almost entirely around the base of the finger," the *Washington Star* reported. "It was an ugly wound to look at." Gabby pulled the finger back into place, had the trainer encase it in plaster, and assured a writer that the injury was nothing serious. "I have been hurt worse many a time and I'll be all right in three or four days."[23] He would repeat similar litanies throughout his career.

The catcher had a strong defensive season in 1909, although with a typically low batting average (.211), while Johnson posted a fine earned run average (2.22) with 164 strikeouts. "But the brilliant feats of Johnson and Street were wasted on a Washington club that lost 110 games while winning but 42 that year," *Sporting News* recalled long afterward.

Johnson followed his 13-25 season in 1909 with a breakout year in 1910, winning twenty-five games then, and again in 1911. Overall, he would amass 414 victories during twenty-one seasons on his way to enshrinement in the National Baseball Hall of Fame at Cooperstown, New York. In Washington from 1908 through 1911, *Sporting News* later said, "The battery of 'Johnson and Street' became one of the most famous in the game."[24]

Gabby probably was the only catcher ever to urge Johnson to throw harder. Fans once watched the catcher stuff a raw steak into his mitt as added protection against the hurler's fabled fastball. "Charley got fans to thinking that no one but Mr. Street could be on the receiving end of the Johnsonian delivery," *Sporting News* also recalled. "It was good advertising, as a lot of bunk is, the thing went over big and Johnson and Street became a big drawing card as [Cy] Young and [Lou] Criger did before them."[25]

The potent battery continued until Clark Griffith arrived as Washington's new manager after the 1911 season. He promptly got rid of Gabby and later, longtime infielder Norman "Kid" Elberfeld as well. Sports pages offered various rationales for the moves.

"Both stunts were charged by friends of the players as being acts of base ingratitude on the part of the Washington owners. Elberfeld was handicapped by an injury to his hip in 1911 and Street was sick during the winter," recalled a newspaper in Chattanooga, where Kid ended up in 1913 as a player-manager. "Griff was after a winner hard last year and gave the two faithful players no time to come back to condition. Street went to New York in a trade for [infielder] Jack Knight. President Taft and all the other Washington notables mourned the departure of Washington's favorite player."[26]

U.S. Vice President James Sherman wrote to the departing catcher. He expressed the appreciation of Washington fans "who have come not only to believe in you as an efficient, reliable and honest ball player, but as an agreeable gentleman both on and off the ball field."[27]

Some sportswriters attributed Gabby's departure, however, to the accumulated strain of catching so many of Johnson's powerful "shoots," while umpire Billy Evans believed the catcher had used his throwing arm too much for too long. "I have always figured that Charley Street worked himself out of the big league about five years ahead of his time. . . . That right arm, once the fear of every base runner, had gone lame; they were running wild. It marked his exit from the big show," the arbiter wrote.[28]

The catcher was angry at having to leave Washington and yield his spot behind the plate to Eddie Ainsmith, who had broken in with the Senators in 1910. "I will make them sorry they ever let me go," Gabby vowed.[29] A Pennsylvania newspaper later cracked, "Charlie Street says that getting away from Washington gives him a chance to get a look at a pennant, something of which he has often heard, but never seen."[30]

The truth was that Gabby wasn't entirely healthy. He later told a sportswriter that "certain sections of his digestive apparatus were out of order and kept him weak and wobbly all the time."[31]

Washington traded him to the New York Highlanders, who would become the Yankees the following year. Gabby played poorly in 1912 and ended the season with the Providence Grays in the Class AA International League. Regaining his health over the winter, he signed to play under Elberfeld with the Chattanooga Lookouts in the Southern Association. *Baseball Magazine* remembered the catcher later in a poem about ballplayers who had dropped from the Major Leagues:

> Street, the gabby one—wherefore and how
> Do names like his drop into the ground?
> We saw them strut on the dusty stage;
> They're out of our heads when they're off of the page.[32]

The catcher flirted with jumping to the new Federal League in 1914 but stayed in Chattanooga to play under new manager and former New York Giant outfielder Harry "Moose" McCormick. Gabby signed with Nashville the following year. The Volunteers had a middling season in 1915 but raced away with the pennant in 1916.

Gabby received a second nickname in Nashville. After a series of earlier offseason jobs in Alabama and Pennsylvania, he began working during the winters for the New York Central Railroad in the Williamsport suburb of Newberry. The *Tennessean* supplemented his familiar moniker by calling him the Newberry Switchman.

The Vols and their popular backstop opened their 1917 campaign with a 9–2 road win over the Birmingham Barons. But Nashville was hampered by injuries, and the Barons turned the tables the next day during the Vols' home opener at their ballpark, the quirky and aptly named Sulphur Dell. "It was Friday. And it was the 13th," Blinkey Horn wrote of the 9–1 loss.[33]

Nashville soon fell into a tie for last place in the eight-team circuit. The Vols climbed out of the cellar but were mediocre the rest of the way. On

Tuesday, June 5, the switchman and his club had a road doubleheader with the Memphis Chicks. This was Registration Day, when American males between the ages of twenty-one and thirty-one had to register for the military draft.

"The twin affair was arranged at the request of the Chick mags, in view of the general closing arrangements of all business houses and industrial enterprises in Memphis on registration day," Horn wrote. "Monday, as is the case in practically all Dixie towns, always produces rust at the turnstiles. Hence the Bluff City moguls secured permission of the Vol moguls to stage the two-ply affair."[34]

Major and Minor League ballclubs playing on the road that day generally ensured that their draft-eligible players registered before leaving home. American men with family obligations or who held essential war jobs could request deferments during registration. Gabby was above draft age and had no obligation, but he had many younger teammates who soon would be in a government lottery to determine who was drafted when.

The Volunteers dropped the first game on Registration Day in front of a crowd of forty-six hundred fans at Russwood Park. Gabby caught the second game, going one for four at the plate in a 3–1 Nashville win. The Vols ended the day as they had begun it, in seventh place with the Chicks two spots higher.

The Vols' season improved only slightly after that. Gabby hurt a finger for the umpteenth time in late June and missed several days. His club limped along, playing neither badly nor well, as the Southern Association gamely stuck to its schedule. The Minor Leagues were in rough shape, crushed by wartime travel restrictions, fan bases diminished by enlistments, daytime war work, and other woes. Only five of twenty-two minor circuits completed the 1917 season intact.

Ballplayers in the first call for the army began receiving draft notices in August, although few were yet ordered to report. The Nashville sports pages printed the names of Vols players and their draft status. Gabby's wasn't among them, since he was nearing his thirty-fifth birthday and well beyond draft age. The club returned to Memphis in mid-September for its season-ending series, which the Chicks swept in three games.

"While the locals fought, valiantly defending their fourth place berth and the Vols fought just as gamely in an effort to regain the coveted place, which they lost the previous day, the game more resembled a spring practice playing than the finale of a season of work," the *Tennessean* said.[35] The Vols returned to Nashville and the players packed to return to their hometowns for the offseason. Gabby chose to drive home to Williamsport, not a quick or easy trip.

"Gabby Street and [first baseman] Dick Kauffman, accompanied by their wives, will leave this morning for their homes in Pennsylvania, employing their flivvers on the journey," the *Tennessean* said. "Equipped with a large tent, the veteran receiver and the Vol doorkeeper will make the trip by slow stages, viewing and wising up on geography. They will go from Nashville to Huntsville, where Gabby Street's people live, from there to Chattanooga, that Mr. Kauffman may lamp the mountains, etc., and from there on up through East Tennessee and Virginia to Pennsylvania."[36]

Although beyond draft age, the catcher also was young enough to join the colors voluntarily if he wanted. Gabby might have decided to enlist in the army even before leaving Nashville, but without a particular branch in mind.

3

....

Frightfulness

The army was actively recruiting men like Gabby Street. He likely read somewhere during October about the Thirtieth Engineers, a newfangled outfit created specially to turn horrifying new weapons and tactics back on the Germans. An advertising campaign that didn't cost the government a nickel brought in enough recruits to meet the regiment's early requirements, after 350 newspapers around America had published articles like this:

> Under the title of "Gas Defense Service," the preliminaries for this "Gas and Flame" service have been under way for some weeks, and this morning, in the seeking of enlistments to perfect the organization, the Army Recruiting Station gave out particulars of the regiment to be formed, which hitherto have been shrouded in such a veil of mystery as to make its work seem likely to resemble the "Black Art."[1]

Kaiser Wilhelm II had been the first to unleash the dark arts on European battlefields, soon after the war began in August 1914. His troops introduced what they called the *flammenwerfer*, which could shoot a pressurized jet of liquid fire nearly one hundred feet. British soldiers ("Tommies") called the weapon a flame projector; today it's known as the flamethrower. Although terrifying, the *flammenwerfer* also had one terrible flaw—men carried it into battle with the fuel in metal canisters strapped to their backs. A bullet or shell fragment could pierce a canister and set the poor soldier alight.

Chemical warfare was generally ineffective during the first months of the war. French troops tried using ethyl bromoacetates (a type of tear gas) grenades when the Germans invaded Belgium, but without much success. British forces investigated other types of tear gas weapons and considered (but didn't approve) unleashing sulfur dioxide clouds on the German lines, followed by advancing British troops wearing protective helmets. Gas attacks from either side were minor affairs into the first spring of the war.

"The French are again resorting to gas bombs at one place on the German front, the exact location of which was not mentioned in the official war office statement," a dispatch from Berlin said in March 1915. "The enemy is hurling shells which develop an ill-smelling asphyxiating gas when they explode. A shower of these shells is followed by a French infantry attack on the German trenches, but thus far this plan has failed utterly."[2]

The German army unleashed the first true poison gas attack the next month, sending clouds of chlorine wafting toward Canadian and French colonial soldiers huddled in trenches near Ypres in Belgium. The Kaiser's authorities believed that by releasing the chlorine from cylinders they were sidestepping a ban on using projectiles to spread such gases, imposed by the First Hague Peace Conference in 1899. On the morning of April 22, 1915, at the start of the Second Battle of Ypres, German troops opened the valves of nearly six thousand cylinders of various sizes, sending 168 tons of chlorine gas into a northeast wind toward the enemy lines.

"Try to imagine the feelings and the condition of the [colonial] troops as they saw the vast cloud of greenish-yellow gas spring out of the ground and slowly move down wind toward them, the vapor clinging to the earth, seeking out every hole and hollow and filling the trenches and shell holes as it came," a British officer later wrote. He added, "The majority of those in the front line were killed—some, let us hope, immediately, but most of them slowly and horribly."[3]

The German newspaper *Frankfurter Zeitung* commented on the attack a few days later, saying that gas also had been delivered in artillery shells. "It is even probable that, in point of fact, projectiles emitting poisonous gases were employed by us, for the German army command has permitted no doubt to exist that, as a reply to the treacherous projectiles of the English and French, which have been constantly observed for many weeks, we on our side also would employ gas bombs or whatever one may call them," the *Zeitung* said. "The German army command, moreover, referred to the fact that from German chemistry considerably more effective substances might be expected, and our army command was right."[4]

The Kaiser's experts were unprepared, however, for the awful success of their gas weapons. "If Germany had been able to follow up its advantage, the history of that war might have read differently," said a U.S. Army manual during World War II. "But, not having large quantities of gas ready for immediate use, the Germans lost their opportunity and gave the Allies time to prepare defensive and counter measures."[5]

Casualty figures have been disputed during the century since the battle, with the opposing sides inflating and deflating the numbers of dead and wounded for propaganda purposes. Still, the shocking German attack brought a swift chemical response.

"The destruction and demoralization which resulted was terrible, but within a week England had plans for gas warfare in retaliation," an American journalist later wrote.[6] *Scientific American* declared after the war, "The introduction of poison gas by the Germans was a military as well as a moral blunder—a moral blunder because its use was expressly forbidden by the Hague Convention; a military blunder because when the Germans decided to introduce this form of attack, they made the mistake of not waiting to accumulate sufficient gas to make a general attack along the whole line."[7]

The British and French armies rushed to respond. First, though, they devised protection for their troops. "When the first wave of gas was projected against the allied trenches, our friends were without any protection," an American engineer officer wrote after the war. "One quick-minded and ingenious quartermaster of a British division took the first step in defense by supplying his troops, within twenty-four hours of the first attack, with a pad of several thicknesses of cotton cloth soaked in hyposulphite of soda which gave them fairly good protection for a short time."[8]

Starting with little more than chemical-saturated veils, chemists and engineers began designing military-grade gas masks and respirators that continually evolved to provide better and longer protection. The British and French armies next pushed to develop gas weapons to turn against the Germans.[9] Here, too, they succeeded.

By the time the United States entered the war in April 1917, the Allies were using several poisonous gases, released from cylinders and artillery shells, as routinely and viciously as their enemy. The Allies also had learned that gas warfare could work against the troops who employed it. This happened in September 1915 during the bloody and chaotic Battle of Loos, when the British Expeditionary Force (BEF) used chlorine against the Germans.

"At Loos, the gas hung about in no man's land or even drifted back into the British trenches, hindering rather than helping the advance," military historian John Keegan wrote at the end of the century.[10] Weather conditions in France, however, generally worked better for British, French, and Belgian troops. "Experts have figured that the gas attack, although invented by the Germans, works to the advantage of the Allies," the *Baltimore Evening Sun* said in November 1917. "The winds over France are mostly ocean winds and drive inland, and as a result 90 per cent. of the days during the year were favorable for the 'gassers' of the Allies and unfavorable for the Germans."[11]

Any new weapons introduced on the battlefield soon brought new defensive tactics, which in turn brought new and deadlier gases. "The history of gas warfare was one of steadily increasing toxicity, matched by a quickly evolving array of defensive measures," observes historian and author Jennet Conant. "By the end of World War I, it had become a kind of technological chess match, with military strategists and scientists devising ways to check each new offensive threat."[12]

The American army's most recent foe was Gen. Francisco Villa's ragtag revolutionary forces along the Mexican border in 1916–17. It wasn't remotely ready for gas warfare. Capt. Archibald Roosevelt, a son of former President Theodore Roosevelt, later authored a blistering attack on America's lack of preparedness. "In spite of the well-known employment of poison gases by the Huns and our allies," he wrote, "not one man in our Army had ever been equipped or trained with the gas-mask until long after our first division had landed in France."[13]

The Yanks scrambled to catch up with the Europeans. "The United States was unprepared for waging chemical warfare even though it had been waged in Europe for over two years," an army history says. "Research on toxics had been begun in the United States only a few months earlier. The nation had no gas weapons, no toxins, no military gas organization, and no protective supplies. It did have some information on gas warfare gathered by War Department observers with the Allies." The authors also comment, "The great paradox of America's wartime gas experience is that in World War I, when the nation was unprepared for it, gas was used, and in World War II, when the nation was prepared, gas was not used."[14]

Surprisingly, the Department of the Interior was the first federal agency to make a useful contribution to gas warfare. In February 1917, two months before America's declaration of war, the interior secretary asked how his civilian workers might assist the War Department during the coming conflict.

Dr. Van H. Manning, a fifty-five-year-old civil engineer from Mississippi, headed the Interior's little-known Bureau of Mines. When Manning put the secretary's question to his own division chiefs, one suggested that the bureau "turn its experience in mine gases and rescue apparatus toward the investigation of war gases and masks."[15] Washington quickly agreed.

"Immediately after the entry of the United States into the war against Germany Dr. Manning began organization of a bureau of experts to study methods of combating the German gas attacks and developing gas as an offensive weapon for the American army," the *Washington Herald* reported. "The body of men gathered in the chemical section is probably the greatest body of experts ever brought together."[16]

Manning would have 1,700 chemists working on war-related research by mid-1918. "The mine bureau, created in peace time to promote safety for miners, extended its operations under Mr. Manning's leadership during the war and developed [the] chemical warfare service, designed delicate instruments for the detection of enemy tunneling operations, increased production of minerals needed for war, improved explosives and many other warfare works," the *Brooklyn Eagle* recalled after Manning's death in 1932.[17] A government history of U.S. chemical warfare flatly declares that Manning "displayed a great deal more vision and foresight than did his military colleagues in Washington."[18]

But most Americans during late 1917 were uneasy over the idea of fielding an army chemical service. The government sought to convince them. "American soldiers will use German tactics, employing gas and flame," the *Washington Times* said on its front page in late September. "War Department orders issued today showed that among special services being organized now are regiments of engineers whose duties will be to adopt the latest gas and flames methods for the new armies."[19]

The *Washington Herald* put things more bluntly. "The United States is going to meet Germany at her own game of frightfulness," it said, "and army men are at work on a plan of making the war so frightful to Germany that the Germans will welcome peace at any price."[20]

Journalist Edward B. Clark was an influential Washington insider and army veteran who often wrote about military affairs. Clark had covered the last "Indian wars" waged against Native American tribes in the West, and later had been a member of President Roosevelt's unofficial Kitchen Cabinet.

"Awful as may be the contemplation of the employment of such agencies for the killing of men, the army that goes up against the German attack is confronted with the simple fact that it either must be wiped out or must wipe out the Germans," Clark wrote. "Armament is powerless if the men to operate it are gassed in their tracks or are shriveled up in flames. . . . The allies are now looking to America to beat the Germans at their own game; and America now calls upon her chemists and her mechanics to accomplish this result."[21]

To catch up with Manning and his brilliant civilian colleagues, the army in October 1917 began recruiting for the Thirtieth Engineers, which assembled at Washington. The army wanted a variety of specialists for the unit. These included chemists and chemical workers; men who knew how to use explosives or manufacture gas; machinists and auto repairmen; anyone familiar with gas or steam engines; and pipefitters, electricians, designers, interpreters, firefighters, carpenters, blacksmiths, plumbers, boilermakers, and chauffeurs.

Officers especially wanted experienced men with years in their respective trades. In addition to its cost-free newspaper ad campaign, the army sent letters and circulars to gas, mechanical, and chemical engineers and to their professional organizations. "The regiment will be required in the field of operation to supervise the American offensive in 'Gas and Flame' service and will be called upon to instruct men all along the front in this most important work," one East Coast newspaper said. "Men who enlist now will be leaders in the spring offensive."[22]

Men volunteered from all over the country. Although many lacked the exact qualifications cited, the army accepted them anyway. Among the enlistees was a competitive swimmer from Hawaii; a cracker-factory foreman from Northern California; a traveling salesman from Oregon; a court clerk from eastern Washington State; a forester from Idaho; a union carpenter from Oklahoma; a school employee from Indiana; a seminary graduate turned chemical-engineering student from Pennsylvania; and a sheet-metal worker from New York City.

Enlistee William L. Langer was a prep-school teacher who later became a distinguished history professor at Harvard University, and during World War II, he was chief of the research and analysis branch for the Office of Strategic Services (OSS). He later described the Thirtieth Engineers' Company E as a motley, congenial group that included "a substantial number of transfers from the Regular Army, several college graduates, chiefly from technical schools, and for the rest an odd mixture of older men, young lads, mechanics, salesmen, and what not."[23]

Many of the regiment's volunteers were above draft age. At least two were newspapermen, who perhaps signed up because they'd been among the first to learn about the unique new outfit. Joining the Thirtieth Engineers wasn't always simple.

A former ship's steward, in Anchorage, hiked with a dozen other men over rugged Alaskan mountains to enlist at Seward. A fellow from Buffalo, New York, previously turned down for army aviation, pedaled a bicycle to Washington DC, shedding so many pounds along the way that he no longer met the minimum weight to enlist. The army still accepted him, an officer saying that "a man who can do what he did is fit, even if he is slightly under weight."[24]

A recruiting officer in St. Louis expressed disappointment at enlisting only twenty men for the gas and flame service. "Applicants for this unit have been few and far between," he said. "The average man seems to have a natural disinclination to being 'gassed.' Then, too, the work is arduous and dangerous."[25]

Gabby Street had no such reservations. He'd once caught Walter Johnson's blazing fastball, so what terror did a *flammenwerfer* hold for him? Besides, his offseason job as a railroad switchman roughly fitted the army's needs; even if it hadn't, no recruiter would have turned away so well-known an athlete. Gabby then, surprisingly, flunked the physical exam.

Neither he nor the army ever revealed why, but the problem likely involved the catcher's mangled paws. The Vols' backstop wouldn't have been the only veteran ballplayer unable to grip the stock or squeeze a trigger of an army-issue Springfield rifle. Henry "Heinie" Groh, the Cincinnati Reds' third baseman, had similarly failed a draft exam in August. "He got away well in the physical test until one of the examiners noted that his fingers were not as straight as they should be. . . . As a result, Groh was rejected by the examining board."[26]

The Cincinnati infielder continued to play big league baseball throughout the war and for a long while afterward. The Nashville catcher, though, was unwilling to return to the diamond. "'Gabby' paid $110 to have an operation performed correcting a physical deformity, presented himself at the recruiting office and was accepted," the *Atlanta Constitution* recalled.[27] The army swore in the Newberry Switchman as a private.

"Charley Street, former Washington American league catcher and lately with the Nashville Southern association clubs, has enlisted here in the United States army and will be assigned to the gas and flame division, he having expressed a preference for that branch of service," the Associated Press reported from Williamsport in mid-November.[28] The army sent him first to Fort Slocum, New York, for processing. There, Gabby later recalled, "everybody interested in baseball thought it was great that I should be on hand to catch the army team. I finally convinced my lieutenant that I joined the army to fight."[29]

Gabby's outfit, the Thirtieth Engineers, was assembling at Camp American University in the District of Columbia. The *Washington Post* jokingly called it "the front-line trenches of the gas and flame division . . . 'somewhere' near the Chevy Chase sector."[30] The university's trustees had offered the army use of the campus soon after America entered the war. With only two buildings, one still unfinished, the ninety-one-acre site at the intersection of Massachusetts and Nebraska avenues was largely rural.

"On the War Department records the battalion is known as the 'Gas and Flame Battalion of the Thirtieth Regiment Engineers,'" the *Baltimore Sun* said. "Throughout the Army they are known as the 'hell-fire boys.' This name is literally true. A group of red-blooded Americans, most of them youths, are daily training in gas and flame fighting and learning how to make a literal inferno in return for German 'frightfulness.'"[31]

Private Gabby Street also would report to Washington, the site of his old glories, wearing his country's uniform for the first time in nearly twenty years. But he would play ball only while off duty, just as millions of other horsehide-loving soldiers did. The Nashville Vols knew the team would miss his talents.

Blinkey Horn wrote in January that "the Newberry Switchman has a contract to peg hand grenades at Fritz attempting to swipe a trench instead of the baseball to head off a would-be diamond theft. . . . And even though 'Gabby' Street was beset with quite a few flaws in his baseball makeup, his absence will slice deep into the vitals of the Vol machine."[32]

Early rosters of the Thirtieth Engineers included the names of at least two other fine athletes. One was 2nd Lt. Joseph T. "Joe" Hanlon, a twenty-four-year-old native of Baltimore, Maryland. He held degrees from the city's Loyola College, where he managed the baseball team, and the engineering school at Columbia University, where he had played ball and won several cups for tennis and swimming.

Joe's father was Edward "Ned" Hanlon, who had played Major League Baseball for thirteen seasons. He also won five National League pennants in seven seasons as a manager for the Baltimore Orioles and Brooklyn Superbas (Dodgers). Among Ned's players during that remarkable run (1894–1900) were managers John McGraw (New York Giants), Wilbert Robinson (Brooklyn Dodgers), and Hughie Jennings (Detroit Tigers), plus future manager William "Kid" Gleason (Chicago White Sox).

Hanlon fils worked for manufacturing giant Ingersoll-Rand before joining the army in July 1917. He was engaged to a young woman from St.

Louis, but they postponed their wedding until Joe returned from the army. He completed the Engineer Officers' Training School at Camp Belvoir, Virginia (later the site of Camp A. A. Humphreys), in October 1917. The army then assigned him to the gas regiment's Company A.

"Now, every Baltimorean knows or has heard of 'Ned' Hanlon, of baseball fame, and a letter received yesterday by Mr. Hanlon from his son indicates it has leaked out in camp that 'Joe' has inherited some of his father's qualities as a baseball manager," the *Baltimore Sun* said in November. "He has, therefore, been appealed to in an effort to form two baseball teams within the ranks of the battalion. Of course, Joe's first thought was of his father, and in his letter he wants him to help fit out at least one of the teams so that it will be known as the crack team of the American Army."[33] Ned gathered enough gear for several ball teams and sent Joe a sizeable check as well.

Pvt. Henry B. LeFort, a former jockey and boxer, also joined the gas regiment.[34] Now thirty-four years old, he had ridden and fought under the name "Jimmie Stevens" to avoid embarrassing his disapproving parents. A native of St. Louis, LeFort had left his job as the International New Service wire editor at the *Dodge City Journal* in Kansas to enlist in late October. The newspaper had declared him "the first man to enlist in the 'Fire and Flame' fighters service in this city and possibly the first man to enlist in that over the water before Thanksgiving company in the State of Kansas."[35]

LeFort took a colorful resumé into the army. According to the *Journal*, he "was at one time considered among the first three leaders of the bantamweight brigade of pugilists in the world and he was a continual runner-up for the championship for four years. He was also right in the front rank of jockeys having rode at most of the prominent race courses of the United States and foreign countries."[36]

The private's Dodge City colleagues exaggerated his ring prowess, but the *Omaha Bee* in Nebraska later attested to his skills atop a racehorse, calling him "one of the best bang-tail pilots in the business. During his career as a jockey LeFort raced on all the big time tracks of the country."[37] After hanging up his gloves and silks, the dapper little man had worked as "a war correspondent in Old Mexico in 1913 and 1914; [and] was one of the American staff with Francisco Villa's army for several months."[38]

Within days of heading east for the Thirtieth Engineers, LeFort wrote to the *Journal* "from 'somewhere in the United States' that the army life is not half as bad as had been pictured to him. The men of his command . . . are well cared for, the food, sleeping quarters and clothing being all that one could ask. The 'Gas and Flame Corps' will soon leave for France according to expectations."[39] Dodge City would hear little more from him during the war.

The officers, pipefitters, carpenters, blacksmiths, plumbers, and athletes of the Thirtieth Engineers shared Camp American University with six hundred of Dr. Manning's chemists and engineers from the Bureau of Mines. The civilians worked at what the War Department called the American University Experimental Station. (The army later changed the name of its part of the campus to Camp Leach to avoid confusion). There the soldiers and the bureau cooperated in experimenting with the new chemical weapons, using stray, lost, and unlicensed animals in lieu of live Germans.

"Dog and cat owners in the northwest section whose favorite pets are missing from their accustomed places by the fireside," the *Washington Post* said in November, "might learn something to their advantage by a quiet snooping expedition in the vicinity of the American University where Maj. E. J. Atkisson's 'Hell Fire' battalion, as the chemical soldiers love to call themselves, is practicing every day with the very latest things from the laboratory and the gas house." An unrecorded number of animals, perhaps a couple hundred, already had "promptly succumbed when brought into contact with the finished product turned out by the bureau of mines, which is working night and day to think up as many devilish things as possible that can be blown through the air or squirted through a hose." The *Post* added:

That dogs and cats are being used in the experiments isn't much of a secret. The 'hell fire' boys are rather cold-blooded about it. Of course, they are using dogs and cats; what of it? Are they not getting ready to asphyxiate what Germans fate may kindly throw in their way a little later on? They certainly are, and make no bones about it. The Germans invented this thing and they are to be paid back in their own coin—with interest.⁴⁰

The Thirtieth Engineers' regimental history says only that "arrangements were made whereby the investigations, experiments, and conclusions of the Bureau of Mines and the Gas Defense Service (then part of the Surgeon General's Department) could be utilized, a step which led to the helpful coordination of useful material."⁴¹ The animal experiments were the domain of the camp's chemists and researchers. "The only gas and flame we have taken up here has been in lectures as we will get all that training over there," a private in Company C later wrote home to Oklahoma.⁴²

The experiments continued and expanded. The *Post* reported that municipal officials it called poundmasters were scooping up strays not only around the capital, but in Baltimore, Norfolk, Pittsburgh, and other cities as well.

"The gas and flame division needs canines if it is to save the lives of American soldiers in France," the newspaper said. "On the theory that an impounded dog will be killed anyhow, they have with the aid of the mayors of various cities commandeered the supply of canines whose owners have refused to take out licenses for them." The Society for the Prevention of Cruelty to Animals and the Antivivisection Society objected in vain, prompting the unsympathetic *Post* to crack, "They made the point, emphatically, that they had not raised their dog to be a soldier."⁴³

Later during the war, the *Post* and other papers would react much differently when scores of dogs confined in crowded crates were mistakenly shipped to the quartermaster corps rather than the experimental station, then left unattended in a warehouse during an August heatwave. The once blasé newspaper bombarded the army, police, post office, and express company with angry calls about the animals' plight.

"What was left of the 90 dogs consigned to the gas and flame division of the American University Training Camp which, through an error, were allowed to remain in crates in the express office all day Tuesday without water or attention of any kind were removed yesterday morning about

9 o'clock," the *Post* finally reported. "Several of the dogs had died and a number were paralyzed."[44]

The Thirtieth Engineers would be in France long before the canine scandal broke. While still training at Camp American University, the regiment was authorized six 250-man companies, comprising three battalions of two companies each, the 1,500 troops assigned to Companies A through F. The army wanted to send at least some of these men overseas as soon as possible. Secretary of War Newton Baker, along with the chiefs of staff of the army and engineers, reviewed the regiment at the War Department on December 22, the *Washington Post* said, "preparatory to their transfer elsewhere."[45]

The first battalion, consisting of Companies A and B, left for France on Christmas Day. "At 3.30 P.M. on December 25, the command was formed on Massachusetts Avenue, and marched through Washington in a snowstorm to the railroad siding."[46] For security reasons, the curtains in the coaches were drawn. The men reached New York City that evening, and the next afternoon they sailed from Hoboken, New Jersey, on the transport ss *President Grant*.

"Now this [gas] regiment is the first of its kind in the service and is composed, with very few exceptions, of skilled men, most of them university men," a Company A private wrote home to Ohio while somewhere in the mid-Atlantic. "Possibly, then, I may be pardoned for saying that the 30th is composed thruout [*sic*] of the highest grade men of any regiment in the service, and for being especially proud of it. Listen for news from us—we are going 'over there' to help, in our own way, to smash that German line and to carve a name—not soon to be forgotten—for the 30th."[47]

A private in Headquarters Company later described the voyage for his father in Wisconsin. "We had quite a lot of sickness . . . and 14 of our boys died on board while we were coming over. I will never forget how they bury a man at sea."[48]

After experiencing several submarine scares and evading a torpedo attack, the transport reached the French port of Brest on January 10. The ship was unable to tie up to a dock for days, however, probably due to overcrowding at the port. The regiment offloaded its equipment onto lighters and small boats to get it ashore. Once they finally disembarked on February 18, the gas and flame men traveled more than four hundred miles by train via Rouen and Calais, headed for training at a British gas school at Helfaut in northern France. Landing at one of the English Channel ports rather than Brest would have eliminated much of their tiresome three-day journey.

Sgt. William Langer would reach France several months later with the regiment's Company E. The future Harvard professor was shocked by the animus many doughboys felt for their vastly more experienced British allies and trainers, whom they called Limeys rather than Tommies. The Yanks especially disliked stiff, formal British officers, although the feeling largely dissipated later during combat. "Common experiences and comradeship at the front undoubtedly did much to destroy prejudice and to further understanding between the traditional antagonists on either side of the Atlantic," Langer wrote long afterward.[49]

Companies C and D, still under strength, moved from Camp American University in mid-December to Fort Myer, Virginia, across the Potomac River from the capital. Thirty-four-year-old Walter Killam, city editor of the *Modesto* (California) *Herald* before he enlisted, was appointed sergeant major (the top enlisted rank) of what was called the provisional battalion. "Killy" described the battalion's new temporary home to his former paper.

Fort Myer, he wrote, "is one of the old army posts and a 'show place' owing to its proximity to Washington. All the big reviews are held here. It adjoins the Arlington cemetery, where the nation's heroes are buried. From our barracks window we can see the fighting top of the USS *Maine*, which was brought here and placed over the graves of those killed in that disaster. It must be a beautiful spot in summer. Everything has been snow covered since we have been here."[50]

Private Gabby Street arrived and reported to Company D. "He came in with a bunch of recruits from Fort Slocum," Killam recalled years later, "and as no one in headquarters at Fort Myer showed any particular interest in recruit Charles Street, he modestly revealed that he was 'the' Charles Street. Street was popular with the men and rose at one time to top sergeant of Company D. He was a good soldier but never took very kindly to the strict Army discipline."[51]

"'Gabby' is strong in his praises for the army for all ball players," the *Washington Herald* said in mid-January. "Street will be stationed at Fort Myer as a sergeant in the Engineers' Corps, to finish his training before being sent over there. Charlie said that fourteen of his seventeen teammates of the Nashville club had joined the colors."[52]

Sportswriter James M. Gould wrote twenty years later of soldier Gabby, "Rather dour of countenance and with a real vocabulary in the two languages required in the Army—English and profane—he was the very pattern of a real, hard-boiled army sergeant."[53] Blinkey Horn updated Vols fans on their ex-catcher's activities in mid-February 1918. "Within the next week Sergeant Street, in company with the Thirtieth Engineers, with which he enlisted back in the winter, expects to sail for France."[54] Gabby wrote to Horn later that month with a message for club secretary Christian Haury.

> Dear Blinkey: Your letter received and glad to hear from some one in Nashville. It was interesting to hear about the new line-up, or rather lack of line-up, I should say.
>
> It will seem awfully strange not to play ball this summer; the first I have ever missed in sixteen years. However, I do not intend to give up my favorite sport altogether, for [Washington Senators manager] Clark Griffith has given me two dozen balls, a mask, a catcher's mitt, a first baseman's mitt and three bats to take along so we can play ball as a diversion "over there."
>
> Tell Mr. Haury that if I develop a phenom among any of the Sammies I'll give him his name so he can draft him.
>
> I like army life fine. The boys are very congenial and Uncle Sam feeds us and keeps us well. Expect to sail mighty soon, although of course will never know the day or hour until some day when we start out on a hike with our packs on our backs we'll just never come back to camp.
>
> We are all anxious to get into active service, and expect to get old Kaiser Bill before we're through.

Regards to all the boys. Send me a paper now and then when I am over in the trenches.

My address will be Sergt. Charles E. Street, Co. D, 30th Engineers, American Expeditionary Forces, Via New York.

Sincerely yours,
"GABBY."[55]

4

....

Winter

Eppa Rixey Jr. first pitched for the Philadelphia Phillies in 1912. The lefthander hadn't spent an inning in the Minor Leagues before going straight up to the National League from the University of Virginia, where he'd starred in baseball, basketball, golf, and tennis. Philadelphia snapped him up ahead of several other clubs.

"He is said to be six feet six inches above the sea level at the surf's edge and looks all of that and more," a newspaper joked.[1] A wire story later called him a "human hatpin."[2]

Sports columnist Bill Phelon of the *Cincinnati Times-Star* is often credited with coining the hurler's nickname, Eppa "Jeptha" Rixey. According to baseball lore, he needed a couple of syllables to fill out a rhyme during the rookie's first swing through the league. A perusal of the paper's sports pages, however, reveals no such poem that week. Reversing the names a few days later, Charley Dryden of the *Chicago Examiner* referred to "Jeptha Eppa Rixey, Jr."[3] Perhaps Phelon had tagged Rixey with the biblical name in Cincinnati, it stuck, then the Phillies repeated it in the Windy City. Sportswriter Fred Lieb wrote long afterward that creating the moniker "may have been a joint effort."[4] "Jeptha" eventually spread so widely that many fans came to believe that it was, in fact, Eppa's middle name. (He had none.)

Any moundsman with a long frame and a catchy handle was irresistible for sportswriters, especially if he could pitch. "He had a fast ball that came down from somewhere like a daring volplaner, a curve that swooped over the plate as unexpectedly as a chicken hawk in a barnyard, and an occasional slow boy that looked as big as a grapefruit and turned into a mustard seed," *Chicago Tribune* sportswriter I. E. Sanborn wrote that first summer of "Jephtha" (an alternate spelling of the nickname).[5] Syndicated columnist Hugh Fullerton in 1915 found Eppa "a strange and peculiar genius. When this fellow Rixey is right no ball team in the world is licensed to hit him or beat him."[6]

Like Gabby Street, Eppa was a proud southerner, a Virginian whose heritage was evident in his speech and manner. But the resemblance went no further. "Quiet, shy and a model of deportment," a sportswriter wrote of Eppa years later. The hurler was always afraid to take the mound, and he considered his fear a blessing. "I really believe it helped me," he said. "It reminded me that I must above all things try my best to win."[7]

Eppa had an unusual pedigree for a ballplayer, especially during an era when baseball was largely a hardscrabble, blue-collar sport. Born in Culpeper, Virginia, reared and educated in Charlottesville, he was something of a southern aristocrat. An ancestor who arrived in America sometime before 1740 had the surname "Riccia," apparently derived from a Ricci family in northern Italy. The Rixeys now counted themselves among the first families of Virginia, the FFVs.

One of the pitcher's uncles was a rear admiral and former U.S. surgeon general. Another had represented a Virginia constituency as a congressman. Eppa, too, was a capable and learned gentleman, who had once taught high school Latin during the off-season. He'd had to lobby his father, Eppa Sr., to be allowed to play professional baseball after leaving the university.

"I know I can't play ball all my life, and when I am through I can fall back on one of the other professions," Eppa Jr. said. "I cannot see why ballplaying should bring any discredit to the family. It is as honorable as any other profession I could choose."[8] In registering for the army draft, he had listed his occupation as "chemist & ball player."[9] His family still hoped he would abandon the diamond for a more acceptable workplace.

Although a fine natural athlete, Eppa had won only one more game than he'd lost during six seasons pitching in Philadelphia. Righthander Grover Cleveland "Pete" Alexander was the club's star hurler. The rawboned Nebraskan had broken in with the Phillies a season before the Virginian. "He taught me many tricks of pitching," Eppa said later, "and I owe what success I have had to 'Alex' and 'Pat' Moran, who was coach for the Phillies."[10]

Eppa became friends with Pete and his longtime catcher, William "Reindeer Bill" Killefer. The Phillies reached the World Series in 1915, lost it in five games with Alexander getting their sole victory, then finished second each of the following two seasons. The team's success was due in no small part to Alexander and Killefer. Quaker City fans had reason to be optimistic about the coming 1918 season. Then two weeks before Christmas, the Phillies shocked everyone by trading their stellar starting battery to the Chicago Cubs, who also played in the National League, for a pile of cash and two journeymen players.

"Thus the Phillies lose their two most valuable players, who constitute the greatest battery in either big league today," the *Philadelphia Inquirer* moaned. Club president William Baker, "in parting with his only famous players stated that he expected to be very severely criticized, but he was sure that time would show that the move was a wise one, even if the Philadelphia team was wrecked for the time being."[11]

The blockbuster deal hinged on the fate of Alexander (and to a lesser extent, of Killefer) in the military draft. Baker calculated that the army would take his pitcher sooner rather than later and thought it wise to get what he could for him now. The Cubs took the chance that Alexander would play for them much or all of the 1918 campaign.

Eppa knew precisely what the Phillies were losing in Alexander. The difference between the two pitchers was an undefinable quality separating talent from genius. (Film critics made the distinction decades later about dancers Gene Kelly and Fred Astaire). During the preceding three seasons, Alexander had won thirty or more games each year, a feat matched only by magnificent Christopher "Christy" Mathewson, the former New York Giants hurler.

"I remember the year I won 22 (1916)," Eppa said decades later. "'Old Alex' won 33 and they didn't even know I was in the league."[12] Fans in Philadelphia and elsewhere across the country, knowing genius when they saw it, hailed the laconic hurler from Nebraska as "Alexander the Great."

If anyone understood Eppa's position on the Phillies, it was pitcher Herb Pennock of the Boston Red Sox. Reared in rural privilege in nearby Kennett Square, Pennsylvania, Pennock was a lefthanded hurler who also had jumped directly into the Major Leagues, with the Philadelphia

Athletics in 1912. His current win-loss record was even more modest than the Virginian's. The unlikely doppelgangers would both find their footing eventually and pitch for other teams during long professional careers. But through the final weeks of 1917, together with Alexander and millions of ordinary American men, they confronted the vital question of what to do about the war, which sooner or later would disrupt their lives.

Alexander stood pat and took his chances. President Baker would be proved correct in the short term—Alexander would pitch only three games for Chicago before the army called him in the spring. But after the war, although greatly troubled, Alexander would continue pitching in the big leagues until 1930, and later enter the Hall of Fame. Pennock, in contrast, chose not to wait. He enlisted in the navy a few days after the Alexander-Killefer deal, glad for a break from the pressures of professional baseball. The hurler would report for duty at Boston in January.

Eppa's situation was somewhat more complicated. His father had died of pneumonia in February 1917. When registering for the draft in June, Eppa had listed his mother and sister as dependents. But as the year wound down, his thinking grew closer to Pennock's. He was as unhappy as any outraged Phillies fan, perhaps even more so, at seeing his friends summarily dealt to the Cubs.

Coincidentally, the War Department in mid-December asked one of his former university professors to recommend two graduates in analytical chemistry for immediate special duty at Norfolk. Eppa was working that winter as a chemist for the Virginia-Carolina Chemical Company in Richmond. When his name was put forward, reports quickly surfaced that the twenty-six-year-old intended to join the army.

"The big twirler has decided to enter the service of Uncle Sam," said an article datelined Charlottesville, "and came up from Richmond last week to procure the necessary papers and recommendations from members of the faculty of the University of Virginia, from which institution he recently was graduated in chemistry and also carried off the bachelor of arts and bachelor of science degrees." The report echoed what was widely stated elsewhere: "Close friends of Rixey here are of the opinion that his decision to quit baseball was hastened by the sale of Alexander and Killefer."[13]

Baker either had miscalculated or ignored the effects of the Alexander-Killefer deal on his club. *Philadelphia Public Ledger* sports editor Robert Maxwell later wrote: "When Alexander was sold, Eppa was depended upon to do the heavy work for the locals, and had there been any idea that he would leave the club Alex would not be wearing a Cub uniform today."[14]

Wesley Branch Rickey—Branch to his friends—had lost the Cincinnati catcher's job to Gabby Street in 1904. Despite his promise to his mother never to play or attend a game on Sundays, which he kept all his life, he broke into the Major Leagues the next season. He made one appearance for the American League St. Louis Browns in 1905, got into sixty-five games with the Browns in 1906, and played fifty-two games with the New York Highlanders in 1907.

Two years later he was a very busy man—coaching baseball and football at his alma mater, Ohio Wesleyan University in Delaware, Ohio; taking night law classes at Ohio State University in Columbus; teaching a beginners' law class at Ohio Wesleyan; and traveling around the state making temperance speeches. When his health broke down, Branch was treated for tuberculosis at Saranac Lake, New York. He later returned to baseball as head coach at the University of Michigan, 1910–13, where he completed his law degree.

Branch seemed always to be juggling several jobs at once. He briefly practiced law in 1911 in Boise, Idaho, where he also headed a rough-and-tumble temperance campaign. (While he lived most of his life no farther west than St. Louis, he went to Boise for its high dry air after recovering from his illness in the Adirondacks.) He had only one court-appointed client in Idaho, a terrifying criminal who promptly fired him. Branch took down his shingle and returned to Michigan.

"A man trained for the law devotes his entire life and all his energies to something so cosmically unimportant as a game," he said ruefully decades later. Yet he never regretted the decision. He returned to the Browns as a scout and assistant to owner Robert Hedges in 1912, while retaining his job as coach of the Michigan nine.

"'Tis said that Mr. Hedges has been anxious for some time to have officiating in the position of secretary, a man with a knowledge of jurisprudence who also is a practical baseball player," a St. Louis newspaper reported.[15] Branch meant to stay with the club only a year, but when it was up Hedges offered him a raise. "There was a new baby at our house. And not much money, new or old," Branch said later. "So I was a moral coward. I chose to stay with the game."[16]

After scouting and working in the Browns' front office, the ex-catcher replaced George Stovall as manager in September 1913. Like an old firehouse horse hearing the alarm, he twice inserted himself into the lineup as a pinch hitter the following season. Three years later, in March 1917, Branch left the Browns and was named president of the cross-town Cardinals, a position he now had held for less than a year after leaving the Browns amid great wrangling. On December 20 he would turn thirty-six years old.

Like President Baker in Philadelphia, Branch faced personnel problems in St. Louis, although none was due to any action or inaction of his own. During the spring, while still employed as the business manager of the Browns, the *St. Louis Star* had called him "the brightest gem in the councils of the American League." The newspaper added, "His greatest asset is his vast knowledge of men. His ability to judge ball players is uncanny. Bonds and sureties are not needed to guarantee any promise he makes. A man of his word, Branch Rickey stands higher in the tribunals of minor league solons than even the magnates of major organizations."[17]

But he had no control over business conditions and pressures affecting ballplayers on every Major and Minor League club in America. With huge cantonments completed across the country, and America finally prepared to train an enormous new army, baseball executives in both major leagues began losing players to the draft and enlistments. Branch saw two good men go before Christmas.

The Cardinals learned on December 1 that their first player would soon depart for military service. Marv Goodwin was a promising rookie right-handed pitcher who had won six games and lost four during fourteen appearances in 1917. He hoped now to earn a commission as an army flier. "Have enlisted in aviation corps reserves," Goodwin confirmed in a telegram to a St. Louis paper. "Expect to be called for training in few days."[18] The twenty-six-year-old was single, without dependents, and subject to the draft. "I don't feel right to stand back and wait for some other fellow to do my scrapping for me," he wrote to a relative.[19]

Goodwin's departure was a blow. "I had every reason to believe that Goodwin was going to be a remarkable pitcher," Branch said. "The fact that four games he won of the six pitched [for wins] were shutout victories, is almost proof alone that the young man had a remarkable assortment of curves."[20] Sports columnist Lynn C. Davis offered a poem for the fledgling aviator:

> Twinkle, twinkle, little star,
> Up above the world so far.
> We will praise your pitching skill
> If you "bean" old Kaiser Bill. . . .[21]

Branch and his Cardinals club sustained an even bigger loss in mid-December, when infielder and captain Jack "Dots" Miller enlisted in the United States Marine Corps from his home in New Jersey. "There goes a shortstop, second sacker, first baseman, captain and potential manager at one crack," columnist Davis wrote.[22] Unlike Goodwin, the thirty-one-year-old player wouldn't have been called for service anytime soon.

"Miller was certified for selective service by the exemption board in Kearny [New Jersey] after declaring that he would not claim exemption on account of being married," the *St. Louis Star* told fans. "He secured a letter from his local board stating that he was not needed to fill quota. Mrs. Miller accompanied her husband to the enlisting bureau and gave her written consent to Miller joining Uncle Sam's forces."[23]

Pearl Miller more than approved of her husband signing up. She followed the ballplayer's example ten days later, when she "joined the Red Cross as a nurse and . . . requested to be sent to France for service," the *Star* said.[24]

The Cardinal president fully understood the couple's sacrifices. He was married, too, with three small children and a fourth on the way. He knew baseball's manpower problem would only worsen. Branch was an ex-player, scout, manager, and executive and possessed a sharp legal mind, even if he hadn't succeeded as a lawyer. He knew that all he could do was patch the holes opening in his club, the same as every other magnate.

"Rickey is far more worried over the future of his club, following the enlistment of Miller than he was after Marvin Goodwin, the crack young pitcher, signed up with Uncle Sam," a *St. Louis Star* sportswriter reported. "While Goodwin will he missed only on every fourth and fifth day, Miller was a daily toiler and the loss of his services may prove fatal."[25]

On the last day of the year, Branch resolved one big concern for the Cardinals, by signing John C. "Jack" Hendricks as their new manager. Hendricks had skippered the Indianapolis Indians in the American Association during 1917. He now replaced Miller Huggins, who was leaving St. Louis after five seasons to begin what would become a legendary stint with the New York Yankees. L. C. Davis was ready with poetic advice for the new Cardinal chief:

> Jack be nimble,
> Jack be quick;
> Jack be ready to turn the trick,
> Jack be foxy,
> Jack be wise;
> Jack jump over those New York guys.[26]

The player exodus continued elsewhere. "Eppa Jeptha Rixey, the big left-handed pitcher of the Phillies, will be doing army duty this summer instead of laboring for the forces of Pat Moran," a wire service said in mid-January. "Eppa yesterday received a commission of first lieutenant in the sanitary corps of the National Army and will probably be assigned to the gas defense section."[27]

The terminology surrounding Eppa's commission in 1918 requires some explanation today. His specialty was not, as a syndicated column mistakenly said, "making the cantonment sanitary."[28] The National Army was a vast, fast-expanding force composed largely of draftees, and it dwarfed the regular army and National Guard. The sanitary corps' name echoed the old-fashioned designations of the Civil War. Established soon after America entered World War I, it included "experts in sanitation, bacteriology and sanitary engineering, and men skilled in the work of supply, transportation and storage required in connection with the work of the Medical Department of the Army."[29]

Gas warfare included both offensive and defensive operations. Officers came either from the Medical Reserve Corps or, like Eppa, were appointed from qualified civilian occupations. None ranked higher than major. Contrary to reports about lab work in Norfolk, Eppa was bound for the field as a first lieutenant, a step above second lieutenant, the lowest commissioned rank. Looking "about nine feet eleven in his puttees, trousers and blouse," he would be involved with gas defense and teaching troops how to defend themselves against chemical attacks.[30]

The former Phillie reported to Camp Bowie, Texas, during the final hours of January 1918. The post on "a wind-swept, untrampled tract of prairie" west of Fort Worth was no one's dream assignment.[31] Conditions at the crowded, hastily constructed camp were so worrisome that in early December the army's surgeon general had made a sudden inspection tour there. Camp authorities were still so unprepared for severe cold weather and resulting illness that the Red Cross "turned over 20,000 blankets to the commandant of the camp, without any cost to the government whatever. Undoubtedly this quick work saved the lives of many soldiers."[32]

"Eppa reached Camp Bowie Thursday afternoon direct from Washington and will be here for two weeks taking the gas defense instruction and practice," the *Fort Worth Star-Telegram* reported as February began. He and other new officers were introduced to gas masks the next morning. Eppa also tried using a shovel-like tool designed to fan poison gas from trenches. The experience wasn't much like spring training with the Phillies.

"This is my first time in Texas," Eppa said. "I didn't know it was so cold down here. I like being in the army all right and am anxious to go to France."[33] He added that he'd never thrown a hand grenade, but probably would be good at it if he got into a tight spot. Although he had always resisted leaving the game, he said he didn't know whether he would pitch again following the war.

American soldiers were popularly called Yanks, doughboys, and Sammies during the war. Eppa and his fellow officers weren't the only ones learning something about poison gas while at Camp Bowie. Other troops training there, mostly men from Texas and Oklahoma, were learning about it, too. The primary lesson was how to don their gas protection quickly.

"The gas defense instruction is one phase of the practice the public never sees," the *Star-Telegram* said. "It sees, if it wants to, the drilling, bayonet and grenade work, but the gas school has been in a secluded spot south of the boulevard. Every man has learned or is learning to put on his gas mask in six seconds. He must not be even seven seconds. If he can do it in four or five his life is that much safer."[34]

Eppa's expected two weeks at Camp Bowie stretched to three, his training covering more than a few poisonous agents, such as mustard gas, that Americans read about in their newspapers. "Rixey tried all sorts of gases, met and conquered them all, including the lachrymal, itching and paralytic," the Fort Worth paper said on February 21. "He was declared a full fledged graduate and visited division headquarters Thursday to bid friends good-bye."[35]

Lieutenant Rixey boarded a train that night with orders assigning him to the sanitary train of the Eighth Division, a new Regular Army outfit beginning its infantry training at Camp Fremont in California. Again, the designation has long since fallen out of common military use. A sanitary train was a medical unit that cared for and evacuated battlefield casualties. A WWI history provides this sketch:

> The 8th Sanitary Train was formed at Camp Fremont the first part of January, 1918, and was composed of field hospitals and ambulance companies that had been formed at the Presidio, San Francisco, California, from May to December, 1917. The nucleus of the train was Field Hospital and Ambulance companies No. 2, which had seen service on the Mexican border.[36]

Eppa's new post, at Menlo Park adjacent to Stanford University, was far more pleasant than frigid Texas. Camp Fremont occupied forty-two square miles of sunny landscape and towering oak trees. Construction disputes had nearly prompted the army to scrap its plans for the camp, which now, however, was finished. Eight thousand troops were training there when Eppa arrived, with room for twenty-two thousand more. The men lived six or eight per tent, with a small wood-burning stove.

"Each tent is set up over what looks at a little distance like an extra well built sheep-pen," the *San Francisco Examiner* said. "It has a smooth board floor, raised off the ground some inches, and wooden walls between three and four feet in height. . . . The two infantry brigades' camp, the camp of the sanitary train known as Base Hospital No. 47, the camp of Cooks and Bakers No. 340, the camp of Motor Truck Company No. 393, and the cantonment of the quartermaster corps all lie between the railroad and the foothills."[37]

Like every military installation in the country, Camp Fremont swarmed with baseball fans. Doughboys played at nearly every organizational level—in company, regimental, and divisional teams, and even in all-star nines. Leagues were formed and uniforms acquired. It was the same throughout the army, navy, and marine corps; each service considered baseball beneficial for morale and physical conditioning. Troops at cantonments in temperate climes, such as Menlo Park's, played ball all year around.

"Followers of the Sanitary Train ball club of Camp Fremont are very happy these days, and they have a good reason for being so," a San Francisco columnist wrote of the unit's talented team in early February.[38] By the end of that month, the "bugs" were positively ecstatic over the arrival of the ex-Phillie, Lieutenant Rixey.

Christy Mathewson, fit and handsome at thirty-seven, was the former pitching star of manager John McGraw's New York Giants. He had left New York in July 1916 for Cincinnati, where he took over as manager for the National League Reds. Newspapers and fans affectionately called him "Matty."

The Reds manager was the second greatest hurler in baseball history, trailing only incomparable Cy Young in total victories with 272. More than a century later, he would retain his place among the sport's immortals, in third place on the all-time winning list behind Young (511) and Walter Johnson (417) and tied with Pete Alexander (373), whom he had trailed until statisticians unearthed an overlooked victory. Admired and even loved by many fans, Matty was better educated than most Major Leaguers of his day, having attended Bucknell University in Lewisburg, Pennsylvania, until he turned professional.

Matty also was known as "Big Six," the origins of which were hazy during a time before players wore numbers on their uniforms. Many people thought the nickname referred to his sturdy six-foot frame. Others held that it came from an African American expression for an unusually powerful and effective man, used by fans in the South who had admired his early performance during spring training.

"Matty, himself, never knew exactly where he got the nickname," sportswriter Bozeman Bulger later wrote. "He had an idea that he was called 'Big Six' when he played football but he wasn't sure. Old friends still insist that he did get the name in football."[39]

The former Giant had a third nickname as well: the Christian Gentleman. Used mostly by the newspapers, it reflected the public perception of Matty's character. He was handsome, confident, athletic, and capable, the seeming embodiment of fictional hero Frank Merriwell. The image obscured the real, more complex man underneath. "If Mathewson was not truly a prince among men—and he had his moments, from punching out a lemonade vendor to 'high-hatting' his teammates—the press was only too glad to fit him into that role, which had been vacant," writes John Thorn, official historian of Major League Baseball.[40]

With such a background, it wasn't surprising that Matty spent part of the winter of 1917–18 mingling with soldiers, too, albeit as a civilian under the auspices of the Young Men's Christian Association (YMCA). He traveled to the army's Camp Sheridan, outside Montgomery, Alabama, shortly after New Year's Day. Ohio National Guard units training there constituted most of the army's new Thirty-Seventh Division.

"All eyes of soldiers Wednesday turned toward Ohio, from whence will come Christy Mathewson, world's famous baseball player, who will spend several days at Camp Sheridan next week," the *Cincinnati Enquirer* said in early January. "Mathewson has notified the Y. M. C. A. that he will come to entertain the soldiers in a checker tournament and in lectures."[41]

Matty was a champion of the popular board game, vice president of the American Checkers Association, and one of the best amateur players in the country. He could easily play and win several games at once. Asking the Reds manager to play checkers with Sammies in a YMCA hut was like asking Enrico Caruso to join a singalong. But Matty did it gladly. "He loved checkers almost as dearly as he loved baseball," the *New York Times* recalled years later, "and many were the games he had with experts from all over the country who came to play with him."[42]

Camp Sheridan greeted Matty warmly. "He has donned the 'Y' army uniform and looks the part of a soldier," a Cincinnati sportswriter wrote, although the Reds' leader more often wore his civilian clothes in camp.[43] As always, Matty was a consummate gentleman, meeting with fans and admirers at a church in town, and at the YMCA and Knights of Columbus huts out at the camp. He chatted with doughboys, shared their meals with them, and cleaned his own mess kit afterward.

"Say, that bird Mathewson is some scout," a sergeant said, "and I'd sure love to see him in my outfit as an officer. He ain't swelled up over his reputation, and he lines up for chow right along with the rest of us."[44]

Matty played pushball and indoor baseball with the troops, as well as a lot of checkers, once on a specially built, eight-foot board. "'Matty' had a large bunch of players engaged in a checker tournament," a Montgomery newspaper said, "and he was just seeing it well done and giving general directions to players, all of whom were very much interested."[45] The Buckeyes were tickled that the best checkers player in the division twice managed to play the Cincinnati skipper to a tie.

The baseball idol disappointed the boys only in declining to toss hand grenades. "You can't tell what might happen, and I might need the old arm this summer," Matty said.[46] He had pitched only once since taking over the Reds, in 1916, but he wanted to be ready.

The Camp Sheridan trip monetarily benefited his club the following month when Matty agreed to shift the Reds' training camp to Montgomery. The previous two seasons the club had trained in Shreveport, Louisiana.

"He was a hero during his visit, and he was such a great attraction for the soldiers that the Y. M. C. A. persuaded Matty to bring the Reds to the camp for their Spring training," said the *New York Times*. "The Y. M. C. A. will bear half the expense of the training season, while the Montgomery Board of Trade will share the other half of the costs."[47] A wire story added:

"Because of the great personal favor with which Matty is regarded, his ball club will have a free training trip while the other major league clubs are expending thousands of dollars to get into shape in the South."[48]

The Reds left for Alabama on the second Monday of March 1918. A large, enthusiastic crowd of fans and soldiers plus a military band met their train the next day at Montgomery's Union Station. The commanding general of the Ohio division addressed Matty during a luncheon at a YMCA hut that afternoon.

"Mr. Mathewson, despite the fact there is a war now on, interest in base ball is very keen with the soldiers," he said. "The boys at the camp are glad you and your players are here and I am sure that you will have a large patronage at the games by the soldiers. Anything that you want while here, and you are unable to obtain it, please call on me, and I will see that you get anything that you want."[49]

The club lodged at the Exchange Hotel and trained at a ballpark four miles away. Matty had agreed to play an army squad several times during training. Cpl. Ralph Sharman of the 136th Field Artillery was the division team's captain. A rookie outfielder who had briefly played for manager Connie Mack's 1917 Philadelphia Athletics, and who coincidentally hailed from Cincinnati, Sharman had various Minor Leaguers and semipros on his roster.

"Mathewson has seen the Division team in action," a local paper said, "and admits that the Reds will have a strong team to win from, when they are clashing with the Soldiers."[50] The doughboys, in fact, did give the Reds a close game on March 17. The teams played at what was called Soldiers' Field, which lacked a grandstand but had open seating for 2,200 troops.

"Captain Ralph Sharman's clever team held the powerful Reds to 4-to-3 count, and would have tied it up in the eighth round and possibly won it out, but for a slight mistake in base running, which cost them at least one run. . . . The Reds played a fast and steady game in true big league style, which makes the good work of the soldier boys all the more noteworthy," the *Cincinnati Enquirer* said.[51]

The Reds thrashed the division nine and a regimental team several times before leaving Montgomery at the end of March for a series in Texas with the Detroit Tigers. The Buckeye troops nonetheless enjoyed these games, which Matty later enhanced with a gift. "Manager Mathewson has agreed to send the old Red uniforms back here for the use of the division team as soon as the Reds reach home and get their new suits," the *Enquirer* said. "The soldier boys have no regular suits, and are now equipped with all sorts of uniforms."[52]

Corporal Sharman barely got to enjoy wearing big league togs again. He drowned on May 24 while swimming in the Alabama River. The army sent his body home to Ohio for burial following the "largest military funeral in Montgomery since the Ohio division came here for training."[53]

5

....

Good Scout

Manager Mathewson was perhaps still the most popular man in Organized Baseball, hailed as a role model for boys everywhere. But the shining image was also protective armor, and the Reds skipper wasn't an easy man to know.

"He turned out to be a most peculiar fellow," a wire story would say after Matty's sixteen-plus seasons with the Giants. "You could meet him socially a half dozen or more times and the next time he never would know you. One couldn't help getting the impression of extreme snobbishness in him. At any rate, during all of the years that adulation was heaped on him by the cartload in the east he formed the habit of extreme shyness. In short, he was absolutely the worst mixer the game ever had seen. He contented himself with playing checkers instead of making even a feeble attempt at good fellowship." But the ex-pitcher realized he could loosen up a bit while managing in Cincinnati, according to the writer. "He found that people were willing to like him not because of hero worship but for his own good qualities. . . . Now Matty can be classified as 'a good scout.'"[1]

Matty's triumphs over the winter and spring at Camp Sheridan had shown both the quiet, shy checkers champion and the newer, more public persona. Once the regular season was under way, the YMCA approached him with a plea to both sides of his personality. The manager received "an urgent appeal from the American Expeditionary Forces to go to France and promote baseball among the American soldiers," the *New York Times* said on April 25. "This message was received yesterday from E. C. Carter in charge of the Y. M. C. A. work in France."

Matty's selection, Carter said, was made by a popular vote, the mechanics of which were never revealed. The *Times* and many other papers also printed the contents of a wire that William Sloane, chairman of the Y's National War Work Council, had sent Matty the day before:

> To meet the imperative demand overseas, the War Personnel Board of the Y. M. C. A. is asked to send this month 1,000 men prominent in business and professional life, including a large number of athletic directors.
>
> Special cables from those in authority urge you to come over with important relation to the promotion of baseball for the entire American Army. Such an opportunity has never been presented to any man. We are hopeful, if this appeal is placed before your management, they will see in it a chance to serve thousands of Americans, now enduring the terrific strain and make a great contribution toward winning the war.
>
> We are not unmindful of the financial sacrifice involved and the difficulty in making the necessary readjustments. We hope that patriotic motives will lead you and your management to accede to this request. When and where could you meet our representative to discuss the entire matter?[2]

With the Reds in Pittsburgh for a series with the Pirates, Matty told writers he would be glad to meet with a YMCA representative. He doubted, however, that the organization needed him. "If they want me as a talker or a checker player I scarcely think I would fill the bill," he said in the *Cincinnati Enquirer*. "As to baseball promotion, I don't think the game needs any special work of that kind." The newspaper said his salary would drop from $2,000 a month with the Reds to $150 with the Y, but Matty said money didn't enter into it.

"The salary part of it does not interest me at all, if I decide that it is my duty to go," he told the *Enquirer*. "But I am in a position where many other people will be affected by my leaving the team at this stage of the season, and it would be only fair to consult with them. I have been with the Cincinnati club for a year and a half and am just beginning to show some results. I do not feel that it would be right for me to leave them flat and go away on the next train."[3]

Garry Herrmann, president of the Cincinnati club, sidestepped the issue. "I am not wholly prepared to give the definite stand of the Cincinnati officials on the matter," he told a Pittsburgh newspaper, "but I feel that Matty and the Reds in general have been paid a lasting tribute."[4] The *Enquirer* added the next day, "President Herrmann thinks that Matty is doing more good for the country here than he possibly could over there in the position suggested, but he will not stand in his way if Matty decides otherwise."[5]

A Reds official pointed out that Matty had sold $150,000 in Liberty bonds since America entered the war and made various speeches. "It is a fact also that almost every American soldier in France knows baseball well enough to get the enjoyment out of the game," this unnamed person said. "By all means help the game over there, but there are easier ways in which it may be helped without causing as much inconvenience."[6]

YMCA officials in France then doubled down, asking that two teams of professional ballplayers be sent over to play games to entertain doughboys behind the front lines. The two requests weren't specifically linked, but newspapers connected them anyway.

John Montgomery Ward had been a great player and player-manager during the previous century, and later a lawyer and baseball executive. He sent Matty a telegram saying he'd like to accompany him to France and assist with the work there. Ward added that he was willing to take the job himself if Matty wasn't interested. "Mr. Ward said that the plan of instructing the soldier boys in the science of baseball appealed strongly to him," the *New York Sun* said, "and he was willing to make almost any sacrifice to get to France and do something to aid the cause of democracy."[7]

The pressures from multiple directions were getting to be a bit much for the Reds manager. "Matty is anxious to do the right thing, at any sacrifice to himself, but he is not going to be carried away by false sentiment into doing something which he thinks is not wise," the *Cincinnati Enquirer* said.[8]

The man the YMCA sent from New York to confer with him was Dr. George J. Fisher, head of the association's War Work Council athletic department and a former head of the Cincinnati branch's athletic department. Fisher hadn't yet arrived in Cincinnati when Matty said on the evening of April 28 that he would stay with his club, "for the present at least."[9]

Papers around the country published the report from the Associated Press. Matty had "definitely decided that he can do more good on this side than he could by going over to France to play baseball with the soldiers, who need no one to teach them the game," the *Enquirer* added. "Matty is of much use to the country in his present position for more than he could be on the other side. He is willing to make any sacrifice for the cause and would go in a minute if he thought it would be a wise move, but he is certain that he can help more by remaining right where he is. In this decision he is backed by all his friends."[10]

An uproar followed, with Matty hearing sharp criticism for perhaps the first time in his career. "Christy Mathewson's refusal to accept the invitation of the Y. M. C. A. to go to France to promote and supervise baseball for the soldiers of the American Expeditionary Forces came as a great surprise," columnist P. T. Knox wrote in the *New York Telegram*. "It was generally imagined and freely predicted that Matty, idol of so many baseball fans, would welcome the opportunity to go 'over there' and do his bit in such a commendable work. But he has missed his chance, and as a result he has lost much of the prestige that once was his."[11]

The *Harrisburg Telegraph* in his native Pennsylvania urged the Reds skipper to reconsider. "Organized baseball, on the whole, has done little enough in this hour of a world's travail," the paper said in an unsigned sports editorial. "Yet it has never turned a deaf ear to a direct call for help. We cannot conceive of one so respected, so honored, so esteemed and so loved as Mathewson proving a nation's idol to have been set up with feet of clay."[12] Other sportswriters and editorial writers echoed the disappointment.

"In fairness to Matty, it should be stated emphatically that he never authorized the announcements from Cincinnati that he thought he could be of more service to the Government by staying here than he could be responding to the call of the men in the camps and trenches of France," Fisher said later.[13] A few columnists understood the spot the Y had put Matty in.

"The Y. M. C. A.'s offer has served to embarrass Mathewson, inasmuch as it was not backed up by an expression of the wishes of the Government in the matter," John Wray wrote in the *St. Louis Post-Dispatch*. "Condemnation of the Cincinnati manager for not at once breaking his contract with the Reds is very unfair and should be withheld until the real situation is ascertained."[14] Such sentiments didn't prevent an avalanche of complaints and second guessing elsewhere, however.

Matty agreed to sit down with Fisher as the YMCA continued its pursuit. The Y man met with National League president and former Pennsylvania governor John K. Tener before leaving New York. "I think Matty can be induced to accept the offer of the Y. M. C. A.," Tener said, "and for the National League I may say that organized baseball appreciates the honor of the call from our soldiers in the trenches."[15] Fisher then spoke with reporters before boarding his train:

> "If there is one name in American sport that stands for clean sportsmanship and clean living, it is the name of Matty. Thousands of those boys in uniform overseas have sat in the bleachers and cheered him when he was in his prime as a pitcher for the Giants. They are 3,000 miles from home. Can any one doubt the enthusiasm with which they would receive the announcement that Matty was coming overseas to them, to be their athletic director and counsellor, to play checkers with them and to inspire them by the very magnetism of his personality? I hope to cable the news to them tomorrow night that Matty is coming."[16]

With the YMCA representative enroute to Cincinnati, the Reds skipper said he hadn't definitely spurned the organization's offer. "Manager Mathewson when interviewed last night said that he would pass judgment on the offer to go to France after he confers with George F. [sic] Fisher of New York, who is expected to arrive in Cincinnati today or tomorrow," the *Cincinnati Commercial Tribune* reported. "'Matty' says he neither accepted nor declined the offer up to last night and if Mr. Fisher can show him where he is needed more on the other side than in Cincinnati he will be glad to serve his country in this manner at this time if it is O.K. with the Cincinnati ball club management."[17]

"Mathewson asserted that he thought well of the idea of sending over two teams from the big leagues to play for the soldiers behind the lines," the *New York Sun* added. "He and Garry Herrmann will confer in Chicago to-morrow with Charles Weeghman of the Chicago Nationals [Cubs] and Charles Comiskey of the White Sox on the matter. If the teams are sent abroad Mathewson will recruit the clubs."[18]

Fisher meanwhile sat down with Matty for a long meeting on the morning of May 1. "Dr. Fisher explained to Matty that the call for him came from the soldiers already over there and that he could do more than any other player on account of his great reputation," the *Cincinnati Enquirer* reported. Matty suggested Honus Wagner, the Pirates' recently retired great shortstop, for the position, "but Dr. Fisher said that Mathewson is the man wanted. . . . The whole matter was left in abeyance until Dr. Fisher returns to New York and gets into communication with the Y. M. C. A. leaders now in France. If they continue to insist on Mathewson giving up his work here and going over he will probably do so."[19]

The *Cincinnati Commercial Tribune* chipped in, too. "Matty would not say he had accepted or that he would not accept the offer, and he is waiting word from E. C. Carter, who is Y. M. C. A. director in France to find out just what his duties would be before giving up his position here," the paper said. "Mr. Fisher left for his home and will wire Mathewson, probably at Chicago. If he accepts, the fans will hear about it, and if he does not, it will be no one's business but his own. The Y. M. C. A. could get many other celebrated players, but the boys want Mathewson and no one else will do."[20]

"Matty himself is coy—says he doesn't know—that he cannot believe himself so important, so worth inviting over," *Sporting News* said. "Therein speaks his well known modesty. Mathewson, the man, is wanted over there, more than Mathewson, the ball player, and his cheering words, his hearty handshake, would be worth a barrel of nerve tonics to the Yankee soldier lads. The question has not yet been definitely decided, but Matty will make up his mind in a day or two."[21] The sports paper added in an editorial, "It seems to be a case of electing a man first and then creating the office he is to fill as a sort of second thought, something that makes it rather confusing and embarrassing to the man upon whom the mantle is to fall."[22]

The *Enquirer* reported that a YMCA worker whom Matty had known at Camp Sheridan advised him not to go. The demand was sentimental, the man said, and Matty could do no real good for baseball in France. The Reds manager seemed to agree. "Dr. Fisher did not give me a single good reason as to what good I could do over there," Matty said. "I tried my best to find out just what was wanted of me and what I could hope to accomplish by going over, but every reply was indefinite. I am open to conviction, but they haven't shown me yet."[23]

The YMCA also now felt heat over the affair. Fisher responded to criticism that the organization had appealed to Matty without proper authority. He produced a general order from American Expeditionary Forces headquarters, which authorized the Y to provide amusement and recreation for the troops. "Therefore, when a telegram was sent to Matty more than a week ago by the National War Work Council, and signed by its Chairman, William Sloane, the appeal contained in that telegram was official," Fisher said. "Defenders of Matty, rushing to his support after the false report of his declination to answer the call had been circulated, overlooked this point."[24]

Days passed while the YMCA and the Reds each awaited Matty's decision. "Much pressure is being brought to persuade Matty that he really is needed in France," New York sportswriter Hugh Fullerton wrote, "and also volunteers are rushing forward eager to take the job. The trouble is that there is only one Matty, and no one else in sport could get the same results."[25] The *Stars and Stripes*, the army newspaper in Paris, knew the result it wanted.

"COME ON, MATTY," said a headline at the top of the sports page. A boxed article below read:

> Cincinnati baseball fans are all worked up because of the rumor that Christy Mathewson, better known as "Big Six," has decided to go over to France and join the American forces.
>
> Matty probably figures that his "fadeaway" would prove of great value in the throwing of hand grenades.

  Baseball philosophers are considerably wrought up by the rumor and hundreds of thousands of words are being written daily as to whether Christy will go abroad or remain at Cincinnati and uphold the national pastime.

  "Big Six" is evidently up against it on the checker end, too; but it would be fine if he could land in the Kaiser's king row.[26]

The furor gradually died as the situation remained unchanged for six weeks. The Reds leader awaited clarification from the YMCA as to what his duties and responsibilities would be in France. A telegram finally arrived on June 25.

"Must defer action regarding baseball," Fisher said. A letter followed from New York, explaining that the Y had received a cable from France, which stated that the proposal was unwise in view of tremendous war pressures. "Then, too, the French people, whose viewpoint in athletics is not in accordance with our own, may possibly misunderstand our whole idea, in which event there is possibility for unfavorable reaction."[27]

  Sportswriter Thomas Rice of the *Brooklyn Eagle* later amplified the second point. "Naboth Hedin, head of The Eagle's Paris Bureau, very frankly pointed out in a number of stories that the increase on French soil of American civilians who had nothing more serious to do than to exploit amusements was causing unfavorable comment," Rice wrote. "Later a story from France stated that because of that growing feeling the offer to Mathewson had been withdrawn, as had the offers to several other non-combatants."[28]

  Sportswriter Jack Ryder of the *Cincinnati Enquirer* broke the story of the YMCA's reversal by adding it at the end of his regular game coverage. "This must make the critics who announced that Matty should have gone on the first boat feel very small," Ryder wrote, adding:

The Red leader has been ready all the time to give up his position and his home here and go to France, but he simply waited until he was assured that he could actually accomplish something abroad, of which he had serious doubts. Now the Y. M. C. A. people themselves come out and admit that he was right in his judgment that he could do less over there than by staying here. Matty felt all along that it was a foolish proposition, but at the same time he stood ready to make the sacrifice and go. His attitude on the matter has been most patriotic, and the Y. M. C. A. men now agree that he was right in his judgment.[29]

Sportswriter Denman Thompson agreed in the *Washington Star*. "Events have justified Christy Mathewson's refusal to be persuaded or forced into accepting the offer of the Y. M. C. A. to take charge of base ball among our soldiers in France," he wrote. "For the present, at least, no one is to be sent overseas for this service."[30]

Johnny Evers, the former Chicago Cubs and Boston Braves star, had recently retired after seventeen seasons playing second base in the Major Leagues. He accepted a position similar to the one the YMCA had offered to Matty, signing up as a uniformed athletic secretary for the Knights of Columbus, which like the Y supported extensive baseball activities in France. "John J. Evers, the famous Trojan, who has long been known as the 'brainiest man in baseball,' will be the generalissimo of baseball in France," said a newspaper in Syracuse, New York.[31]

Evers indeed later sailed to France, came under fire during the course of his duties, and was highly popular among the Sammies he met over there. He even taught the rudiments of the game to French soldiers, known as *poilus*.

Matty was now free of the unwanted pressure that the YMCA had exerted upon him, unwittingly or otherwise. But the Christian gentleman couldn't ignore the moral weight that he shouldered upon himself. With other Americans engaged in the war raging across Europe, Big Six felt a growing obligation to participate. The feeling only intensified over the summer.

6

....

CWS

The burgeoning American army was no more ready to wage gas and flame warfare than any other type of combat. Assignments and responsibilities were hopelessly scattered among the Bureau of Mines, the army's medical and ordinance departments, the Signal Corps, the Corps of Engineers, and the Gas Service with the American Expeditionary Forces (AEF) in France.

"The War Department was alive to the futility of the existing disar-rangement," journalist Edward B. Clark later wrote. "None of the agencies connected with gas service with the exception of the chemical warfare troops and the Ordnance Department had any understanding of the military value of the work they were doing. The conditions verged on the chaotic."[1]

The War Department appointed Maj. Gen. William L. Sibert to organize all these efforts as director of the new Chemical Warfare Service (CWS) in May 1918. General Sibert had built locks and dams for the Panama Canal before the war. Once America entered the conflict, he went to France with General Pershing and commanded the army's First Division. He also had five sons serving in uniform. General Order No. 62 activated the new service on June 28, with Sibert becoming its chief on July 1. Colonel Amos Fries was promoted to brigadier general and kept in command of CWS operations in France.

Fries, an able engineer and graduate of the United States Military Academy at West Point, had served in the Philippines under General Pershing. He had supervised early construction of Los Angeles harbor before the war and built roads in Yellowstone National Park. Setting aside the traditionalism of his service, Fries had made himself into a gas expert in France. He later would head the CWS for a decade following the war and later still, establish a reputation as a virulent anticommunist.

"The feeling in the Chemical Warfare Service, A.E.F., that our troubles in the United States were mainly over with the appointment of Sibert, proved absolutely correct," Fries wrote in 1919.[2] The army also placed a gas officer and assistants on the staff of every division, corps, and army commander. "It soon became apparent that an efficient gas officer must become a versatile man," the CWS later informed Congress. An efficient gas officer, it said, not only had to be knowledgeable about his own army's capabilities, but "a walking encyclopedia on the characteristic of German battle gasses."[3]

"The responsibility of providing chemicals for all branches of the government and assisting in the procurement of chemists for industries essential to the success of the war and government has been entrusted to the chemical warfare service," Secretary of War Baker said. "All chemists now in the army will be removed from their units and placed under the authority of the chemical warfare service. Newly drafted chemists will be assigned to the chemical warfare service."[4]

The reorganization also affected the Thirtieth Engineers. The army officially redesignated it the First Gas Regiment on July 13, 1918—"we have at last got our right name," a Company C Sammie wrote home to Missouri.[5]

"We have been at last transferred from the Engrs. and are now in the Chemical Warfare Service and are part of the first army, but are a special unit and are not attached to any division," Private Henry "Bun" Bunnell of Company C wrote to friends in Pennsylvania. "They assign a company or part of a company to any division needing our services and at times one company will be separated into two sections and work sixty miles apart.... This is a lonesome place and only the large amount of work which our department is doing, keeps us from a lingering death of loneliness."[6]

Soldiers wore a patch on their uniform's left shoulder to identify their unit. The CWS patch was a shield divided diagonally, the upper half blue and the lower half yellow. The collar insignia looked more scientific, a benzol ring superimposed on two crossed chemical retorts. The *Stars and Stripes* newspaper later said that the insignia was "so highly symbolical that it didn't hardly symbolize anything to unscientific and war-hardened minds. Its two crossed chemical retorts looked to the uninitiated like the irons of golf sticks, and were reminiscent of ancient pottery and clay pipes of the mound builders."[7]

Many CWS officers agreed, and unofficially adopted an insignia of a dragon's head above crossed six-inch gas artillery shells. The First Gas Regiment had another version, a Company F bugler writing home that "our collar ornament has two stokes mortars and a dragon curled around the mortars."[8] The regiment's shoulder patch was a simple blue numeral "1" on a yellow shield. When in the field, however, the gas troops stayed anonymous, and wore neither insignia nor unit patches.

The chemical service was authorized nearly twenty-four hundred officers and over twenty thousand enlisted men, numbers that would substantially increase near the end of the war. "The fact of this organization, with half as many officers as there are in the whole ordnance department of the Army, indicates the size of the undertaking assigned to it," the *Washington Star* commented. "In effect it has become practically an independent organization like the Army Engineer Corps and with corresponding powers."[9] The army quickly began recruiting CWS officers to fill the new billets, all around the country, and not among chemists alone.

"The chemical warfare service, which has charge of defensive and offensive gas and flame work, will commission fifty to sixty high class men in the grades of second lieutenant, first lieutenant, and a few captains, for work in developing and perfecting methods of chemical warfare," said an article in the *Cleveland Plain Dealer*. "These men will go to France within two weeks after medical examination. This service is rapidly coming to the front and the opportunities of advancement are excellent." Local applicants were tested in Cleveland, then sent to Chicago for a final test. "The chemical warfare service wants only high grade men with college education and military training if possible," the *Plain Dealer* added. "In the language of the army officers in charge of this particular recruiting, men of inventive genius are especially desired, even though these men may be considered to be 'cranks' in their local communities. This does not, however, mean men lacking in sound education and judgment."[10]

Although popularly known as the gas and flame outfit, the First Gas Regiment did little or no flame work in France. Its primary business was gas.

Like allies and enemies alike, the regiment relied on three primary gases: chlorine, phosgene, and mustard.

Chlorine, the war's first chemical weapon, had a familiar smell in small doses, as it often was used to sanitize swimming pools. "Chlorine was the only war gas produced on a commercial scale in America prior to the war," says one history. "At the ordinary temperatures chlorine is a greenish-yellow gas of strong, suffocating odor."[11] Exposure to high concentration of the gas profoundly affects the lungs, causing pulmonary edema (swelling caused by trapped fluids) that can kill within a day.

Phosgene was similar to chlorine, but five times deadlier. "Upon meeting moist surfaces it is broken up and hydrochloric acid is liberated," a U.S. Army memo explained. "It excites less spasm than does chlorine in the upper respiratory tract, and so can penetrate to the innermost recesses of the lungs, where it causes an irritant edema which may be a little delayed in its development."[12]

Finally, there was dichloroethyl sulfide, also known as mustard gas. It inflamed and burned skin and tissues, clung to clothing and equipment, lingered longer than chlorine or phosgene, and sometimes collected in shallow pools. When German troops began using the gas in July 1917, British Tommies coined its nickname because it smelled of mustard or garlic. The Germans themselves called it *Gelbes Kreuz*, or Yellow Cross. General Fries later described mustard as "probably the greatest single development of gas warfare."[13]

"Mustard gas, the deadliest instrument of warfare yet devised, is not a gas but an amber fluid of a faint, sweetish, not unpleasant odor," said a newsletter for American gas workers. "It is no more volatile than turpentine. It kills by inhalation and maims, or blinds by contact. In one recent attack, lasting fort-eight hours, it was estimated that the Germans used 7,000 tons of it."[14] General Sibert told an interviewer, "Mustard gas lasts a long time; it takes days to get away, and if an area is soaked with it, it is not safe for troops to go in for several days without their gas masks on, and if they stay in any length of time the stuff will go through the clothing and burn the flesh."[15]

The American gas troops had a simple arsenal for shooting gas at the Germans. "We used three kinds of weapons, the 'projector,' containing thirty pounds of gas; the four inch Stokes mortar, firing gas of various kinds, and the cylinder, weighing 130 pounds and carrying from sixty to seventy pounds of liquid gas," Maj. John B. Carlock explained after the war.[16] The projectors and mortars fired gas shells (sometimes called bombs or melons), while cylinders released poisonous clouds. A shell contained no actual gas, only powder or liquid that vaporized when it exploded.

The Livens projector, first used in the Battle of Arras in April 1917, was devised by Capt. William H. Livens of the British Army. It was an "exceedingly crude weapon, the first ones being made simply by sawing off the tops of gas cylinders," a gas officer wrote.[17] Later projectors weren't much more elaborate. "They resemble great iron test tubes, four and a half feet long with an eight-inch smooth bore, weighing some one hundred and forty pounds," says a history of the gas regiment's Company E (largely written by Sergeant Langer).[18] Projectors were short-range weapons, reaching eight to seventeen hundred yards, which had to be half buried in mud or dirt to make them stable.

It took time, stealth, and backbreaking effort to carry the tubes forward and ready them for firing. Scores, hundreds, or thousands of projectors might be used during a gas "show," all fired simultaneously in a deafening barrage. "With that projector eight-inch drums containing thirty pounds of liquified gas were hurled into the enemy trenches by high explosives, electrically fired. Upon landing among the enemy the drums, or bombs, were exploded by a timing device."[19] Gabby Street later said that gas troops could hear shells "knockin' together up there in the air."[20]

The Stokes mortar was another British innovation, introduced in 1916. Gas troops used a version with a four-inch-diameter barrel, up from three inches in the infantry's model. "One can follow the flight of a Stokes bomb just after it leaves the muzzle of the piece," a Company E second lieutenant later wrote, "the weapon is not rifled and consequently the bomb turns over and over on its high trajectory flight, it is thrown more than fired."[21] The mortar was far easier than the projector to transport, set up, and fire—repeatedly and rapidly.

"A Stokes mortar looks like a soda fountain carbonater [sic] with one end open. This pipe is set on its legs and thirty-pound shells of gas or smoke placed in the open end," a private in Company A wrote home to Iowa. "This shell is allowed to slide down at the will of the firer. It strikes a pin and jets toward the Hun with a maximum range of 1,200 yards."[22]

Gas cylinders, in contrast, were one-piece steel containers with valves at the top. When the wind and weather conditions were both right, troops released deadly clouds to waft across enemy positions. "The cylinders usually weighed about 130 pounds and held from sixty to seventy pounds of liquid gas," Major Carlock said in 1919. "We would put into action from 500 to 5,000 of these deadly charges on one front and hurl them simultaneously into the enemy lines. They were used for trench warfare."[23]

In addition to gas shells, the First Gas Regiment fired thermite shells from mortars to eliminate small tactical targets such as machine gun nests. White-hot particles of molten steel rained down once the shells exploded above a target. In a letter to his parents in Pennsylvania, Sgt. George E. Herbst of Company D described a thermite attack on German gunners hidden in barns and nearby woods.

"Now, a thermite bomb is filled with iron oxide, tin and chloride which when exploded combine to form molten iron such as is poured out of a blast furnace," Herbst wrote to his sister in late July. "Can you imagine what Fritz did when about 300 of such bombs came down on him? The effect was wonderful. We saw the Boche climb out of trees and jump out of barn doors, windows and any hole through which their bodies would go. . . . So much for Fritz."[24]

The Yank gas men operated close to German lines, in companies or platoons, usually at night to avoid detection. The regimental history describes a show in early August that involved five hundred projectors in two emplacements, plus seven Stokes mortars firing three hundred shells. One projector position was camouflaged at the edge of a wood, while the other was "just forward to the front lines trenches in wrecked and battered ground that had once been a forest. Though the enemy was not more than 180 yards away, French outposts intervened between us and him."[25] Reaching such advanced positions sometimes entailed long hikes under heavy burdens of weapons and ammunition.

"I have been up to the front a few times and I sure was glad when I got back to my billet. (A barn. Ha! ha!)," a Company D sergeant wrote to friends in Indiana. "Going up and coming out is the most dangerous part of it all, as it is the back areas and roads also the artillery Fritz keeps shelling at intervals and you can never tell where they are going to land."[26] Regimental surgeon Capt. Phil J. Keizer likewise wrote, "We surely have had lots of excitement and one never knows in what shape he is coming back, for there are so many heavy trucks and things on the road all the time, if your feet slip and a truck runs over you, you would be killed and buried all at once."[27]

The weapons, gases, and their many variants had steadily advanced the dark art of chemical warfare since 1915. Chemical warfare was an all-around terrible business. Gases could choke, burn, blind, sicken, and kill unprotected troops and civilians. A first lieutenant from Company A described enemy actions: "The attacks are usually at night or at dawn, and you can't see the gas, and as for smelling it—one good whiff and you wish you were dead, for in gas warfare there are only two classes of people, the quick and the dead."[28]

"The most terrible sight ever witnessed was that of a man dying of gas," said a French army doctor who had seen every horror on a battlefield.[29] The gas masks designed to protect troops on both sides constantly evolved during the war. Again, the United States had successfully scrambled to catch up.

"The American gas mask is, I am quite sure, better than that produced by any other country, and we are continually improving it," General Sibert would say in September. "So our people can rest assured that our soldiers in France have at least as good a protection as those of any other nation.... In the beginning a good many of our masks were bought in England, but we are now meeting the demands of the army for masks for both men and horses."[30]

The U. S. Committee on Public Information assured Americans of the masks' effectiveness. Often called the Creel Committee after creator and chairman George Creel, the far-reaching body was "America's first dedicated ministry of propaganda."[31] The committee supplied domestic publications with photos showing doughboys working and playing in their masks. Articles explained a mask's operation and construction in detail. A full-page ad appearing in numerous industrial magazines noted that a gas mask easily "fits over the head like a baseball catcher's mask."[32] A widely distributed image showed soldiers at the Gas Defense Plant at Long Island City, New York, playing baseball while fully masked.

Sammies quickly learned to trust their masks—they had no alternative. "Notice the gas masks are worn at the alert position like we wear them on the line, and we put them on in six seconds or less," a Company C corporal wrote home during the summer. "Our mask is a better friend on the line than our rifle or the tin hat."[33]

Each mask needed a substance to filter the poisons from the toxic air the soldiers breathed. Washington would launch a program in September 1918 to collect mountains of fruit pits, which were cleaned, dried, and subjected to high temperatures to produce granulated charcoal used in filters for gas masks and respirators. "It has been found that the coal from the shells of certain seeds and nuts, among them cocoanuts, chestnuts, horse chestnuts, as well as peach stones, has a much greater power of absorbing poisonous gases than ordinary charcoal from wood," *Popular Science Monthly* explained.[34]

"The Government needs carbon," said one of countless newspaper articles about the push. "It asks the boys and girls of America to save: Peach pits, apricot pits, plum pits, cherry pits, prune pits, hickory nuts, walnuts, butternuts and shells of these nuts. . . . Two hundred peach pits or seven pounds of nuts produce enough carbon for one gas respirator. Carbon is made from fruit stones and nut shells."[35]

American authorities hoped to collect a hundred million pounds of shells and fruit stones. The Boy Scouts, Campfire Girls, the Red Cross and other organizations, along with children and adults around the nation, rallied to the call, with stores in cities and towns everywhere serving as collection points.

"We are told, that six or seven years ago the women and children of Germany collected the stones of fruit and shells of nuts, in order to have them converted into carbon for the making of gas masks," a large department store in Bridgeport, Connecticut, said later in a newspaper ad. "This proves how carefully Germany got ready for this war. We must be equally industrious here to gather the materials in the same way for the protection of our own soldiers."[36] An Omaha store commented in another ad, "Women's war work clubs or associations can render very valuable help to the government by appointing 'Peach Stone Committees' and using every means to collect as many stones as possible."[37]

Early results proved disappointing. "The people, because of the smallness of the task asked them, failed to realize its importance and did not respond well to the appeal made during the fruit season," the Associated Press reported the first week of November 1918. "What the help of each person means is shown by the fact that two peach stones or two large nuts turned in each day by each person in the nation would supply the needs."[38]

Governors in several states declared November 9 as Gas Mask Day for the collection of fruit pits, seeds, and shells. "We are informed that the losses by gas are greater than those by the guns of the enemy, and even when death does not ensue the effects are much more horrible than wounds inflicted by shells," Maryland's governor said.[39] But the armistice signed in Europe soon eliminated the need for pit collections.

7

....

France

The American Expeditionary Forces would be authorized three gas regiments before the war's end, "each to consist of six battalions of three companies each, and totaling about 5000 men per regiment."[1] Of these, only the Thirtieth Engineers/First Gas Regiment ever reached France, at a maximum of half strength, with Companies G through M still training in Ohio at the armistice.

The regiment had a chaotic, disjoined existence. Its three battalions arrived overseas separately, a few months apart, never all to reunite during the fighting. Once fully trained, Companies A through F operated mostly independently, widely separated, sometimes down to the platoon level. No other American fighting regiment was so scattered. "This is the real outfit, it gets more Germans per pound of equipment and cost than any other method of warfare; in fact, it has revolutionized warfare," a senior master engineer wrote. "I feel very proud to belong to it."[2]

Sgt. Gabby Street had left Fort Myer for France in late winter with Company D, which with Company C comprised the provisional battalion. "On Monday afternoon, February 25, at 3.30, the companies assembled with full equipment, and after roll-call, marched to the Roslyn Station, near the Potomac Bridge, where they entrained with neatness and dispatch," the regimental history says. "The train left at 5 P.M. and reached Jersey City at 2.30 A.M. After four hours of waiting and a brief ferry trip, the battalion was reassembled on the pier at Hoboken, and before 11 A.M. had embarked on the U.S. Transport Agamemnon, 22,000 tons, once the Kaiser Wilhelm II."[3]

"The time has come," a Company D private wrote home to Kansas. "Am leaving soon. Do not know what day. Can't write much so do not know what to say except I will be careful."[4] Escorted by armored cruiser USS *Seattle*, *Agamemnon* sailed at 6:30 that evening and steamed eastward in convoy with two other German liners confiscated when the United States entered the war, *Mount Vernon* (ex-*Kronprinzessin Cecilie*) and *America* (ex-*Amerika*). Another Company D doughboy described the crowded conditions in a letter home to Indiana:

> The only disagreeable feature was that safety precautions made it impossible for us to have but little air in our apartments. Our bunks were arranged in sections with 12 or more to a section, usually they were four deep. They had a maximum width of approximately 18 inches. My bunk was an upper one which was both good and bad—good when all were seasick because then I was not below the sick man, above, bad because of the air.
>
> We messed in cafeteria style, men fell into long lines and then passed rapidly by a table from which the chow was served. We ate standing at other long tables. Our chow was not bad—but it did seem to me that we had brought the available liver supply of the world with us and that we consumed it at a very early date.[5]

Agamemnon reached Brest the morning of March 10, the battalion going ashore the next afternoon. "We had a very nice crossing, nice smooth water and very little wind, and I was only sick about one day," the Kansas private reported home. "We landed in an old French town by the sea and it looked very pretty from on board the ship, but on closer inspection proved to be very old. We were marched to a group of old buildings formerly occupied by Napoleon. Our beds are very funny things, will tell about them in the next."[6]

The battalion spent two days in Brest before boarding a train for Langres, over five hundred miles to the east. Arriving on the morning of March 16, the Yanks then marched the last few miles to Humes, a village on the Marne River. There they would receive five weeks' training in offensive gas warfare from British royal engineers.

"I would like to be back in the old place and put in a few nights of pinochle and bridge again; don't get much time for cards here but bet I could outwalk any of you boys," Private "Bun" Bunnell from Company C wrote at the end of March to his old buddies in a Pennsylvania bicycle club. "Can do eight or ten miles in the evening very nicely now with a full pack, and a full pack with side arms and guns and gas masks and blankets is some load to drag. We have not seen any Boches yet but when we get our gas and flame on them we expect to hear ''em fall.'"[7]

Although not much of a correspondent while in France, Gabby Street dashed off a few lines to his old manager back in Nashville. "Skipper Ellam received a letter from the former receiver advising him that he was 'somewhere' about the fighting zone, and next to aching for a crack at Fritz, about to go mad for a chew of tobacco. Sergeant Gabby wants some 'Honest Scrap,' a favorite cud of ball heavers, and the Vols plan to send him twelve pounds of the weed immediately."[8] A Company C doughboy from New York wrote home, "Charlie Street, the famous old Washington catcher who made Walter Johnson famous, is in our regiment in D company. He is some soldier, too."[9]

Companies A and B, meanwhile, had trained extensively in offensive gas operations with experienced royal engineers. "Have not seen any other U. S. troops over here but our own and we are working with the British army, eating British rations, smoking their tobacco and in fact, as far as we are concerned we are the only U. S. troops here," Captain Keizer, regimental surgeon, wrote home to North Bend, Oregon, in early February.[10] Various platoons from the first battalion went into action with British forces in late March and early April, during a large and dangerous German spring offensive.

The battalion suffered sixty-five men wounded, one killed, and one mortally wounded by shellfire on April 9. "Our companies over there have already seen action, and some of the men have already met their end," Sergeant Major Killam wrote to his former newspaper back in Modesto.[11]

"The Thirtieth will always be grateful to the First Battalion for having launched its reputation on a high level, and maintained it under hard conditions," the regimental history says. "And that gratitude can never be separated from our gratitude to the British for having done everything to hasten the day when the American Army could begin to use its own Gas Regiment."[12]

Companies E and F, comprising the Second Battalion, sailed for France aboard *President Grant* on June 30 and landed on July 12. The men of the

Thirtieth Engineers' first five companies (A–E) were all volunteers, while the sixth, Company F, was half drafted men. These Sammies soon would launch their own gas "shows," independent of the British, while supporting Allied and American forces wherever they were fighting along the front that stretched from the Swiss border to the North Sea.

"Am in a different place than I was when I wrote you last, so you see we don't stay in one place long enough to vote or even to pay poll tax. . . . The weather is getting much better now, with lots of sunshine, but when it rains here, it makes up for lost time," a Company C private wrote home to Oklahoma. "It rained two and twenty hundredths inches last night, and it reminded me a little of the flood we had at home when we lived in the dugout on the farm, except that I was sleeping in the loft of a barn last night."[13]

"It was a kind of secret service," a Company A sergeant later recalled. "Even the fellows in whose companies we were attached did not know what we were doing. We were constantly shifted from one division to another so the enemy could not keep tabs on us—sometimes we were with the French, sometimes English, with colored regiments of the French, and with our own American troops." The gas troops didn't reveal their regiment's identity. "We would tell them [we were] with the engineers, or that we were repairing barbed wire or put off the question in some other way."[14]

The gas troops had to overcome traditionalism within their own army, however, which hardly knew how to deploy them. "Our first rôle in this great forward movement [after Chateau Thierry] consisted of the repairing of roads and the burial of the dead—necessary tasks for which no other troops were then available," the regimental historian wrote.[15] A corporal in Company B said in a letter home to Nebraska that "they had us build roads or rather fill up shell holes so that 75s [artillery pieces] could get through."[16]

Col. Amos A. Fries, chief of the AEF Gas Service in France since 1917, lamented that "the first regiment of gas troops was raised under the Corps of Engineers, and what happened? They were put on road work following the beginning of the Marne offensive and only relieved after their Colonel begged that they be given the chance to clean out German machine-gun nests that were killing our boys by the hundreds."[17]

The AEF had its headquarters at Chaumont, which sprawled on a high plateau between the Marne and Suize Rivers, 165 miles southeast of Paris. The town had been "pillaged to death during the Hundred Years war," a major wrote to a newspaper. During the Napoleonic wars, "the prince of Schwarzenburg tried to take it by crossing the bridge [at] Choignes, . . . and after a hard fight managed to get across the Marne and walk in on Chaumont, and take full possession, including the lives of hundreds of the French."[18]

The Thirtieth Engineers set up headquarters at Choignes, some two miles from Chaumont. The Sammies pronounced it "Swang."[19] Historian Sergeant Langer later wrote that "not a few of us were struck by the remarkable beauty of the landscape, for the surroundings of Chaumont, with its wooded hills, green meadows, and the winding Marne Canal are eminently picturesque."[20] The army created what it called an experimental field up a hill from Choignes. More than two thousand American officers would receive specialized training there in defensive and offensive gas warfare on twenty square miles of ground.

"On the field are physiological and pathological laboratories. Trench systems and artillery batteries are laid out. All ideas are tested on a full battle scale," a Stateside newspaper said later.[21] The fifty-plus homely wooden buildings included barracks, mess halls, a machine shop, ammunition magazines, and shops for opening and filling gas shells. Many of the officers based or trained there were college educated.

"It is worth noting . . . that very little of the specific information learned in the university could be applied by these men in their work," a professor-turned-CWS lieutenant colonel said after the war. "No one in the Gas Service, for example, had ever studied gas warfare at college. The experimental and engineering and tactical problems involved were entirely new, no text books existed which prescribed their solution."[22]

Lt. Joe Hanlon probably spent little time at the field, if he saw it at all. Much respected in the regiment, the devout Catholic officer managed to find a spiritual side to army life. He had written to his mother about the prospects of the unit securing a Catholic chaplain. (The Thirtieth Engineers instead received a Protestant clergyman, 1st Lt. James Thayer

Addison, who later became the regimental historian.) Joe said more about his worship and circumstances in a letter to a former professor back in Baltimore.

"Father, even if we could get a Chaplain, he would be able to do little for all of us," he wrote to the Loyola College priest. "We are forever split up, and while some will be in northern France, others will be in southern. It is the special work again, and while it does that, it also lands us near a village for billeting. Thus I have been able to get to Mass nearly every Sunday. An English Chaplain said the Mass in a certain village where I was. I had the pleasure of being his altar-boy. It was quite an allied combination. The church, built in 1664, was French; the priest was a captain in the English Army, and the server, myself, a lieutenant in the American Army." Joe also shared with the priest various details and doubts that he hadn't mentioned to his mother:

> When we first reached France, we spent a month and a half getting our elementary training in our special game. Then we were all parcelled out to other companies; one platoon of us to one company, and have thus been trained more deeply in the details of the work.
>
> In less than a month I have been with three such companies in different places and so, Father, I learn a great deal about the geography of France. . . . A real military decision seems quite impossible to me. Another queer thing that quickly comes to all is the feeling of fatalism. If the bullet has your initials on it, it will get you. So the boys go out, enter zones of danger and are able to laugh at the quips that are all ready to spring. "Getting the wind up" sounds odd to the uninitiated, but it is quickly understood when a man has once been under danger. . . .
>
> Father, remember me to all of my old friends of the Faculty and students, and many thanks for your prayers.
>
> These are the greatest helps, though letters are the greatest pleasure; and may your prayers bring peace to the boys who survive, and peace also to those whose lads "go West."[23]

Junior gas regiment officers like Joe exerted an unusual degree of authority in France. Most other Yank army officers knew little about gas warfare. "But on the other hand when the value of gas troops had become fully known the requests for them were so great that a single platoon had to be assigned to brigades and sometimes even whole division," General Fries wrote. "Thus it fell to Lieutenants commanding those platoons to confer with Division Commanders and Staffs, to recommend how, when and where to use gas and do so in a manner which would impress the Commanding General and the Staff sufficiently to allow them to undertake the job."[24]

On the night of June 18, assigned now to Company B, Lieutenant Hanlon participated in a massive dual attack to support American and French troops in the relatively quiet Toul sector. The Thirtieth Engineers used Livens projectors to shell German positions with over thirteen hundred gas bombs, without losing a man to heavy enemy counterfire. Joe was among twenty-six officers and men awarded the French Croix de Guerre, medals that the regimental history acknowledged were "given frankly for a job well done and not for marked valor."[25] He later wrote to his parents that he had been awarded the decoration, but didn't say how or why.

The First Battalion, Companies A and B, then shifted on July 3 into the Chateau-Thierry sector. The Allies had blunted the German Army's spring offensive with the help of American doughboys and a legendary stand by United States Marines at Belleau Wood. The regiment now expected to launch its first independent offensive gas and flame operations.

"Partly, however, because of the unstable and informal condition of the front, partly because the probability of both a German offensive and an Allied counter-offensive was in the air, and partly because plans for gas warfare seemed to many to be novel and even trivial, no practical opening was given us; and two weeks slipped by with our powers regretfully unused," the unit history says.[26]

Finally, at the end of the month, Joe Hanlon went on another nighttime operation for the newly designated First Gas Regiment. During the predawn hours of July 31, accompanied by a captain from the Royal Field Artillery, he led forty men from companies B and D out from Villers-sur- Fère, on the Soissons-Rheims front. Their mission was to carry forward weapons and ammunition for a planned Stokes mortar attack. Pvt. John J. Twohig of Company B later wrote a long account to Joe's father, Ned Hanlon, about what happened:

We traveled in trucks to a position in the woods about one mile from the town of Villiers-Sur-Fere and prepared our guns and ammunition for carrying into position. The Boche was shelling very heavily. With Captain [J. T.] McNamee of the British army leading the platoon and Lieutenant Hanlon assigned to bring up the rear; walking two at a time and with 30 pace intervals, we passed through the town, which was being bombarded with gas and high explosive shells. It was very dark and hard to see the men ahead. Suddenly high explosive shells dropped very close to those at the rear end of the column. The last men, including Lieutenant Hanlon, were in danger. All except Joe and two runners were carrying 90-pound shells and it was hard trying to get ahead.

Then Lieutenant Hanlon proved that he was the gamest officer in our outfit. Without thought of his own safety he was helping the men to adjust their shells on their shoulders after they had thrown themselves to the ground to avoid injury. He was continually encouraging them to keep cool under the strain. It seemed as if the last 10 men were receiving the concentration of all the enemy's fire. Every time we tried to get ahead exploding shells menaced us.

We crossed a footbridge and were then in the front line. The doughboys of the old Sixty-ninth New York National Guard [165th Infantry, Forty-Second Division] were lying in "fox-holes" in the ground. Some of them told us to take shelter, but we had to press on to reach our position and we soon left them behind. We were to proceed to a little wooded plot in front of No Man's Land. Suddenly the rain of shells was redoubled and they began to fall thick and fast about the last 10 men in the line.

As the first shell exploded Private [George T.] Panuska fell forward saying, "Oh, my God! I am hit." Then Private [Harry H.] Guilefuss was killed. Lieutenant Hanlon saw Panuska fall and went to aid him, thinking he was alive. From a lad who was close to Lieutenant Hanlon at the time I learned what happened. This lad was beside Panuska when the shell exploded; he escaped uninjured, but was so nerve stricken that he could not move.

He saw Lieutenant Hanlon rush past him toward Panuska saying, "Men, here is a man that is hit." Lieutenant Hanlon saw that Panuska was dead and ran to help Guilefuss, who had just fallen. As he did a shell exploded very near him and he fell injured. Private [William F.] Fischer, the medical man and I ran to him, bandaged his wounds and tried to get him to a first-aid station.

Joe had already given us proof of being the gamest officer we ever had, but while lying on the stretcher, wounded, is where he gained my admiration. Not once did we hear him groan. He did not fear death and passed out very peacefully before we could get to the dressing-room, a mile away.[27]

The regiment buried Lt. Joe Hanlon two days later with full military honors in the officers' cemetery at Chaumont. A Columbia classmate, serving as a private in Company E, attended the rites. "An English-speaking priest conducted the service and spoke feelingly of the dead, whom he knew personally," he wrote in the university's alumni bulletin. "The service impressed all, and to me, one who had known him for four years in school, it was doubly so."[28]

Joe's was the first combat death of a Chemical Warfare Service officer. Calling him "an officer of unusual promise, great ability and high ideals, and one who, while every inch a soldier, was loved by all who knew him," the army changed the name of the experimental field at Choignes to Hanlon Field.[29] Ned Hanlon, the dead officer's father, was a park commissioner in Baltimore. In 1920, the city would rename a hundred-acre city park in Joe's honor.

The lieutenant's death "was a loss that hurt keenly," the regimental history says. Among his soldiers, Joe Hanlon had earned "a greater devotion and affection than were accorded to any other officer—an affection which spread beyond his own unit to the whole regiment. Men, on every hand, were prompt to say and to write of how deeply they felt so sudden a loss."[30] A private first class in Company B later remembered Joe as "a soldier and a man, courageous and helpful, admired, and respected and followed by all—a man among men."[31]

Fig. 1. Charles "Gabby" Street, catcher, Washington Senators,
1910. Courtesy Library of Congress, Bain News Service
photograph collection, LC-DIG-ggbain-07988.

Fig. 2. Sgt. Gabby Street
before going overseas.
Author's collection.

Fig. 3. Eppa Rixey,
pitcher, Philadelphia
Phillies, 1913. Courtesy
Library of Congress,
Bain News Service
photograph collection,
LC-DIG-ggbain-12267.

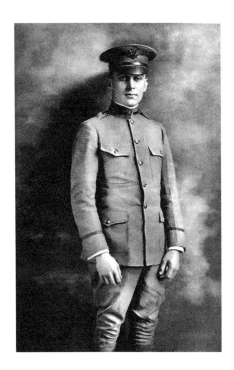

Fig. 4. Lt. Joe Hanlon,
U.S. Army. James Thayer
Addison, *The Story of the
First Gas Regiment* (1919).

Fig. 5. Branch Rickey,
business manager, St.
Louis Browns, 1916.
Author's collection.

Fig. 6. Christy Mathewson, manager, Cincinnati Reds,
1916. Courtesy Library of Congress, Bain News Service
photograph collection, LC-DIG-ggbain-22415.

Fig. 7. The YMCA hoped that Christy Mathewson would head its baseball operations in France. *Cincinnati Enquirer* Archives, April 26, 1918.

Fig. 8. Ty Cobb, outfielder, Detroit Tigers, 1910. Courtesy Library of Congress, Bain News Service photograph collection, LC-DIG-ggbain-08006.

Fig. 9. Percy D. Haughton, football coach, Harvard University, 1916. Courtesy Library of Congress, Bain News Service photograph collection, LC-DIG-ggbain-20818.

Fig. 10. Maj. Gen. William Sibert. National Archives.

Fig. 11. Brig. Gen. Amos Fries, France, after the armistice. National Archives.

Fig. 12. Maj. Gen. Charles Richardson (right), Tours,
France, following the armistice. National Archives.

Fig. 13. Chemical Warfare Service poster for troops.
Courtesy Library of Congress, LC-USZC4–11179.

Fig. 14. Soldiers playing ball in masks, Gas Defense Plant,
Long Island City, New York. National Archives.

Fig. 15. Gas troops preparing Livens projectors; work usually done
at night. Victor Lefebure, *The Riddle of the Rhine* (1923).

Fig. 16. Company C, First Gas Regiment, firing phosphorus and thermite shells, France, October 1918. National Archives.

Fig. 17. Doughboys entering gas chamber, France. National Archives.

Fig. 18. Pfc. Gabby Street, Baccarat, France, summer 1918. National Archives.

Fig. 19. Maj. Branch Rickey's AEF identity card. Courtesy Patrick Kerwin, Library of Congress Manuscript Reference Librarian.

Fig. 20. Capt. Christy Mathewson, on board ss *Rotterdam*. National Archives.

Fig. 21. Capt. Ty Cobb, wearing cws collar insignia. National Archives.

COBB, MATHEWSON, RICKEY AND HAUGHTON WILL NOT ENJOY SOFT BOMBPROOF PLACES

Fig. 22. Authorities countered criticism that CWS officers occupied "soft berths." Author's collection.

Fig. 23. Lt. George Sisler served Stateside, didn't
make it "over there." *Baseball Magazine.*

Fig. 24. Lt. Eppa Rixey (second from left), at First Army HQ, the day after the armistice. National Archives.

Fig. 25. Authorized cws insignia (top) and an unofficial insignia
adopted by many gas troops (bottom). Author's collection.

8

Summer

Tigers outfielder Tyrus Raymond Cobb might have read an account of Joe Hanlon's death. If so, he didn't mention it to sportswriters. The war in France nevertheless had weighed heavily on his mind since winter.

Ty was hardly a youngster now, although he was four years younger than Gabby Street. He had broken into the Major Leagues a season after the catcher, at Detroit in 1905, and had terrorized opponents and thrilled fans ever since. Ty had led the American League in batting average ten times and in stolen bases six. Fans who loved him called him the Georgia Peach, while those who despised him considered him hell on the basepaths. The Tiger lived during the offseason at his home in Augusta, Georgia, near the army's new Camp Hancock.

"Ty Cobb is in Augusta, having returned from a hunting trip to Maine," a local newspaper said in November 1917. "He will supervise the laying out of baseball diamonds at Camp Hancock and the distribution of baseball equipment which has been shipped here."[1] Ty was known to pick up the checks of Sammies dining in town and hand out boxes of cigarettes. He spoke at the opening of a YMCA building at the camp in February 1918 and posed for photos there with the boys.

Along with players on every American League club, Ty had learned military exercises and drills under an army drill instructor in 1917. Everyone had marched and drilled in squads, first at spring training shortly before America entered the war, then well into the regular season. "The Georgian was a little awkward at first, but was game and soon mastered setting up exercises, in which base ball bats were used for rifles," the *Houston Post* said in March that year, as the Tigers trained in Waxahachie, Texas. "If [the sergeant] enforces discipline Cobb will probably be in the guard house tonight, for he cut the drill this afternoon and beat it to Dallas for a game of golf."[2]

Both major leagues had made it through their seasons without major disruption to their rosters. The same wasn't true in 1918, though, when seventy-six players in the armed forces were missing from spring training. Friends speculated early in the year that Ty might enlist in the U.S. Marine Corps. Former Detroit and Cleveland catcher Jay Clarke, already in the corps, visited the Tiger at his home in Augusta.

"He is just itching to get into harness with a gun and bayonet or cheese knife and get at the Germans," Clarke said. "He kept me busy showing him all the bayonet exercises and manual of arms, always watching me like a hawk."[3] Ty, he added, planned to visit him the following week at the marines' training base at Parris Island, South Carolina.

But with a wife and young children, Ty wasn't yet prepared to exchange his baseball flannels for khakis, nor was he obliged to do so. He denied reports that he would soon join up. "The Georgia Peach stated today that he may enter the army late in the summer or next fall but does not contemplate joining the marines," the *Detroit Free Press* said in early January.[4] Later that month his Georgia draft board classified him Class 1-I, the lowest category in the highest of five draft classes. In other words, Ty was listed among the last of the first to go.

"It is probable, however, that Cobb will not be called soon, for it is held that those who have reached 31 since registering and have not been called shall be exempted temporarily," the *Augusta Herald* said. "Ty will be excluded from the next call, as he was 31 on December 18th, last."[5] Ty returned to the board several days later to contest his classification.

"In passing on his questionnaire the board discovered that although he had classified himself in Class Two he had failed to answer the questions as to dependency," the *Herald* said. "Cobb told the board yesterday that this was due to a misunderstanding and asked that his case be re-opened."[6] The board accepted his explanation and dropped Ty down into Class 2-A. He might still be called, but no time soon.

The Georgia Peach didn't enlist in the marines, but his younger brother did. Paul Cobb signed up with the "devil dogs" in late April 1918. A career

Minor Leaguer, Paul soon began playing ball on a very good Marine Corps team, whose roster also included Clarke, Cardinals captain and infielder Dots Miller, and ex-Yankee and future Phillie Mike Cantwell. Their club played numerous games over the summer in Washington DC. Paul and his teammates would ship out for France in October 1918 with the Eleventh Marine Regiment, Fifth Marine Brigade, too late to see combat.

Perhaps Ty feared being sidetracked while in the armed forces, as Paul was. Many popular big leaguers in the army, navy, and marines (but certainly not all) played safely on service teams across America. Understandably, the war and navy departments used these men to boost military and civilian morale, and as part of recruiting efforts. But if he enlisted, Ty wanted to be assigned to a combat unit.

The government in late May 1918 issued a "work or fight" order, which required most draft-age American males either to serve in the military or take work-related jobs. One big question was if and when the ruling applied to professional baseball.

"I am ready to answer when Uncle Sam calls," Ty said in June, when it appeared the leagues might soon lock their turnstiles. "But I hate to see baseball pass out. Don't think this will happen if I should be called, or that they will have to close the gates. They played before I started and will continue after I am gone." He added:

> "But baseball should not be stopped because of the war. There will be many left here, and they will want to go to the games to forget the horrors of the war and also to get some fresh air. Baseball players are public entertainers and are essential to the country, and our national pastime should be continued. But when players are called they should answer their country's call."[7]

After considerable wrangling and uncertainty, the work-or-fight rule would bring an early end to the regular season, followed by a World Series in September. The Tigers rolled into Washington in mid-July for a series with the Senators. Ty had made a decision, which he announced not in the dugout, locker room, or press box. He spoke instead to journalists at the

White House, while visiting Joseph P. Tumulty, President Wilson's private secretary. Ty told the press there he planned to enlist at the end of the season. The news made the front page of that evening's *Washington Times*.

"Every time I look at the American casualty lists I feel mean," the Georgian said at the executive mansion, his eyes misting. "I am in a deferred class of the draft because I have a wife and three children, but I feel that I must give up baseball at the close of the season and do my duty to my country in the best way possible. Baseball is good for the entertainment and morale of the people, and I love the game, but the close of the coming season will see me out of it until the war is over."[8] Ty didn't say—and perhaps didn't yet know—what the best possible military service meant for him.

Two weeks after Ty's announcement, the *Boston Globe* reported that Percy D. Haughton, of 364 Washington Street, Boston, had been commissioned a major in the army's Chemical Warfare Service. For the uninitiated, the paper explained elsewhere that the new officer was "P. D. Haughton, the old Harvard football coach, and now president of the Boston [Braves] National League Baseball Club."[9]

The fellow pinning a major's insignia onto his collar was an unusual baseball man. Haughton was far better known as a collegiate gridiron coach than a Major League executive. Standing six feet one inch tall and weighing 180 pounds, recently turned forty-two years old, the new major had a wife, a young daughter, and two older stepdaughters. With a broad open face and an amiable expression, he looked like the golfing and racquets champion he also was.

Haughton was born in Staten Island, New York, and reared in tony Brookline, Massachusetts. He starred in football and baseball at Harvard University, class of 1899. He afterward succeeded Glenn S. "Pop" Warner as head football coach at Cornell University, where his record was 17-5 over two seasons. Haughton then returned to Boston, where he became a banker and helped coach the Harvard football team. In 1908, the school named him head coach. He got no pay and continued working as assistant secretary of a city trust company. By the time he finished at the university, he not only would receive a salary, but a hefty one.

"Haughton's career as Harvard's football coach stands out as has the career of no individual in the football history of any college or university in the country," the *Boston Post* said later. "Until his advent as the Crimson's coach Harvard's football prestige was almost always at a very low ebb, particularly as it concerned the Harvard-Yale contests."[10] Biographer Dick Friedman writes, "During the next nine seasons in Cambridge, his ability to divine exactly the right moment to insert a substitute or trot out a special play would be instrumental in bringing him a 71-7-5 record and three national championships."[11]

Harvard players were intensely loyal to Coach Haughton. "He had three qualities to a remarkable degree—thoroughness, imagination and leadership," one said. Another recalled his sense of humor. Once, when a scrimmager suffered a bloody nose, Haughton shouted, "That's it! That's what we want—blood! You can't play this game without blood. It's good for you." When a player then accidentally trod on his toe, the coach grabbed his shoe and cried in mock anguish, "God! Fellows, this is a rough game! What do you want to play it for anyway!"[12]

In January 1916, Haughton joined a syndicate of local businessmen who purchased the Boston National League club that had won the World Series in 1914. His only recent baseball experience had been as temporary, unpaid coach of the Harvard nine in spring 1915. "PERCY HAUGHTON BUYS BRAVES," the *Boston Globe* proclaimed—which, while not strictly accurate, made a fine page 1 headline.[13] Haughton was elected club president. "If the Braves and Harvard win the baseball and football championships next fall," *New York Tribune* sportswriter Grantland Rice wrote, "Percy Haughton will have to be crowned Sporting Emperor of the U.S.A. There will be no one else even close enough to be ranked second."[14]

"While I had charge of football, I was probably a bit distant and uppish," the new Braves chief told scribes. "That's all past now, however. I realize that I am a servant of the public and having invested all the money I could scrape together, I am naturally out to do what I can for everybody."[15]

Neither the Braves nor the Crimson won a championship that year, but the Braves played well and finished third in the National League behind Brooklyn and Philadelphia. Heavily involved with the front office, Haughton left field operations to Braves manager George Stallings. He didn't return to the Harvard eleven until October 1916, taking a large cut to the $15,000 salary he had earned a year earlier. The Crimson had a disappointing 7-3 season playing mostly for field coach Leo Leary, losing to archrival Yale University for the first time during Haughton's tenure.

Harvard and other universities canceled their 1917 football seasons for lack of players after America entered the war in Europe the following spring. The school did arrange informal games with nearby teams, "there being about 20 old varsity, substitute, scrub and former freshmen players on the field and 63 youngsters from this year's entering class."[16]

Without a contract with the Crimson, Haughton volunteered to coach the army's Seventy-Sixth Division football team at Camp Devens in nearby Ayer, Massachusetts. The soldier squad scheduled one game at Cambridge with the Harvard "Informals." A Boston sports columnist wrote, "What a strange sight it will be if P. D. Haughton leads the following line-up of Camp Devens soldiers against Harvard. . . . Whoever thought Percy Haughton would be guilty of coaching a football team to lick Harvard?"[17] A mere four hundred fans watched the teams play to a scoreless tie at Harvard's large stadium.

Haughton's Boston Braves performed poorly once the 1918 baseball season began. Headed for a seventh-place National League finish, they were in sixth place and falling, with 41-52 record, when he resigned on July 29. But the record almost surely had nothing to do with Haughton's departure. The war department needed his services more than his club did. The coach had many high contacts within the army, any of whom might have convinced him to accept a commission.

His connections traced back to an army training program begun at Plattsburg (spelled then without the concluding *h*) in upstate New York. It had since evolved into the Plattsburg Movement, a national military preparedness program for business and professional leaders. Theodore Roosevelt, the former American president; General Leonard Wood, the army commander in the East; and many other influential citizens supported the movement.

Thirteen hundred men attended the first Plattsburg camp in August 1915 as the world war raged in Europe without American involvement.

Haughton was a trainee. A Boston newspaper described the eclectic group: "Bankers, lawyers, doctors, merchants, artists, brokers, policemen and clerks will be there. . . . Nearly every polo player and steeplechase rider in the country will attend, also former stars of the gridiron, among them Percy Haughton, the Harvard coach, and Frank Butterworth, still remembered as the greatest Yale fullback."[18]

Plattsburg was a sort of adult Boy Scout camp with a deadly serious purpose. The khaki-clad men lived in tents, marched and drilled across the fields, fired on the rifle range, and went out on exercises and maneuvers. Haughton qualified as an expert rifleman. The camp garnered a lot of attention around the country with the Harvard coach's picture running in many newspapers identifying him as a Plattsburg rookie. "Percy D. Haughton, Famous Football Coach, Now a Rookie at Plattsburg," read the headline. The caption below told readers:

"He is an apt soldier, with plenty of 'push' in him instilled by his long experience on the football field. The famous football hero is seen here pulling on a tent rope at the Military Instruction Camp, where he is being taught the rudiments of a commanding volunteer."[19]

Haughton told an army officer later that the experience had helped improve his Crimson football team. "We never really knew at Harvard what discipline was until after some of us had been at Plattsburg. . . . At Plattsburg, however, a few of us learned that orders are meant to be obeyed, and we learned, too, how to impress that fact upon others."[20] He echoed those sentiments that December at a large preparedness meeting of Harvard men.

Plattsburg became an officers' training camp after America entered the war. It was no surprise that the war department wanted Haughton as a gas officer in 1918—certainly, he had much to offer the army. His coaching methods alone were invaluable. "Why, our scouting system in football was nothing more or less than a polite espionage system," he once said. "The more you elaborate the more you realize the similarity between football and war."[21] Sportswriter Grantland Rice, an artillery officer in France during 1918, had described what was called the "Haughton System" in November 1916. Anyone reading it again nearly two years later would have realized why the army wanted someone like Haughton on the front lines. Rice might almost have composed the piece for a manual on military tactics:

> The bulk of [the system] amounts to this—to launch a deceptive attack, so well covered that no defense can be braced to meet the rush.
>
> An eleven might face Harvard with a strong, powerful defense. But unless this defense was also exceedingly alert and quick to diagnose a play, it would be of little value.
>
> For Haughton puts through few direct, non-deceptive plays. There is, in most cases, a threat one way and a rush the other. And to vary this he uses the direct attack only often enough to keep the guessing contest under way.
>
> In this manner Haughton prevents any defense from becoming set for his charge. He always takes away quite a bit of any opposing aggressiveness, for there is no great elation in charging forward to spill a play when one has a hunch that he is probably charging in the wrong direction. The moment a defense becomes bewildered, its efficiency is destroyed. For, after this, it will probably fail to charge forward in any direction at all. No man in football has developed this combination of threat and deception upon attack as well as the Harvard mandarin. In this respect, at least, he has no equal. . . .
>
> A team can fight doggedly enough against a powerful attack that is driving in straight and hard. But an attack that bewilders more than it overwhelms is sure to do far greater damage.[22]

Haughton's teams could adapt to changing conditions as well as attack. Harvard once played a home game versus the fabled Carlisle Indian Industrial School from Pennsylvania. The school's backfield players had sewn pads onto their jerseys in the exact shape and color of a football—a clever tactic that violated no known rule. It was difficult for a defending team to know who had the ball. Haughton, however, ignored suggestions to protest. "The home team, however, which furnished the ball for the game, in due course produced a ball painted black, against which also no specific rule could be found."[23] Carlisle removed their pads and lost.[24]

A postwar piece by St. Louis sportswriter John Wray also indicated, if unintentionally, another reason why someone with Haughton's skills was so valuable to the CWS. "'Haughton's system,' was merely organization and attention to detail," Wray wrote. "It involved alumni help in obtaining material—a nation-wide recruiting force which kept in the Cambridge confines the finest lot of football talent that could be gleaned from the East and Middle West."[25]

Haughton's exceptional connections, in sports and other fields, likewise helped the war department reach the caliber of men it most wanted as gas and flame officers. He resigned as Braves president two days after the announcement of his commission.

"Major Haughton will report at once in Washington to assume his duties with the National Army chemical warfare service, in which he was recently given a commission," a wire service said. "He expects to be assigned overseas in the near future."[26] He later attended a special meeting of the National League club presidents on August 2 in New York. "Haughton, who appeared in the uniform of a major, stated that he was taking the opportunity to bid his former fellow magnates good-by, as he was taking up his military duties."[27]

New York City became the center of CWS officer recruitment. Maj. Charles E. Richardson headed the effort there, although initially his name was withheld from the public.

"There is an uncommonly modest major with an office at 19 West Forty-fourth Street, who since July 15 has been recruiting officers for this branch," *New York Tribune* sportswriter Louis Lee Arms later wrote. "So successful has he been that the roster of the officers who are to be, or have been, sent overseas might be fictionally utilized for a modern Knights of the Round Table." Arms added:

"We got most of the men we went after," said the major, much as a college senior and moving spirit in fraternity life might speak. The

major, and we are pledged not to mention his name, then produced
a list of officers that have been recently inducted into service. One
glance at it was sufficient to prove that from now on the activities
of the Chemical Warfare Service in faraway France will be closely
followed by professional and amateur sport fans.[28]

Christy Mathewson had now made up his mind to enlist. He paid a quiet
visit to West Forty-Fourth Street while the Reds were in New York during
early August for a series with the Giants. The CWS office occupied the
same building as publisher Henry Holt & Company; the back door to the
Harvard Club was only a short way up the street. Matty never said whether
someone had directed him to the address or if he had gone on his own.

General Fries had dispatched a staff officer from France to the United
States in May to recruit technical personnel as gas officers. Major Richardson followed the next month to recruit nontechnical men like Matty
for the service. Fries later described Richardson's mission:

> What was wanted were good live men for staff positions with Divi-
> sions, Corps, and Armies. Men with experience in dealing with and
> handling other men were not only highly desirable but absolutely
> necessary. Men charged with the training of troops in Gas Defense
> did not need a knowledge of chemistry nor indeed of any other
> science. What those men did need was good health, energy, ability
> to handle men and above all to have good personalities. For that
> reason Major Richardson was instructed to take men from any
> walk of life.[29]

Matty was an ideal candidate. Richardson refused to confirm that the
Reds manager was receiving a commission, but journalists already had
sniffed out the story. "The offices of the Chemical Warfare Service are at
19 West Forty-fourth street, and Mathewson called there last Thursday
to make formal application for enlistment," a wire report said on August
10. "The game between the Reds and the Giants at the Polo Grounds
prevented Matty from completing his application and he has taken his

papers with him to Cincinnati, whence he will return them to the officers of the Chemical Warfare Service."[30]

It surely was no coincidence that the Forty-Fourth Street address had another strong connection to athletes. The National Security League, an important organization in the prewar preparedness movement, also had its headquarters in the building. The group had announced the formation of two hundred committees across twenty states in March 1918 to conduct a campaign for physical improvement of civilian men and women. Walter Camp, a former Yale University football star and trainer, had directed the campaign. The U.S. Navy had since appointed Camp as the service's commissioner of athletics. Sports, business, preparedness, and the old-school-tie network all overlapped on West Forty-Fourth Street.

The war was very much on Branch Rickey's mind as well. He was making $15,000 a year as president of the Cardinals, but a sign he had noticed in a downtown St. Louis storefront during the season had humbled him. "Closing up after six months in business," it read. "I am going to war."[31]

By late summer his ball club had lost fifteen players to the army, navy, or marines and another to a job in a munitions plant. Despite opposition from his wife, Jane, whom he often called "Mother," Branch grew increasingly determined to do something in the war himself. "'War overshadows everything,' he must have repeated to himself again and again," Rickey biographer Lee Lowenfish writes.[32]

Branch left for the East Coast on August 9, without telling sportswriters his business there. "President Branch Rickey of the Cardinals, who has been away on a mysterious trip for a week, did not return today as expected," the *St. Louis Star* said later.[33] The purpose of his trip became clear the next day when Branch announced his intention to enter some sort of war work overseas. He told the *St. Louis Globe-Democrat*:

> "I am going to France. I am not saying that with any other idea than that of having it materialize. Whether I go as a private or as one who is engaged in one of the several war activities, I do not know, but I am going. I have been for the past year engaged in an occupation

that the government has adjudged nonessential. Now the only way that I see to equalize matters is to engage in the greatest of essential occupations, namely to enter the service in some way. My wife and children will be able to care for themselves for the period that I am away, so there is no restraint. I am going to France."[34]

"Rickey has applied for Y. M. C. A. work," the *St. Louis Post-Dispatch* added, "but there is a strong possibility that he will switch in favor of entering the service."[35] Branch soon made up his mind. He was aided by Major Haughton, who helped bring other well-known figures from the sports world into the cws.

According to Arthur William Mann, an author and baseball writer who later worked for Branch in Brooklyn, Haughton made a strong pitch. The major explained to the Cardinals chief that Americans were following a Canadian example in involving coaches and other non-engineers in devising new ways to use gas on European battlefields.

"Branch, I've just come from an important meeting in Washington on this very matter," Haughton said. "They have asked me to recommend intelligent leaders to take charge. You're my first nominee." Branch was more interested in traditional combat arms, however, and responded that he hadn't thought of fighting in that way. "You're nearly thirty-seven, Branch, with four little children," Haughton countered. "Let husky kids do the fighting. This calls for brains and leadership."[36]

The major added that Branch could help as well by suggesting other qualified men as cws officers. His arguments carried the day. Perhaps Haughton succeeded in part because Branch as an Ohio schoolboy had taken a congressman's competitive examination for an appointment to West Point.

"There was one branch of mathematics I hadn't had in school, so I took a special course in it for six weeks," Branch remembered years later. "When the examination came, I passed in that subject with flying colors, but found my specialization had resulted in neglect of other essentials. I was the second alternate, at that."[37]

According to Arthur Mann, Branch and Haughton left immediately for Washington. The Cardinal president filled out paperwork there on

August 13 for a commission as a CWS major. Ty Cobb, in the capital with his Detroit club for a series with the Senators, penned a brief letter of recommendation the same day. The Tiger outfielder wrote, having been acquainted with Branch for fifteen years, "I believe he is in every way qualified for whatever commission his judgment may lead him to seek."[38] Branch's statements about YMCA work once back in St. Louis likely indicated only that he was waiting for his application to be approved. The *Post-Dispatch* broke the news to St. Louis fans on August 24.

"Rickey today said he had not been active in seeking an army commission and he believed his appointment was due to the efforts of Percy D. Haughton, former president of the American League Boston team, who is an officer in the chemical section."[39] Following Haughton's example, the CWS's newest major promptly recruited the Tiger star who had recommended him for gas and flame duty.

"As soon as I got in touch with the Chemical Warfare Service in Washington," Branch said, "I found that it offered real action and thought it would be a great field for Ty Cobb. I phoned him and brought him to the attention of the War Department. He filed his application and I am hopeful he will soon receive a commission. I would like to have him with me."[40]

Ty passed the physical exam on August 16 to join the gas and flame service while in Washington, where the Tigers were wrapping up a three-game series with the Senators. "He has been pronounced in perfect condition in every particular," an Associated Press dispatch said.[41] Authorities called and wired his local draft board in Augusta that same day, to confirm his registration status.

Detroit Free Press sportswriter Joe S. Jackson, perhaps unaware of the call from Branch, wrote that the CWS hadn't been the star's original choice. "Ty Cobb's first love was the aviation corps, but he will serve his country in the gas and flame division of the army, because he couldn't qualify to go up in the air."[42] Jackson later added, "Cobb may steel himself now for the surprise shown several thousands of soldiers in the customary remark of a fan seeing him the first time: 'Gee, I thought he was a big fellow.'"[43]

In addition to the familiar names of baseball men, Louis Lee Arms shared a long list of polo players, football stars, track and field men, a rower, and a fencer recruited by the Chemical Warfare Service. One also snapped up was Marion L. J. Lambert, a thirty-seven-year-old St. Louis socialite, sportsman, and businessman who may well have been known to Branch Rickey.

L.J., as friends called him, had been a track and football star at Smith Academy prep school in St. Louis, and later was a keen boxer and big-game hunter. At eighteen, he had overcome his guardian's objections to marry a socialite from Richmond, Virginia. They were now divorced, and his former wife was remarried to Adolphus A. Busch III, scion of the prominent St. Louis brewing family.

Lambert was a graduate of the McGuire School of Chemical Research in Richmond and vice president of Lambert Pharmacal Company, manufacturer of Listerine antiseptic and toothpaste. Shortly after America entered the war in Europe, he and three other well-to-do St. Louis men each donated an ambulance to the American Ambulance Field Service. The quartet also joined the service, accompanied the vehicles to France, and drove them under German shellfire.

The forty-five-man ambulance unit operated twenty vehicles. During five and one-half weeks in the Verdun sector, in July and August 1917, the drivers shuttled sixty-five hundred wounded men from the front to dressing stations and base hospitals in the rear. Upper-cruster Lambert later called Germany "a rowdy intruder at a polite party where the gentlemen present are called upon to bounce him. . . . Our work was mild in comparison with that of the soldiers who stand for weeks in the trenches, the direct targets of German kultur. We simply relieved men who were eager to undertake more heroic work."[44]

Lambert doubtless had an accurate idea of what service in a gas and flame unit entailed, having seen first-hand the effects of gas warfare. "We had gas masks, of course, and wore them, as 60 per cent of our wounded were victims of this mode of warfare," said Harry Blackwell, another donor-driver.[45]

Two months after returning safely from France in November 1917, Lambert got into a very public fight in the lobby of a St. Louis hotel. He slugged an ambulance driver from another unit who had questioned his service. In February 1918, a month after the scandal, the *St. Louis Globe-Democrat* reported that Lambert was now "a student in the School of Machine Gun Fire at Princeton, N. J., in which his brother, Gerard B. Lambert, is a lieutenant. Lambert expects to go to France as a member of a 'Suicide Club,' as the machine-gun squads are known, as soon as he completes his course in gunnery."[46]

The following July, however, the same paper said Lambert, now a member of a machine gun company in Texas, had received a first lieutenant's commission in the CWS.[47] L.J. was the fourth brother to become an army officer, along with Maj. Albert Bond Lambert, Capt. Gerard Lambert, and 2nd Lt. J. D. Wooster Lambert.[48]

Athletes and socialites weren't the only men of interest to the gas and flame recruiters. Sportswriter Arms also named architects, writers, painters, physicians, merchants, ranchers, and chemistry professors. Among them was Henry F. Hornbostel of Pittsburgh, a flamboyant and highly respected architect known for his colorful silk bow ties and a distinctive Van Dyke beard.

Born in Brooklyn of a German father, Hornbostel included among his famous designs the State Educational Building at Albany, New York, the City Hall at Oakland, California, and the imposing Soldiers and Sailors Memorial Hall in Pittsburgh. An aide later called him "the George Bernard Shaw of architecture."[49] His brother was a marine recruiting sergeant who recently had received a commission.

"The opportunity came to me of being an officer in the army, although I was an architect and architects were considered absolutely useless at that time," Henry Hornbostel recalled years later. "Through some curious coincident [*sic*] and the fact that I had quite an imagination—I knew how to get along with young men, of course, I have taught them all my life—they gave me a major's job in the army."[50]

Edward B. Clark, the newspaper correspondent who had written about chemical warfare the previous fall, became a gas officer, too. A West Point cadet before serving as an enlisted man in the regular army during the previous century, Clark secured a commission as a captain in the National Army. Positively elderly for a junior officer at age fifty-seven, he had gone to France and served five months before receiving a promotion to major in July 1918. Clark shifted now into the CWS, as did Lawrence Waterbury, another wartime officer.

A New York City financier and a world-class polo player, Waterbury had first entered the war as a naval reserve lieutenant and intelligence officer. He switched services to become an army captain and, like Clark, a chemical officer. The move was unusual but lateral, since a navy lieutenant and an army captain held equivalent ranks.

Clark wasn't the only Washington insider to enter the CWS. Politicians joined the new service as well; one current and one former congressman got commissions. Both were middle-aged, and neither would get farther than Camp Humphreys before the war ended. To Louis Lee Arms, such appointments, along with those of leading men from business and sports, "serve to show the range of professional life from which the men have been drawn."[51]

9

Final Innings

Lt. Eppa Rixey trained with the Eighth Division into summer 1918 while playing army baseball on weekends and holidays. The Bay Area lost its two professional teams, the Oakland Oaks and San Francisco Seals, when the Pacific Coast League closed in mid-July, but numerous good service teams kept the fans entertained.

Eppa pitched for three teams: the sanitary train, the division, and an area nine called All-Army, which he also briefly coached. He threw the first four innings of an All-Army versus All-Navy game in late July at Camp Fremont. Among his teammates was Private Larry Chappell, former Chicago White Sox and Boston Braves outfielder, now serving at the army's Letterman Hospital in San Francisco. Twelve thousand Sammies cheered the team on.

All-Army trailed 3–1 in the ninth. Chappell, the team's heaviest hitter, was due up with two outs and the bases loaded, but he had already changed into his service khakis. After a rhubarb, Chappell wasn't allowed to bat. A pinch hitter fanned to end the suspense. "The boys at Camp Fremont will probably charge Larry Chappelle [sic] of pulling the prize bonehead stunt of any of the army or navy games," the *Oakland Tribune* said.[1] The game was Eppa's last in Northern California.

The lieutenant received new orders in late July, about the time P. D. Haughton got his commission and not long after the army had shifted all its chemists into the new Chemical Warfare Service. A San Jose newspaper said Eppa's loss to Camp Fremont's baseball team was "irretrievable." It added that "the sight of that towering, smiling cool-mannered giant of the box occupying the center of the infield, is something which cannot be fully replaced. To hear 10,000 of his fellows chorusing as one 'Rixey, old boy!' during the intense moments of some big game, is something never to be forgotten."[2]

The former Phillie was fortunate to leave the Eighth Division. As he headed for the East Coast and France, nearly two thousand of the division's troops were sailing westbound across the Pacific Ocean. These men were the first of five thousand doughboys from Camp Fremont sent to Vladivostok, Russia, as the vanguard of ill-conceived Allied support for anti-Bolshevik forces fighting in Siberia following the 1917 Revolution.

Dubbed the Polar Bear Expedition, the mission would drag on until 1920, sustaining losses seemingly with no clear aim or purpose. The rest of the division kept training at Camp Fremont. Its engineering units would reach France before the armistice, but most of the division wouldn't head toward the embarkation ports until mid-October.

"The journey . . . occurred in the height of the influenza epidemic," a history says. "Many a man was taken from the trains of the Eighth Division to hospitals along the route, and many a one who entrained at Camp Fremont was dead before his comrades saw the Manhattan skyline."[3] Armistice day would find some elements of the division still on the East Coast, never to sail for Europe at all.

Lieutenant Rixey boarded the transport uss *George Washington* at Hoboken, New Jersey, on August 18. He reached the French port of Brest nine days later, a week ahead of Major Haughton. The army's strange amalgam of new gas officers—the athletes, architects, chemists, polo players, wealthy socialites, and others—would somehow work well for the cws. But the arrival of famous ballplayers seemed to surprise General Fries in Paris.

"I was forced to get personnel from the Army everywhere, and not succeeding in getting enough there I sent my own officers to the United States to get personnel," he later testified. "We wanted about 20 per cent chemists, and the rest of them good live men, so that we had men from all over the United States. The officer that I sent over got two or three baseball players, and got quite a little notoriety out of that."[4]

The situation seemed less surprising on the other side of the Atlantic. "An unusual number of players have gone into this service because the first players who were taken in, after becoming acquainted with what they were to do, were asked to name other men of similar ability," explained an officer involved in recruiting.[5] Nonetheless, some Americans objected to the athletes' commissions. The author of a letter to the editor of the *Cincinnati Enquirer* said he didn't intend to cast any aspersion on Matty's character, but added:

> Personally I believe all the ball players and other professional men who are qualified to enter the real army and navy and fight with a gun or some other weapon have a sneaking feeling that they are cheating. . . . Ball players and others of known qualifications who have received unearned commissions to do their bit behind the lines should be ashamed to again make a public appearance. They are worse than slackers, because a slacker is usually rounded up and put where he belongs—but you can't get these fellows because they are "different."[6]

After the war, a South Dakota congressman would seek a special committee to investigate political "pull" in granting commissions in the CWS, Quartermaster Corps, and Judge Advocate General's Department. "In the chemical warfare service," he said, "all of the baseball players, football coaches, polo players, golf experts, mile runners, painters, architects, brain specialists, merchants, fencers and clubmen received high commissions, while the real chemists were fortunate if they could become sergeants."[7]

General Sibert tried to assure skeptics in September 1918 that the athletes would serve in France like everyone else, and that they wouldn't be slotted into what critics called bombproof jobs. "The men were not commissioned because they were ballplayers," Sibert said, "but because they were healthy, live specimens of American manhood and the type of leaders we need in the service. They were not selected because of any knowledge of chemistry, but will be used solely as leaders with gas troops or with organizations having gas administering units."[8]

An interviewer pressed the general about army commissions for Matty, Branch, Ty, and P. D. Haughton. "Can you say what specific duty those men are to perform, or is that a tabooed subject?" the journalist asked.

"Our troops are not chemists," Sibert replied, "—that is, the gas troops are not chemists and the officers that go with the divisions teach the men how to use the gas mask and stay with them through the engagements. These officers are not chemists and it is for work of that kind that these men are taken. They were not taken because they are baseball players; we simply want to get strong, robust fellows that have good average common sense and these men wanted to come in and we took them. They will go over in the gas troops as gas officers."[9]

Maj. Edward B. Clark, the former newspaperman in the CWS, later argued that the army did, in fact, have good reason for sending celebrated ballplayers to France. "These men were known undoubtedly to every soldier in the American expeditionary forces," Clark said. "A gas officer has services of a peculiar kind to perform. It is necessary for him to have the close attention of his men when they are under instructions and it is necessary also that the instructor should be a man well qualified physically to do things well, and in a hurry, and should so impart the lessons to others that they will be equally capable and alert."[10] Clark and others also must have appreciated any professional baseball man's understanding of strategy, deception, and the effects of wind across open spaces.

General Fries later pointed out the breadth of the information new CWS men had to absorb, since "the thoroughly trained gas officer needs a wider knowledge of all military tactics, of meteorology and the topography of the battlefield than any other officer . . . that the weather, the woods, the knolls, the ravines, the wind and the sun must be taken into account, not only with gases in general, but with each new gas in particular."[11]

Although never overtly acknowledged, commissioning famous athletes in the CWS also helped the government make gas warfare more acceptable to the American public. Consider the key figures involved: Major Haughton, the highly respected Harvard football coach; Major Rickey, the equally well-regarded Cardinals president, widely known for observing the Sabbath; and Captain Mathewson, baseball's revered Christian Gentleman. The unspoken message was that these three men would not only keep America's sons safe overseas but would help turn detested and feared poisonous weapons back against the Germans who had used them first.

Add a fourth, more profane name to the mix. During an offensive campaign, who better to have standing beside your son, father, or husband than Captain Ty Cobb, the most notoriously aggressive batter and baserunner in all of baseball? Unquestionably, commissioning such major sports figures for their battlefield presence was brilliant public relations, and it perfectly suited what the new gas officers wanted to do anyway.

Christy Mathewson was busy wrapping up the season before going into the army. The Reds' 1918 campaign would have been difficult even without the early YMCA controversy, since Matty also had faced two other great problems. Pitcher Fred Toney had been one of them.

The tall righthander from Tennessee had won twenty-four games for the Cincinnati club the previous season, second in the National League only to Pete Alexander with the Phillies. But two days before Christmas 1917, federal authorities had arrested him for draft evasion. Toney claimed his wife, child, mother, stepfather, and sister were all dependent on what he earned with the Reds. The government thought otherwise.

Toney's trial in April at Nashville ended in a hung jury. His trouble continued, however, when a federal grand jury indicted him under the Mann Act (also known as the White Slave Traffic Act), for taking an underage woman across state lines for what the law deemed immoral purposes. Toney posted bond and tried to get his job back. The Reds put the hurler on waivers but reluctantly took him back in May; no other club had picked him up, he hadn't yet been convicted of any crime, and Matty's pitching staff was weaker without him. Toney was performing poorly when the Giants purchased his contract in late July, eliminating one embarrassment for the Reds skipper. In a long and detailed critique of the state of the Major Leagues the following month, sportswriter J. B. Sheridan dismissed Matty and his club with a single sentence: "The Cincinnati Reds have not shown a very patriotic spirit."[12]

Matty's other headache during the 1918 campaign concerned Hal Chase, perhaps the best first basemen in the National League. The manager thought his first sacker had been dogging it for weeks, and suspected he was throwing games.

"Hal Chase will never play another game for the Reds so long as Matty is manager or at any other time," the *Cincinnati Enquirer* said on August

10. "His in and out work for the past few weeks led Manager Mathewson to investigate his actions, and he found that Hal was playing very indifferently at times and not going at his best speed on several occasions. He waited until he became firmly convinced of what was going on, and then suspended the crack first baseman indefinitely." The paper added that Matty was "very bitter on the subject. Most of the players have been wise to Chase's methods for some time, and they are tickled to death that he is through with the club."[13]

Matty concluded after the club's investigation that "Prince Hal" had approached teammates and New York Giants players about fixing games. "President Herrmann and Manager Mathewson were busy all yesterday morning in collecting the evidence in the Hal Chase case, which will be submitted to the National League for review," the *Enquirer* said on August 16. "In case the charges against Hal are sustained he will never play another game of ball with any organized club."[14]

The Reds neared the conclusion of their disappointing season. Matty believed his club would have finished second in the National League, and perhaps had a shot at the pennant, "had it not been for the way Chase handled himself during the past two months. Matty could hardly believe that a man like Chase, getting a big salary and possessed of great ability and popularity, would stoop to such methods, but he has the goods and the Cincinnati Club is going to be very firm in the matter."[15] The team tossed Chase from the roster.

The season wound down toward the early end on Labor Day, with the early World Series to follow. Matty had hoped to make a memorable exit by taking the mound for the Reds for the first time in two years. Major Richardson wrote to him on August 19, however, "to notify you that your papers have been put through the Adjutant General's office and your commission should be issued in a few days' time."[16] Events began to move quickly.

His captain's commission, issued August 22, "will interfere with plans that had been made for the closing National League game of the season here next Monday," the *St. Louis Star* said a few days later. "Matty was to have pitched against the Cardinals, while Manager Jack Hendricks of the St. Louis club was to have played right field." Matty sent a friendly message to his new superior officer, the *Star* added. "If there is a chance to have a big game 'over there' for the entertainment of the boys, I hereby challenge Maj Rickey to come out and catch my delivery. I know he can catch just as well as I can pitch, and we'll show the soldiers that the Chemical Warfare Service is the real home of baseball."[17]

Weather then ruined Matty's expected departure from the Reds in Cincinnati. Fans got no opportunity to say goodbye when rain washed out the scheduled game with the Braves at Redland Field on August 27. After the rainout, Matty planned to motor six hundred miles from southwestern Ohio to northeastern Pennsylvania before reporting to the army.

"I'll drive east to my old home in Factoryville, Pa., then go to Washington to start wherever they send me," the manager said as he cleaned out his desk. "I'm not thinking about coming back as a general or with any added decorations. That's just the luck of war opportunities and help from the boys around you. All I'm thinking of is the chance to do whatever I can and do it to the best of my ability. I've had a splendid time in Cincinnati, and I hope I leave some loyal friends behind me. Good-bye, everybody!"[18]

"He will drive as far as his old home . . . where he will leave his boat [car] for use of Mrs. Mathewson while he is overseas," the *Cincinnati Enquirer* said. "He has set a hard first day's program for himself, as he will set out before dawn to-day with the idea of making Pittsburg by evening. This is a drive of more than 200 miles, and he will have to keep going at a fast clip to live up to his schedule, but if the roads are not too muddy from the two-day rain he is likely to sleep in Smoketown to-night. If he can make Factoryville in two days he will be in the same class with Barney Oldfield as a driver."[19]

But Matty first went to the train station that night to say goodbye to his players as they left for a series in Chicago. "The boys all shook hands with him and wished him the best of luck in carrying out his military duties. He said he would watch the Red scores with the greatest interest and would be pulling for the team every day."[20] The clubs would finish the season in third place, behind the Cubs and Giants.

The manager then hit the road for Pennsylvania. Matty, Jane, and Christy Jr., spent Sunday, September 1, visiting his parents' home in

Factoryville. Later in the week they all headed a hundred miles south-west to Lewisburg, Pennsylvania, which was Jane's hometown and where Matty had attended college. The captain's wife and son would live there with her parents until his return from France. "The giant baseball star makes a fine appearance in the uniform of his country and his many friends here were glad to see him."[21]

Matty afterward went to New York City to await a troopship overseas. He visited a small gas mask factory on Jackson Avenue, Queens, on Saturday morning, September 7. "Captain Mathewson was known to many of the soldiers detailed at the plant and soon word was passed around among the thousands of employes [sic] who gave the celebrated visitor the 'ounce [sic] over,'" a newspaper said. "'De chances are that Matty culd tell yer more about baseballs and bats than he could about the stuff in here,' continued the kid whose hangout is near the Gas Mask plant."[22] The youthful skepticism was shrewd and justified. A week later Matty sailed for France.

The St. Louis Cardinals' president had now also departed for duty. Branch turned over the team's affairs to club treasurer Hiram Mason and put his eleven-room home on Bartmer Avenue up for rent. "President Branch Rickey appeared at his desk today in the complete uniform of a Major in the United States army," the *St. Louis Post-Dispatch* said on August 26.[23]

The new major briefly addressed the future of first-year manager Hendricks before leaving town. The Cardinals had finished last in the National League, losing fifteen players to the armed forces and getting a disappointing year from star shortstop Rogers Hornsby, who had feuded publicly with Hendricks.

"I am going to France," Branch told sportswriters. "When I return I will be identified with the Cardinal in the highest possible capacity. I consider a manager's job 90 per cent of a baseball club," the *St. Louis Post-Dispatch* said. It added, "Asked if that meant, point-blank, that he would manage the club, Rickey refused to supplement the statement."[24]

The newspaper inferred, however, that after the war Branch would occupy the dugout bench rather than the president's chair. Hendricks had a son in the army and would soon sail to France himself, as a uniformed athletic secretary for the Knights of Columbus.

Branch left St. Louis on Tuesday morning, September 10, due to report to the army five days later. His family had departed ahead of him. "Accompanied by Scout Charley Barrett and William De Witt, Maj. Rickey's stenographer, Rickey is motoring to Lucasville, Ohio, his parents' home," the *St. Louis Star* said.[25]

The major's family would stay with his parents at their farm at Duck Run, outside Lucasville, while he was overseas. The kids had spent summers there, swimming, riding horses, and playing tag in the barn. Branch's drive to southern Ohio in his 1910 roadster was about five hundred miles, depending on his route. He motored across Illinois and Indiana, through Indianapolis where he had friends, and perhaps as far east as Columbus before swinging south. *Sporting News* described the trip:

> If Rickey was looking for a hardening process he got it en route. It took the major and the scout about four days to make the trip. They got stuck in the mud, they had tire trouble, and they were held up by the no-automobiles-on-Sunday rule East of the Mississippi, something they had entirely forgotten about. Only Rickey's uniform and declaration that he was on urgent war business saved them from going to jail in a cross roads [*sic*] town, according to Barrett. . . . Well, anyway, they got to the Ohio home place, where Rickey had expected to spend a few days, but he found orders awaiting him to come on to Washington and he was away again within a few hours.[26]

"Looking as neat and trim as when he wore an American league base ball uniform, Major Branch Rickey arrived in the city from St. Louis Thursday afternoon," said a newspaper in Portsmouth, Ohio, on the Ohio River a dozen miles below Lucasville. The paper added, "Major Rickey's mission here is to say good-bye to his many relatives and friends before leaving an Eastern port for 'Somewhere in France.'"[27]

The Cardinals' chief was soon on his way again, to report for duty at the Chemical Warfare Service headquarters at Seventh and B Streets

Northwest in Washington. The trip took two days. He took the soldiers' oath to support and defend the Constitution against all enemies, foreign and domestic, on September 16. "And there ends the first chapter of Branch Rickey's going to war," *Sporting News* said. "He has his faults and he has made his mistakes, but may God bless him and keep him and return him safe."[28]

Ty Cobb wasn't expected by the army before October 1. The Tiger great recently had been making noises about 1918 perhaps being his last season. Unlike for Matty, the stars twice aligned for him to end it with something special for the fans. The first opportunity came on August 24 in New York City, where twelve thousand enthusiastic Yankees fans turned out for a doubleheader with the Tigers.

"Perhaps they came out to take a farewell peep at Ty Cobb, at least for the period of the war," sportswriter Fred Lieb wrote in the *New York Sun*.[29] The crowd called for Cobb to make a speech during a War Saving Stamps drive between the games.

"Tyrus climbed onto the roof of the Detroit bench and made a simple, impressive plea for the stamp drive, and when he said that he would soon be on his way to France, he got as big a hand as he ever did for the longest hit that ever bounded from his prolific bludgeon," the *New York Times* said. "Cobb said that he had bought $250 worth of war stamps, and pleaded with the fans to buy and buy and buy. The more they bought, said Tyrus, the sooner the war would be over."[30]

The second special moment came on Sunday, September 1, in St. Louis. The Browns were slated to host Cleveland, but the Indians had refused to finish their schedule and had gone home instead, freeing the date for the Tigers. With Detroit losing the second game of the unexpected doubleheader, outfielder Ty took the mound to pitch two innings in relief. The Browns reciprocated by sending out first baseman George Sisler. The versatile young player fans called the Sizzler had occasionally pitched legitimately for St. Louis.

"Ty pitched two innings while Sisler pitched one, Detroit's half of the ninth," the *St. Louis Globe-Democrat* said. "The performance of the Georgia Peach justifies the assertion that as a pitcher he is without doubt the peerless outfielder of baseball."[31] Syndicated sports columnist L. C. Davis saw Ty off to the army with a poem:

> Ty Cobb says he's through with the pastime forever,
>   But though he's retired and scored his last run,
> In war as in baseball, the Peach will endeavor
>   To lead all his comrades in batting the Hun.[32]

The Tigers then ended their season at home on Labor Day, with a doubleheader sweep of the White Sox. Ty lingered in Detroit for about a week before heading south to his home on Williams Street in Augusta. Whether he drove or went by train is unknown, but he put his seven-passenger 1907 White steam car up for sale soon after arriving.

"Many will be the friends to tell Cobb good-bye before he leaves Augusta for the army, and to wish him all kinds of good luck while with the colors and a successful return after the last inning of the 'world's series' being played over there is won in favor of the allies, and his friends believe that he will distinguish himself on the fields of France as he did on the diamonds of America," the *Augusta Herald* said.[33]

Fans still didn't know whether he would give up baseball once he entered the army. Perhaps he didn't know, either. "Cobb himself is something of a fatalist," *Detroit Free Press* sportswriter Joe S. Jackson wrote. "He doubts that he will come back—but in a sense other than the one being discussed. Perhaps he figures that he will be unable to restrain himself from his old chance taking, and that the battle field will not be so kind to him as the ball field has been."[34]

Ty stayed in Augusta with his wife and children until the last day of September. "This morning the Georgian was saying good-bye to his numerous Augusta friends. 'Good-bye, until I see you again,' he would say," the *Augusta Herald* reported. "And his friends wished him all sorts of good luck for a safe journey overseas, for even brighter laurels upon the fields of France than he won upon the diamonds, and for a safe return 'after the war is over, after the war is won.'"[35] Ty would be in uniform before he learned he had won his eleventh American League batting title.

"With Ty Cobb, Branch Rickey and Christy Mathewson in the gas and flame division it looks like the Kaiser is in for a pretty hot time," columnist Davis wrote at the end of August.[36] The trio would soon discover whether his crystal ball was foggy or frighteningly clear.[37]

Charlie Lombard Cobb, Jane Moulton Rickey, and Jane Stoughton Mathewson, meanwhile, settled in to rear their eight children, who ranged in age from two-month-old Mabel Rickey to soon-to-turn-twelve Christy Jr. They would soldier on alone, without their husbands, none of whom had been obliged to enlist.

10

....

Shipping Out

With Maj. P. D. Haughton and Lt. Eppa Rixey now in France, baseball's other Chemical Warfare Service officers wrapped up their affairs and headed over as well. Capt. Christy Mathewson was next to sail. Some observers believed he, too, might never return to the professional game.

"Matty, even if the war ends suddenly, will stick to army life and strive to rise in his new profession," *Sporting News* reported. "Letters from Matty to a New York newspaper man seem to show that Big Six has little thought of returning to the game. He declares himself wrapped up, heart and soul, in army life." The sports paper ascribed this attitude to the criticism he'd heard over the YMCA offer:

> There can be little doubt that Mathewson was alienated from baseball and made doubly eager for army ventures through the unjust criticism heaped upon him in many papers during the summer—at the time when he failed to accept the call from the Y.M.C.A. These critics panned Matty savagely without in the least understanding what they were talking about.
>
> Matty, even at that time, had dreams of a commission—talked about army aspirations.[1]

The new captain headed overseas from New York City on September 14. He went as a "casual," a soldier traveling apart from his unit. The nearly six thousand passengers on his ship included elements of the Eighty-Sixth Division and women from the Army Nurse Corps.

Matty surely dreaded the sailing; he was horribly prone to seasickness. A storm off Cape Hatteras while headed toward spring training in 1905 had left him a physical wreck, and a day's fishing off Sheepshead Bay,

Brooklyn, could cause him agony. The great pitcher had skipped the Giants' and White Sox's world tour in 1914 because he hadn't wanted to travel by sea. "In sailing for France as an army officer," sportswriter Maj. Bozeman Bulger later wrote, "it took a great deal more nerve on Matty's part than to have gone over the top in the face of heavy fire."[2]

The Reds skipper sailed on SS *Olympic*, a sister to *Titanic* and one of the world's great liners before its conversion to a British troopship early in the war. Gone were the luxurious accommodations and the White Star Line's bright peacetime livery. The liner's hull, superstructure, and four raked stacks were painted now in a crazy-quilt "dazzle" scheme, a pattern of black, blue, and blue gray meant to obscure heading and speed from any stalking German U-boat. The ship's best defense against a torpedo attack, however, was speed—*Olympic* could dash across the Atlantic without a convoy, escorted only by a few equally quick destroyers.

Some transports sailed directly to France. Others went to Liverpool, where the troops disembarked and entrained for England's southern coast, there to board other ships for the short crossing to France. *Olympic* did neither, steaming instead directly to Southampton on the English Channel, a great passenger port during peacetime. (*Titanic* had begun her fateful voyage there.) "Landing was made at South Hampton [*sic*], in the evening of the twenty-first, during a heavy rain," a newspaper reported.[3]

At first Matty seemed fortunate to sail on such a large, stable vessel. Unluckily, as the government said later, "a severe epidemic of influenza . . . blazed out during the last days of the voyage."[4] The Great Britain Ministry of Health said *Olympic* landed "573 cases of influenza and pneumonia; within a week about 1,000 fresh cases occurred among the troops that had come by the 'Olympic.' There were about 300 deaths in connection with the outbreak among the American drafts landed from this vessel."[5]

One of the casualties was Cornelia Elizabeth Thornton, the first U.S. nurse to die following America's declaration of war. Authorities moved *Olympic's* ailing passengers to nearby army hospital camps and quarantined the others on board for a few days. Matty finally was allowed to cross to France, where he also fell ill. Sgt. George V. Christie, a former *Brooklyn Eagle* sportswriter, found him hospitalized at Base Hospital No. 15 at Chaumont.

"Matty must be addressed as 'Captain,' though I confess he looked more like a big boy in bed for punishment," Christie wrote. The pair chatted about the ballplayers serving in France and joked about the conversion of Ebbets Field, home of the Brooklyn Dodgers, into a government cold storage plant for the duration of the war. Matty said he had seen none of the Chicago Cubs–Boston Red Sox World Series before leaving America.

"No, I was in Washington and New York and all around," the captain said. "I didn't have much chance to look in on them. One thing, though. Cincinnati finished third, you know, and there is still a couple of hundred dollars coming to me for that. They let the first, second, third and fourth teams in on the prize money last season, and my boys were in on the deal." Sergeant Christie's story minimized the danger of Matty's illness, which had killed so many fellow passengers from *Olympic*:

> Aside from his little cold, the big manager of the Reds looks in prime fettle. I cannot tell you of his work, or anything like that, but he seems on edge to get to it again. He is a hero among the sick and wounded officers here, and for that matter, the boys are pretty much excited about having him around.[6]

The illness kept Matty hospitalized for eight days. Jane Mathewson would repeatedly mention his bout of influenza as her husband coped with another serious illness a few years later. The seasickness that he had dreaded before boarding *Olympic* would have been easier on his body than the flu, which ravaged fighting forces on both sides of the front in Europe and killed millions of civilians across the world. But Matty apparently didn't reveal his health troubles to his family back home.

"Relatives of Christy Mathewson in Pennsylvania last week received brief letters from him," a Cincinnati newspaper said in late October, "to the effect that he had arrived safely in France without having any particular experiences, and that he was already taking 'lessons' in chemical warfare work."[7]

Maj. Branch Rickey departed for France on September 23 from Hoboken, New Jersey, a main troop embarkation port. He sailed on board *President*

Grant, which earlier had transported the Thirtieth Engineers' first battalion. "Rickey said he had arrived in New York from Washington with the understanding that he would have three days in which to purchase some necessary equipment and say goodbye to friends, but he was met there with orders to sail the next day, so he was writing a few notes of farewell before hustling to the dock."[8] He lacked time even to write a goodbye letter to his wife in Ohio.

Branch's experience at sea proved far worse than Matty's. "Three days into the weeklong voyage to Europe, the dreaded influenza bug swept through the ship. . . . Rickey was one of the ailing soldiers. He grew delirious and was placed on an upper deck of the ship, kept away from his fellow servicemen," writes Rickey biographer Lee Lowenfish.[9]

The convoy steamed slowly across the Atlantic to Saint-Nazaire, France. Of nearly twenty-five thousand passengers on board eight transports that arrived there on October 6 and 7, almost three thousand suffered from flu during or within five days after the voyage. More than five hundred died, including 130 on *President Grant*. The navy buried their bodies at sea rather than return them to the United States, for lack of embalming fluid. A sailor on one transport watched as the weighted canvas sacks were solemnly dropped into the Atlantic as the convoy neared France.

"I confess I was near to tears, and there was a tightening around my throat," he wrote. "It was death, death in one of its worse forms, to be consigned nameless to the sea."[10] The government said later that the death rate was "without parallel, and . . . will give an idea of the gravity of the situation and the severity of the influenza epidemic at the time."[11]

Branch felt relatively lucky, though. A ship's doctor examined him at sea and diagnosed pneumonia, which often followed influenza. "And you're going to get well," the medico added.[12] The major was carried ashore at Saint-Nazaire on a stretcher and admitted to a British hospital, a story that according to biographer Lowenfish he didn't share with his wife for decades afterward. If accurate, Jane apparently had no access to St. Louis newspapers in isolated little Lucasville. The *Star* and the *Post-Dispatch* both printed portions of an October 18 letter that her husband sent to Cardinals treasurer Hiram W. Mason from a hotel in Tours.

"I have been in the hospital three weeks—bronchial pneumonia. . . . I became quite ill the first day on the boat, was in the hospital from that day until a couple of days ago," Branch wrote. The major's legs were so weak he could walk only about a block, but he didn't feel that fate was against him; he wrote that "if you knew how fatal this influenza-pneumonia has been you would understand how very fortunate I have been."[13]

Branch added elsewhere, "After I regain my strength, which I expect to do within a week, I will be on my way to my training school. It is a hard, bitterly hard course ahead of me and I must master the work within six weeks. . . . Maj. Percy Haughton is now at the front, while Mathewson is in a hospital somewhere over here. Capt. Cobb has not yet shown up."[14]

The army planned to give Captain Mathewson and Major Rickey most of their gas training in France, but ordered Capt. Ty Cobb to Camp Humphreys, Virginia, which today is called Fort Belvoir. The new installation sprawled beside the Potomac three miles below George Washington's home at Mount Vernon.

"Tyrus Cobb, the Mary Pickford of the baseball world, is expected to transfer his activities from the diamond to the strenuous life of an army training camp early this week," the *Washington Post* said in late September. "The celebrated center fielder of the Detroit baseball team is due to arrive at Camp Humphreys, near this city, within a day or two, it is reported."[15] A Virginia paper added, "Already there are some of the leading stars of the country in their line at this big camp. Cobb, however, will be the first of the baseball stars to take up training at this camp."[16]

But the new captain, being Ty Cobb, had other ideas. "If I go to Camp Humphreys, I may be immured there for six months and miss all the fun overseas," Ty said. "So I've asked to be sent to New York for a brief stay before being shipped directly to France."[17] The Tiger star was more expansive in a Washington DC interview with sports editor Robert W. Maxwell of the *Philadelphia Public Ledger*:

That report about my going to Camp Humphreys is all wrong. I'm not going there because it would take months to finish the course.

I object to that. I joined the army to fight and do my bit, and the sooner I get "over there" the better I will feel. I am ready and anxious to see active service, and would rather resign than stay in this country while the fighting is going on.

I expect to be in France within three weeks or a month. I have been ordered to go to New York for further training and it will be only a short time before I sail.

I am in the field offensive service and my work has to do with the practical application of gas on the enemy. We first study the lay of the land and then determine the method of applying the gas to the enemy. It's very interesting work and I enjoy it. The officers are kind and considerate and are taking special pains to teach me the work properly.[18]

Ty got his way. "If Capt. Cobb makes as good an officer as he was a ball player, the war ought to be over by Christmas," a syndicated sportswriter chirped.[19] As he prepared for overseas duty, the Tiger met a doughboy who earlier had assisted Lieutenant Rixey and Captain Mathewson before they shipped out. "I fitted all three with gas masks, as I had charge of the 'gas chamber' in Long Island City, N.Y.," the man wrote to a Philadelphia newspaper more than forty years later. "This is possibly information you may not know concerning these three fine gentlemen."[20]

Ty sailed from New York three weeks after Major Rickey on board the British transport RMS *Baltic*. This same small liner had delivered General Pershing and his staff to England in June 1917, soon after America entered into the war. Among the nearly 2,500 troops on board *Baltic* were elements of the Thirty-Fourth Division, including an ambulance company from Waterloo, Iowa. Having learned from its disasters the previous month, the army had lowered the number of men sailing on each ship and held back some units before letting them embark.

"The influenza epidemic at that time placed that part of the [Thirty-Fourth] division which had not already sailed under quarantine for one month and delayed the sailing of the ambulance company until Oct. 12, 1918. . . . They were transported to England on the S.S. Baltic in a convoy of 13 ships with other units of the division, landed at Liverpool Oct. 25,

1918," an Iowa paper reported.[21] Ty would then have crossed the country by rail, and the English Channel by ship, before reaching the gas school at Choignes during the final few days of October.

Major League Baseball's last gas-and-flame officer almost didn't make it into the army. The circumstances were complex, but George Sisler had only himself to blame for much of the uproar that briefly tarnished his reputation.

After pitching against Cobb near the end of the season, George went East to play for Washington manager Clark Griffith in a seven-inning All-Star Game on September 7 in Baltimore. The stars included pitcher Jim Shaw and third baseman Eddie Foster of the Senators and third baseman Frank "Home Run" Baker of the Yankees. Twelve thousand fans, mostly servicemen, saw the professionals shut out a picked military team representing the Army and Navy League, 2–0. George drove in both runs, one a solo homer to left field.

The first baseman then planned to start work three days later at a steel plant in Lebanon, Pennsylvania. He also expected to play ball on weekends for the plant's team in the Bethlehem Steel League, probably the strongest of more than a dozen steel mill, shipyard, and industrial leagues scattered across the country. Men working in essential war jobs were exempt from the draft, and ballplayers starring in the so-called paint and putty leagues often heard catcalls about not serving in the armed forces. The games nevertheless were well attended and popular with fans.

George was twenty-five years old; college educated; married, with a baby son; and clearly eligible to accept war work. The Bethlehem circuit was sometimes called the Steal League because of the numerous players it signed from the Major Leagues. The league had attempted to sign George near the end of the curtailed regular season, as the *Philadelphia Public Ledger* had reported in mid-August:

Before departing for Shibe Park yesterday to play the final game with the Athletics, First Baseman George Sisler and Pitcher Allan [*sic*] Sothoron, of the St. Louis Browns, were approached by George [*sic*] Kelchner, a former big league scout, now acting for the Lebanon club, and made offers to jump to the Bethlehem Steel League. Neither player would give Kelchner any definite answer, and they both left with the Browns for Washington, where they play today. This is the second attempt Kelchner has made to land St. Louis American League players. They were all willing to listen to the propositions, but none of them flopped. Sisler and Sothoron are two of the American League stars, and their presence on the Lebanon team would make that club a formidable one in the Steel League.[22]

"Dixie" Sothoron stayed with the Browns the rest of the season, and later landed a job and played industrial ball in the Triangle Factory League at Dayton, Ohio. George didn't jump, either, although he promised Kelchner in Lebanon "that should he decide to work instead of fight he would accept employment here and play with the local Steel League team."[23] Kelchner had been known as "Pop" when he had scouted for the Browns and the Cardinals. According to *Sporting News*, he was now an "employment agent for the steel mills."[24]

But Major Rickey wanted George to accept a CWS commission instead. Eleven years older, Branch had coached George for a season at the University of Michigan. He had become a mentor and friend, whom the younger man would call "Coach" for the rest of his life. While managing the Browns in 1915, before joining the Cardinals, Branch had snatched George away from the Pittsburgh Pirates. The first sacker had starred for the team ever since.

Branch appreciated George's zest, a quality he valued in other great ballplayers, such as Ty Cobb. He valued him as a man and a player and had once said he wouldn't sell George's contract for $80,000. "Like Rickey, George had chosen a life that placed clean living, gentlemanly tactics, and sportsmanship on the highest plane," biographer Rick Huhn writes of Sisler. "In his young, energetic performer, Rickey must surely have seen himself, and vice versa."[25]

The major appeared to have succeeded in recruiting the first baseman as a gas officer when George informed Kelchner he was entering the army. "George Sisler has done what a star should do—decided to join Rickey, Cobb and Matty in the chemical service, after having listened to an offer from Lebanon, Bethlehem Steel league," the *Detroit Free Press* said. "This may cripple production, but will win Sisler new friends."[26]

Sporting News added: "George Sisler, who had joined a steel mill ball club, changed his mind and took service in the chemical warfare department. It is understood Major Branch Rickey was influential in getting Sisler a commission and that the southpaw first baseman will be attached to Rickey's staff."[27] The St. Louis-based publication (mistakenly) also had the pair sailing together for France.

The feel-good story went up in smoke, however, during the first week of October. *Sporting News* rolled out two unconfirmed reports about Sisler into one damning article, which was quickly reprinted by newspapers around the country. The story hit the ballplayer's reputation like a *flammenwerfer*.

> Praises sung for George Sisler, former first baseman of the Browns, will have to be revised a bit, in light of later developments. . . . When Sisler learned that he would be commissioned a second lieutenant only, to start with, instead of a captain, and that the pay of a second lieutenant is only $1,700 a year or so, and out of that he would have to buy his uniform and equipment, his war spirit cooled. He turned his back on the service and at last accounts had turned to the prosaic but well-paying business of working in the big Hog Island ship yard and playing ball for "bonus wages" on the side. . . .
>
> Turned down a commission in the Army! Why, there are a lot of youngsters of Sisler's age in this country, with everything that money can buy at their command, who would give it all and sleep in a ditch full of water seven nights a week for one of those second lieutenant's commissions![28]

It was hard to say which charge was worse—that George had turned down a commission because he didn't want to pay for his uniforms, or that he was working and playing ball for a Philadelphia shipyard instead. The source of neither tale was ever clear, but reaction was swift and brutal.

Under the headline "The Manager Always Supplies the Uniform," the *New York Tribune* sputtered, "The reason ascribed by St. Louis correspondents to Sisler's refusal of a commission sounds unbelievable. It is that he balked when informed that he would have to withstand the cost of his uniform, the same as all army officers."[29] Louis A. Dougher resorted to sarcasm in the *Washington Times*. "If this story is true, Sisler should not be blamed over much," Dougher wrote. "He is a professional baseball player, therefore accustomed to being coddled and mothered for six months of the year and feted and lauded for six more."[30]

George refuted both aspects of the story, but his denial took time to filter into the nation's sports pages. The *Free Press* in Detroit, where George was spending time with his family before leaving for the army, led the counteroffensive.

"Somebody in the shipyards, which have gotten a lot of ball players in badly by offering temptations that they could not resist, has more to answer for now, and in a different sort of way," the newspaper said. "There seem to be two somebodies, or two sets of the same, in this case. Lebanon and Hog Island are their residence, and George Sisler the sufferer. . . . Anyway, very shortly George will board a train headed east and south for Camp Humphreys. He has his second lieutenant's commission, and must report by October 10, under order of the war department."

"I was very much surprised to read the article saying that I had passed up a chance to become an officer in the United States Army and preferred to play baseball for a shipbuilding team," George later wrote to the *St. Louis Star*. "As I wasn't near Hog Island, I naturally was surprised to read that I was playing baseball there. On leaving St. Louis at the close of our baseball season, I went direct to Washington to file my application for a commission in the Chemical Warfare Service."[31] Learning that he had been accepted, he said he went to Detroit to await his call and stayed there except for a short trip to Mackinac Island.

The new second lieutenant reported to Camp Humphreys for training in defensive gas warfare as ordered. Some scribes who had slammed him now obliquely apologized. Dougher acknowledged that the Brown had been "placed in a wrong light by some unknown masquerading under his name." Working hard at Camp Humphreys, George was "praying night and day that the war won't end before he can get one crack at the Huns. . . . He denied ever playing with a shipyard team and rightly scorned to reply to the second rumor [about the uniform]. . . . It's really too bad!"[32]

George wrote a long, somewhat rambling piece about the affair later, saying he had studied chemistry at Michigan and had registered for the draft when required. He added that he'd had no qualms about continuing to play ball for the Browns during the 1918 season while caring for his young family.

"But when the season was terminated by Secretary Baker's order although I had plenty of opportunity to enter some industrial pursuit closely allied with war service, in fact was offered a large salary to sign up with such a concern, I determined to enter military service and immediately applied for admission into officer's training." Sisler also explained why he hadn't joined Major Rickey:

And now that I look back upon my experience I regret that I failed to act a little quicker, before luck broke against me. Branch Rickey my old college coach and former employer tipped me off. There was an opening, so it seemed, to get quick action, in short to be sent almost immediately for service overseas. But at the time I was mainly concerned in fitting myself for an officer's commission at which, heaven knows, I had little enough training. And when I decided to embrace the opportunity he spoke of, the chance had gone.

At the time, however, I wasn't greatly disappointed. The end of the war seemed far off and I had no doubt that I should see my full share of it.[33]

11

Autumn

The Thirtieth Engineers/First Gas Regiment fought well that summer, showing the rest of the American army what it could do all along the front. Sgt. George Herbst of Company D described moving into the line on July 3.

"The long train of motor trucks which transported us moved up to the line of fire so quietly that Fritz never suspected our presence, or if he did he did not open fire on us," Herbst wrote home. "On the morning of the fourth, however, we were quite conscious of the fact that some had their guns trained on us and that they meant to make life miserable. . . . One's first desire when the cannon began to roar is to run. But how foolish to run! Can a human being outrun bullets and shells? There was only one thing to do; remain cool and trust to fate for luck. . . . Not a man in the Thirtieth was harmed beyond, being 'orfully skeer't,' Ha! Ha!"[1]

The gas soldiers often reaped what they sowed. "The attention of all ranks is called to the increasing importance of gas warfare," a staff memo declared. "Failure to understand the modes of employment of gas and the necessary measures of protection against it will have most serious consequences."[2] Pvt. Irl Rogers of Company D, who had worked with Sgt. Maj. Killam at the *Modesto Herald* before the war, fell to mustard gas during a German barrage in June.

"Heinie sent over gas shells and high explosives mixed," the former linotype operator wrote from a base hospital. "The high explosive is to scatter the gas. It does—it also scatters anything else it happens to hit. The bombardment lasted two hours and I was in my mask during that time. At the end of the two hours the mask becomes so uncomfortable that a fellow debates with himself whether he will take it off and die at once or keep it on and die by degrees. I waited too long for the former but thought I was due for the latter." Rogers wore the mask but removed the face piece, which let the mustard gas reach his eyes. "You can see that army life has its ups and downs."[3]

Private Rogers regained his eyesight, returned to the line, and survived the war. But like every frontline doughboy, he knew the incalculable value of luck. A third ex- *Herald* employee in the regiment, Pvt. Carl McIntosh, was first detailed to dangerous duties as a dispatch rider. He later reported to a seemingly safe billet in the circulation department of the *Stars and Stripes* newspaper in Paris. McIntosh died in the French capital on October 4 of influenza. He had often corresponded with the *Herald*, which after his death hailed him as "a man among men."[4]

Sgt. Gabby Street was still with Company D. "While the First Battalion was at the front during March and April, Companies C and D had been spending their first two weeks at Humes (near Langres) in becoming adjusted to their new quarters and in continuing the usual drills and 'hikes,'" the regimental history says.[5] Gabby's unruly nature soon landed him in hot water.

"I went over as a first sergeant, but after having a row with my company commander over how to run the war, was reduced to private," he said years later.[6] In the same account, Gabby said he had quickly regained his stripes, only to lose them again. Various records indicate his situation was a good deal more serious. He was court martialed in April, broken to private, and confined to two months' hard labor.

His battalion played a series of six baseball games while in training, the companies vying for a cup offered by Colonel Atkisson. Although Company D took the prize, Gabby likely wasn't in the lineup. The *Stars and Stripes* noted his absence from a ballgame in May, saying only that he was "unable to play."[7] Gabby got into more trouble in June, with a fine and another fifteen days' hard labor. The regiment also shifted him from Company D into the First Replacement Company, informally called Company Q.[8] He rebounded during the summer, and in July retrieved one of his lost stripes with a promotion to private first class.

A Signal Corps newsreel crew filmed Gabby in mid-August at Baccarat, in the Lorraine sector, playing ball with other Sammies while wearing catching gear over his army uniform. He later told *Washington Times* sportswriter Louis Dougher how soldiers had mixed athletics with their regular duties during the war.

> We were kept pretty busy, of course, preparing for gas shows here and there, but we did manage to play baseball. I caught sixteen games last summer [1918] in France, generally near Chaumont, where general headquarters was stationed. We'd prepare our gas and then duck up, say, to Soissons or Verdun, and then come back to prepare some more, generally taking about four days to get ready for the next show. That was when we played our baseball.[9]

John Kieran of the *New York Times* years later recounted a good-natured exchange between Gabby and Hank Gowdy, the Boston Braves catcher who had been the first active big leaguer to enlist in 1917. With the columnist giving him an exaggerated southern accent, Gabby named places he had fought and units he had supported before the final big push in the fall. They included Château-Thierry with the Marines, Belleau Wood with the army's Second Division, and an unspecified battlefield with the Forty-Second "Rainbow" Division. "We was [*sic*] tear gas and mustard gas, but mostly we used phosgene," the Alabaman said. "That was our real bad medicine."[10]

Gabby shifted from the replacement company to Company C in early September and sewed on a corporal's second stripe. He never regained his lost third stripe, but he remained forever a sergeant to loyal sportswriters. The gas and flame regiment now began preparations for a push involving nearly half a million American troops. Their goal was the elimination of the German salient at St. Mihiel, less than twenty-five miles south-southeast of Verdun.

An army historian writes that the offensive would "not only serve as a baptism of fire for the [U.S.] First Army but also demonstrate to the Allies and the Germans alike that the Americans were capable of operating as an independent command."[11] The First Gas Regiment history notes, "Though a gas regiment had never before operated as part of an army in an offensive, we had already won, upon a smaller scale, sufficient experience to make our duty clear."[12]

The battle opened with an intense artillery bombardment at one o'clock on the morning of September 12, 1918. The regiment divided up Company C among the Eighty-Second and Ninetieth Divisions at the extreme right of the line; we don't know which division Gabby and his platoon supported. The artillery thundered and boomed until five o'clock in the morning—zero hour, the time of the attack. The gas regiment troops then kicked off operations everywhere they were positioned along the line, supporting infantrymen going over the top.

Company C alone launched nine "shows"—four smoke screens (two for each division); three "fake flashes" to simulate a projector gas attack; and two real projector attacks supporting the Ninetieth Division, a hundred rounds altogether. The regiment's handwritten war diary says that during the four-day offensive, Company C backed the infantry "by throwing Thermite on enemy's machine gun nests and strongholds, also encircling with smoke screen, obscuring enemy observation during Infantry advances."[13]

The regiment's five other companies were equally active. The operations plan was for the gas troops to launch shows whenever and wherever the infantry bogged down. The regimental history explains why they weren't necessary:

> In these offensives our gateway to usefulness opened and shut automatically. If the infantry were checked by prolonged enemy resistance, we could carry forward in time to help them. When they were not so checked and we failed to keep pace with them, they did not need our help. . . . The Army encountered not merely far less resistance than it had planned for, but even far less than it had genuinely expected. Compared with what might have been, the advance was a "walk-over."[14]

Cpl. Robin Day of Company E later described the fight for an Oregon newspaper. "The barrage, said at the time to be the heaviest ever put over in the war, permitted the gas men and doughboys to advance over wire entanglements, shell holes and wire netting of all kinds," the *Salem Capital Journal* said. "The advance was steady and for five days Mr. Day's regiment went ahead so far of the mess wagons that the eating of regular meals was out of the question. At the end of five days the Huns had been cleaned out of the famous sector."[15] The army declared the battle at St. Mihiel over on September 16.

Two days later, Company C took trucks seventy-five-miles northwest to Les Islettes. The move was part of the army's massive relocation for the Meuse-Argonne offensive, which would prove to be the last great push of the war. Zero hour was set for early on September 26. Once begun, the fight would rage across northeastern France for forty-seven days. "To call it a battle may be a misnomer," General Pershing later wrote, "yet it was a battle, the greatest, the most prolonged in American history."[16]

The gas troops again supported the U.S. First Army, headquartered at Souilly near Verdun. The regiment shifted its own headquarters to nearby Lemme and reorganized the three battalions. Companies C and E now formed the First Battalion, B and D the Second, and A and F the Provisional. The six companies dispersed, as ordered, among various American divisions. Corporal Street and Company C reported to the Thirty-Fifth Division, composed mainly of national guardsmen from Missouri and Kansas. The Thirty-Fifth was known as the Santa Fe division because the troops had trained near the Santa Fe Trail.

Gabby waited with Company C's second platoon near Hill 253. Officers had checked that each man carried a full canteen of water and wore his identity disk. "At the instant of 'zero' . . . our companies, all along the line, launched sixteen separate attacks," the regimental history says. "Two of these were projector attacks with high explosive bombs. All the others were strictly smoke barrages, or combinations of smoke and thermite."[17] A captain serving with a machine gun battalion later wrote a vivid account of waiting for the fighting to begin:

> We got into position about dark and got everything set. Our work was to begin at 5:30 a.m. About three or four hours earlier the artillery opened a barrage and kept it up until 5:30. It was a terrific bombardment, yet a beautiful sight. In a large semi-circle behind us it seemed there was nothing but guns. The flashes were continuous

and put a glow in the sky like early dawn. The light artillery close up and the heavy back of it according to the range of the guns. All the shells seemed to go over our heads and there was a continuous roar and swish. At the appointed hour the machine gun barrage broke loose. . . . The sharp cracks of the bullets mingled with the artillery like tenor does with bass . . . a song of death. There was a gas regiment on the same hill with us. . . . I was talking with one of the sergeants and found he was Gabby Street, the baseball player. . . . After the infantry went over the top we followed them with carts and animals. They went so fast the first day we couldn't catch them.[18]

The gas regiment's official history states that Company C was attached to the 140th Infantry. But the 140th went into the line behind the 138th Infantry, which Gabby and his men helped support instead. He always spoke highly afterward of the 138th, composed largely of St. Louis men. Conditions that morning weren't right for the planned firing of phosgene gas, but the ex-catcher and his men helped lay down heavy smoke to mask the infantrymen's advance. The gas and flame troops then leapt up to follow them. Gabby blew his whistle and bellowed, "C'mon, men! Let 'er go!"[19]

"Vauquois Hill is a huge fortress a hundred feet high and ten times as long, which dominates the country for miles around," says the 140th Infantry history. "The Germans had held it since 1914, it was thoroughly mined and completely fortified. Time after time the French had stormed it in vain. 'Dead Man's Hill' they called it and vowed it could not be taken. It fell to the 138th in an hour, and as we followed them to clear up the ground, we were impressed by the trenches."[20]

Gabby later called the 138th "as fine an outfit as I ever saw, and I was proud to be attached to it. The men were badly officered, but they were real fighters!"[21] After leaving the 138th, he and his men supported the Sixteenth Infantry, a regular army regiment attached to the First Division, the army's "Big Red One." The Sixteenth had advanced toward Cheppy the night of September 27.

"As they were passing along the valley that night, a group of soldiers met them, who had been evacuated from the 35th Division, which was about to be relieved," says the Sixteenth's regimental history. "One boy, with a wild light in his eye, told of the terrors up yonder on the hills, summing it all up by saying: 'Oh, it's one hell up there.' 'Cheer up,' came the prompt response from the ranks of the Sixteenth, 'We were fighting the Boche before the Draft Board ever gave you a number.'"[22]

Many postwar profiles (and an Alabama state record) say Gabby was wounded in action on October 2. But army records indicate that all of Company C's officers were wounded early that day by a gas shell that hit their dugout, and the company was subsequently withdrawn from the line to reorganize. Contemporary accounts and Gabby himself said he fell twelve days later, on October 14. The regiment's official history offers scant details of that week: "On October 12th, after the 1st Division was relieved by the 42nd Division, Company C was attached to the 165th Infantry of the 83rd Brigade."[23] The circumstances of the old catcher's wounding must be pieced together from accounts published months and years later.

Gabby said he was lying on his back in a shell hole, firing with three fellow doughboys up at a strafing enemy plane. The likelihood of bringing down a low-flying aircraft with rifle fire was slim, but Sammies from Company D had already done so twice. "Finally this bird gets kinda annoyed, I guess, so he just swoops down and pours it onto us, and old Gabby is the only one damaged," the former catcher told Hank Gowdy in 1933.[24] According to one account, the German pilot flew upside down to strafe Gabby and his companions.

Sportswriter Bob Pigue of the *Memphis News Scimitar* wrote shortly after the war that the corporal was "hit by a machine gun bullet, which plowed a furrow across his nose. However, the wound is not very deep. To make bad matters worse, Gabby was struck with shrapnel, several pieces of metal finding their way into his intestines. The big drive was at its height when Gabby was hit, and consequently he lay 14 hours before found by stretcher bearers."[25]

Sporting News also reported that "while he was lying on the field the enemy sent over a liberal supply of mustard gas, the effects of which prevent the growth of the beard on certain parts of his neck and chin."[26] *Little Rock Arkansas Gazette* sports editor Henry Loesch added, "He was able to get on his mask, but still he was burned in several places about his body by the fiendish stuff."[27] Finally rescued from the field, the sergeant began a long journey through army hospitals.

The First Gas Regiment's losses during October were four dead, forty-three wounded, forty-nine gassed, and one man missing in action.[28] The best athletes in the outfit were now all out of action: Lt. Joe Hanlon dead, Cpl. Gabby Street wounded and gassed, and Pvt. Henry B. LeFort in even worse condition than Gabby.

LeFort, the ex-jockey who had boxed professionally as "Jimmie Stevens," had landed in France with Company B in January. Like Gabby and many other athletes, he pursued sports while in the army. LeFort also had an unexpected reunion at Lens with a peacetime friend, Frank Murray, who served in the Signal Corps.

"They were separated a short time later when Murray was shifted to Paris. His old 'buddy' obtained leave during the month of February, 1918, to box Benny Marks, featherweight champion of the Canadian forces," the *St. Louis Star* said later. "The bout was staged in the French capital, and naturally Murray had to serve in Le Fort's corner at the Palace De Grace. Le Fort won the battle easily, putting his opponent away in 1 minute and 32 seconds."[29]

The tough little gas soldier afterward hung up his gloves, to begin the far deadlier fight at the front. LeFort took several hard blows from the Germans. He was "gassed at Chateau Thierry, stopped a bullet's flight at Lens, picked up a piece of shrapnel in the Argonne and got in the way of a shell at Verdun. He came home a hero, but a badly battered wreck," the *Star* said. "He spent months in hospitals and time after time was given up as lost, but on each occasion managed, somehow, to avoid the military funerals which were being planned."[30] LeFort mentioned none of his injuries in a letter to friends back in Kansas shortly before the war's end.

"This is one of the most active and aggressive branches of the service in the army (any army)," he wrote of the First Gas Regiment. "We have operated on about every front of importance in Western Europe and believe me we have accounted for many, many of the kaiser's degenerated subjects. . . . While many, many sorrows and hardships of course is our lot, Uncle Sam sure certainly takes mighty good care of his boys fighting over here."[31]

LeFort went home the first week of March 1919. He returned on the transport SS *Leviathan*, part of a casual company of walking wounded.

Lieutenant Eppa Rixey also had reached the front, although he saw nowhere near as much fighting as Gabby or LeFort. Maj. Edward B. Clark, the former journalist, wrote an appreciation of Eppa for American newspapers, calling him "a fine type of soldier."[32]

Clark met the ex-Phillie in October at General Pershing's field headquarters at Souilly, while waiting for transportation to Maj. Gen. Joseph T. Dickman's First Corps, which was heavily engaged in the Meuse-Argonne offensive. As Clark explained in his long article, the two chemical officers journeyed a hundred miles together across the backwash of the clashing armies.

> Along came Captain [*sic*] Rixey in an open motor with his bedding roll, his gas mask and his tin hat. He had been ordered to proceed to the far front to act as gas officer of one of the fighting divisions. . . .
>
> It was some ride that Eppa Rixey and I undertook that day. It was as cold as France in October knows how to be, as windy as it was cold, and most of the time it was raining harder than both.
>
> I came pretty near freezing, because my bones are not clothed with as much flesh as Rixey can boast. Moreover, I am old enough to be his father, and then some. That day he looked after me much as a good son looks after his father, and this was not due to the fact that I ranked him in the army.
>
> From out of many a hole into which the motor plunged and stuck did Rixey's big shoulder and hard muscles pull us, or rather shove us. He was the skirmisher-in-chief for food, and when night fell and the incoming and outgoing artillery and munition and food trucks cluttered the way it was he who, in the blackness of the night, felt out the course for us and enabled us to get somewhere when getting there seemed impossible.

For a considerable part of that journey we watched the flashes of the big guns on the hillsides. At night we ran dark because of the presence of German airplanes. Rixey found food for us when the finding seemed impossible, and finally, late at night, due to his piloting, we reached a haven of rest in a shell-torn, roofless structure at Buzancey. There we slept in our bedding rolls, he on the floor and I in a flea-ridden Boche bunk. The next day at breakfast we learned that 100 pounds of high explosives with a fuse attached had been found in the basement of the mess building.

Rixey and I separated at General Dickman's headquarters. He went to his division and made good.[33]

12

Choignes

Maj. Branch Rickey and Capts. Christy Mathewson and Ty Cobb had yet to reach the front. They were still learning how to be officers and gas experts, stationed together at Hanlon Field during what proved to be the war's final days.

"On overseas duty at Choignes, . . . the three officers were inseparable and became known as 'The Three Musketeers of Baseball,'" the *St. Louis Star* said later.[1] The trio was a mutual admiration society, each man admiring the abilities of the others. Branch, for one, considered Matty the greatest pitcher he had ever seen, equaled in his estimation years later only by Dizzy Dean. The Cardinals chief, meanwhile, wrote from France that he expected within six weeks to be "in the game as a player, and not a spectator."[2]

Matty and Ty felt the same. The *Detroit Free Press* went so far as to declare of the Georgian, "Ty felt, when he enlisted, that his baseball days were over—that he never would return alive."[3] Although they had arrived at Hanlon Field about three months behind the first gas officers, the three baseball men were no better trained or prepared to perform their new duties on French or Belgian battlefields.

"The first lot of about 100 officers were sent to France in July, 1918, with only a few days' training, and in some cases no training at all," General Fries wrote. "Accordingly, arrangements were made to train these men in the duties of the soldier in the ranks, and then as officers. Their training in gas defense and offense followed a month of strenuous work along the above mentioned lines. . . . The work as laid out included squad and company training for the ordinary soldiers, each officer taking turns in commanding the company at drill. They were given work in map reading as well as office and company administration."[4]

Even ordinary Sammies were extremely aware of the dangers posed by German gas attacks. They saw posters to remind them everywhere they went in France. "Nothing can give a stronger warning than to contemplate them," a wire report told Americans at home. "You cannot approach any of the three fronts in France without reading, in great black letters, on high, broad, special billboards: 'Precaution against gases. From this point do not circulate without your mask!'"[5]

Authorities behind the lines used bells to warn civilians of gas attacks, many of them salvaged from war-ruined churches. Matty, Branch, and Ty would have known all the warnings as they learned their gas duties. The trio was conspicuous among American troops, but received no favors or privileges—except, perhaps, during a few pickup baseball games.

"I have always felt that a man who rose to eminence even in professional base ball as did Ty Cobb and Christy Mathewson, had the ability, energy, and probably the personality to make a successful officer," General Fries wrote. "So far as we had gotten I saw no reason to change that opinion. Indeed Captain Christy Mathewson was making a most excellent impression with every one who met him."[6] A regular army colonel later told sportswriter Major Bozeman Bulger that "Mathewson was one of the best teachers he ever knew, because of the immediate confidence he inspired in the men."[7]

Sergeant Major Killam would recall a group of experienced gas regiment noncoms, training for commissions, who met the two famous captains at Choignes. "Mathewson was the more popular, as he was modest," he wrote. "On the other hand, Ty Cobb demanded the deference he believed was due Ty Cobb. He got it to his face, being a commissioned officer, but not behind his back."[8]

The CWS made good overall use of its athletic stars and officers from other industries. "Someone conceived the idea of taking natural quick thinkers and forming a 'strategy board' to 'think up' new methods of coercing Jerry [the Germans] out into the open for American gas displays," the *Pittsburgh Press* said after the war. "So Tyrus Cobb and Christy Mathewson, baseball artists, and Percy Haughton, football coach, and Henry Hornbostel, architect, were formed into a board 'to wander up and down the lines doping out strategy.'"[9]

The presence of the famous baseball trio in France generated considerable publicity, which no doubt was part of the army's purpose in sending them there. But the key event during their weeks together at Choignes was a gas accident involving only Ty and Matty. Ty described it decades later in *My Life in Baseball*, an autobiography he produced—"wrote" doesn't accurately describe his role—with sportswriter, ghost writer, and freelancer Al Stump.

According to the Cobb-Stump book, published shortly after Ty's death in 1961, a group of doughboys was marched into a sealed gas chamber for training. They were supposed to don their masks once toxic gas was released, but most missed the signal. So did Ty and Matty. The mistake sparked a frantic, deadly scramble to pull on masks and rush safely outside. Ty said in his account that he was sick for weeks afterward, suffering from a hacking cough and a clear discharge from his chest. Big Six, he said, was worse.

"Ty, when we were in there, I got a good dose of that stuff," he quoted Matty saying, "I feel terrible." Ty added that his fellow captain had "inhaled just enough chemical gas to weaken his lungs. It left him wide open."[10] Tragically, according to the book, eight doughboys lay dead on the ground, with eight others injured.

What seems an unconscionable action today—exposing troops to poison gas, rather than using tear gas or some other irritating but nonlethal substance—was commonplace during the war, both Stateside and overseas. Many Sammies described their exposure to mustard or chlorine gas in what they called the Chamber of Horrors.

"We have just returned from a gas mask test," a private from Brooklyn wrote home from France. "We remained in a gas chamber while chlorine was released from a tank. The test was just to make you feel confident in your mask."[11]

The army boasted that it had equipped its doughboys with the best gas masks issued by any army. But even three years after the first German gas attack, despite continual evolution and improvements, the masks still were bulky, claustrophobic, and uncomfortable.

"They are made of rubber, and fit tight around the face; they have goggles and have a tube which runs to a tin box containing cloth saturated with acids which neutralize the different gases," former linotype operator Pvt. Carl McIntosh wrote to the Modesto newspaper soon after reaching France. "Then there is a mouthpiece which we breathe through. We have a clip which closes the nose so there will be no danger of getting any gas that may leak through the mask."[12]

Army gas instructors sometimes intentionally but briefly exposed doughboys to toxic fumes, to familiarize them with the smell of mustard gas; failure to react quickly enough would kill them in the trenches. "The smell wasn't so bad," a corporal from Delaware wrote from France, "but for a half hour after we all looked as if we had lost near relatives judging from the tears in our eyes."[13] Fifty soldiers training to be instructors at Camp Zachary Taylor, Kentucky, in early 1918 likewise had "passed through the gas chamber with their gas masks off and with the gas strong enough to kill in five minutes. . . . It is a safe wager that some of these soldiers broke world's records in adjusting the masks."[14]

A gas chamber wasn't necessarily a large room specifically built for training. Rather, it might be any suitable space or void, or even a trench filled with heavy gases. A New England clergyman working in France with the YMCA described his own unique indoctrination. "An old sergeant, who had been to the 'gas school' gave me a half hour's schooling last week, showing me how to adjust the mask, put it on quickly," the pastor wrote home to Connecticut. "He ended by taking me down into a cave filled with poison fumes where I had to stay for several minutes just to teach me, as he said, to have confidence in the mask."[15]

A mask test could be terrifying for young doughboys. One Sammie fainted twice—once while preparing to enter the chamber, once after leaving it—before he managed to stay on his feet the whole way through on his third attempt. And his company was facing only nonlethal tear gas.

"Many have 'the wind up' (i.e., they are afraid inside, but are ashamed to show it)," a YMCA worker wrote after the war. "Reliance on the guide, the expert who has been through it all, and the sense of companionship, the stronger ones unconsciously strengthening the weak, have a steadying effect upon all the men."[16]

One superbly disciplined group of U.S. Marines, in contrast, made a name for themselves—and nearly panicked their trainers—by remaining in a gas chamber for fifty-five minutes. When anxious American and French officers finally opened the doors, "there, sitting on the floor, midst swirling clouds of gas, sat the company of marines, playing blackjack!"[17]

Gas chamber tests inevitably caused casualties, both at home and overseas. Fingers fumbled, straps broke, seals failed, valves stuck, and men missed or misunderstood their orders. One soldier collapsed in a gas chamber at Camp Cody, New Mexico, while wearing a faulty mask. Another doughboy who picked up the mask to inspect it was sickened, and later was discharged with heart trouble. (The incident sparked an unlikely report that the mask had been "tampered with by a spy.")[18]

The Boston Globe reported that a Haverhill, Massachusetts, man was still suffering several months after exposure during a mask test. "Four days after he went through the gas chamber he became ill and was sent to the hospital, remaining in hospitals in France until he was invalided home."[19]

The army no doubt believed that such casualties were unfortunate but acceptable, the cost of preparing troops for German gases that nearly all would face in the frontline trenches, and which the First Gas Regiment would unleash in return. Sending forward doughboys who were unready to react immediately and accurately to gas was unthinkable. A captain from Baltimore wrote home about being blasted from his dugout bunk by a shell that hit his trench at 6:10 in the morning.

"I hated to lose those 20 minutes' sleep," he wrote, "but my 'room' was immediately filled with mustard gas (it was a gas shell), and it was a case of dressing with a gas mask on and getting out of that regular gas chamber, as that stuff burns worse than a hot poker. I got two whiffs of that gas before I could get into my mask and did not get over the effects until the next day. It's a great life if you don't weaken."[20]

The account of an accident at Hanlon Field that sickened Captains Mathewson and Cobb and that killed or injured sixteen other soldiers is still widely believed today. But it's problematic, mainly because of Ty's coauthor, Al Stump.

Stump's work on Ty's autobiography, as well as a later *True* magazine article and his book *Cobb: A Biography* (which led to the 1994 movie *Cobb*), is widely criticized by baseball historians. They find the accounts full of inaccuracies and distortions, such as a tale that Ty had killed a man in Detroit in 1912. "Such a remarkable assertion should have a solid, accurate factual basis for its foundation," writes Doug Roberts, an attorney and former prosecutor who investigated the story. "Neither Stump's book nor the movie does."[21]

Cobb biographer Charles Leerhsen describes Stump as "a quantity, not a quality guy. . . . He resented being thought of as just a guy grinding out stories for hairy-chested barber shop monthlies like *True*." Aging and in failing health, Ty perhaps didn't know—and his publisher perhaps overlooked—what Leerhsen calls Stump's "reputation for inventing scenes and dialogue and otherwise stretching the truth."[22] Charles Alexander, another Cobb biographer, writes of *My Life in Baseball*, "Factual mistakes abounded, as did distortions and half-truths."[23]

Leerhsen and Alexander don't seriously dispute the biography's account of Ty's and Matty's gassing, however. But Branch Rickey did. Throughout his career, and still today, the CWS major enjoyed much more respect than Stump. He likely would have known of any accident at Choignes, but flatly declared that the Cobb-Stump account was untrue.

"I went through the exact training with Matty and was with him immediately afterward," Branch wrote (with no mention of Ty, who had since died). "He had no mishap after the final field-training exposure. In fact, Matty took part in an impromptu broad-jump contest and out-leaped everyone in our group who cared to try, and by a comfortable margin."[24]

Neither Matty nor his wife ever mentioned a gas accident, either, and no army record regarding one has yet emerged. Matty did speak several times about brief exposures to gas during his service in France—while opening gas shells for troop lectures, for example. "Less than two weeks after leaving the hospital he was in the gas house teaching gas non-coms how to distinguish various kinds of poison gas by their odors," a United Press correspondent wrote in 1921. "Four hours a day for four months he inhaled small quantities of the deadly gases."[25]

Matty echoed the account two years later. "We were careful, but there is no doubt the accumulated gases affected my lungs," he said. "For instance, if you stayed in this room long enough and mustard gas was released only a little at a time, eventually it would get you."[26]

It's also possible, of course, that an accident *did* occur at Hanlon Field, and that the army suppressed any report or investigation and ordered all soldiers involved never to speak of it, even later as civilians. Obeying such an order would have been characteristic of Matty and Branch, although perhaps not of Ty, from whom we get the story. That still leaves Branch's denial several decades later.

Staying mum about a catastrophe differs greatly from falsely claiming that it never happened, which would be uncharacteristic for a man who kept a promise to his mother never to play baseball on Sundays. It's difficult to imagine why Branch might have done so. It therefore seems unlikely that the training accident recounted in *My Life in Baseball* ever happened. Stump might have exaggerated real training methods shared by Ty, or simply invented the disaster. Nonetheless, such an accident *was* possible, and there's some evidence to support it.

The *Boston Globe* mentioned—again, without confirmation—similar gassing deaths while reporting on the return of Maj. P. D. Haughton in December 1918. Haughton had served at Hanlon Field for two weeks before Ty or Matty arrived, and later as an assistant division gas officer with the Twenty-Sixth Division and a staff officer at Fifth Corps headquarters.

"The gas school attended in France is no playground," the *Globe* said. "Sixteen men were killed there during one school, but during Maj Haughton's session there none was seriously injured."[27] Interestingly, the number of casualties cited by the *Globe* matches the Cobb-Stump account.

Whether or not there was an accident, Matty and Ty, along with Branch, continued their duties at Hanlon Field. Only Matty ever reached the front, receiving orders the first week of November assigning him as an assistant gas officer with the Twenty-Eighth Infantry Division. Like Matty, most of the men in the "Iron Division" were Pennsylvanians. "It was at his request that he was attached to a division from his native State," the *New York Times* said.[28]

The captain later recalled that he was "just about to get to the front when they signed that bit of paper which the Germans have found it impossible so far to tear up."[29] Some accounts say he reached his division at the front on November 11, 1918, the day the German army signed the armistice.

Matty came excruciatingly close to seeing combat. But despite his best efforts, like Ty and Branch, he simply had arrived in France too late. "We are sorry we could not get into action," he said, "but that was the fortune of war."[30]

13

....

Homecomings

Baseball's gas and flame officers had shipped overseas individually and would return individually. Former star second baseman Johnny Evers, serving as a uniformed Knights of Columbus athletic secretary in France, saw them all in late November, although apparently not at one time.

"A few days before I left Paris, I saw Ty along with Matty, Percy Haughton, president of the Braves, and Branch Rickey at the army headquarters at Chaumont," Evers said. "None of them at that time had any idea of leaving for home."[1] The men appeared well, he added, except for Matty, who was still convalescing from his flu—or, some might argue, from a gas accident at Hanlon Field.

The four CWS men didn't know when they would receive orders back to the United States. Ty, for one, wasn't eager to leave. He wrote to Tigers owner Frank Navin that if the war hadn't ended, he would have completed his gas course on December 7 and been assigned to a unit. He didn't foresee heading home now before mid-January.

"Also Ty told of his wishes to join the army of occupation [in Germany] and his failure to be a party to it," the *Detroit Free Press* reported. "His next hope was to get a few days' leave and survey the place, or part of it, where the battle line was pitched."[2]

In the unfathomable ways of armies everywhere, Ty became the first to go home instead. He arrived from Brest at Pier 4 in Hoboken, New Jersey, at 8:45 on the morning of December 16, on board the gigantic transport SS *Leviathan*. Evers, who had started before him, arrived later that same morning with other returning KofC men and troops on SS *Lorraine*.

Any suspicion the Detroit club had pulled strings to secure an early release of its star were perhaps diminished by the presence of other CWS officers among the nearly nine thousand joyous soldiers jammed on board

Leviathan, the ex-German liner *Vaterland*. The doughboys knew the Tiger was among them; Ty had spoken to them during a minstrel show at sea.

"Capt. Cobb said that he was happy to think that he was able to take part in the fighting and that he considered it a high honor to fight for his country," the *Brooklyn Eagle* said. "He extended then and there an invitation to all on board the big liner to attend some baseball game in which he takes part, adding that all those accepting his invitation would have to say was that they heard Ty trying to make a speech and that would be sufficient to admit them to a seat in the grandstand."[3]

One Sammy remembered the Georgia Peach's exact words: "If I'm stealing second, and it flashes on any one of you who I am just as I'm sliding to the base I want you to stand up in the bleachers and yell out, 'Hey, Ty, I'm a guy that was on the Lee-vy!' And I'll run right off the baseline and over to wherever you are in the bleachers and shake hands and sit down and have a talk about this trip. T'ell with whether we win or lose."[4]

Ty's remarks during the voyage, however, differed from what he said upon landing. "I'm going down to my home in Augusta, Ga., and rest up for several months," he told reporters. "I intend to break away from baseball. I'm tired of it. I've had fifteen years of it, and I want to quit while I am still good. There is the danger that the fascination of the game has its hold on me, but I shall make every effort to tear away from it, and not sign with any club again."[5]

The *Detroit Free Press* quickly surmised that the outfielder was kidding. It added that Ty would hang up his spikes only when he was "too old to hobble around or somebody passes a law prohibiting the use of a bat against a pellet."[6]

Major P. D. Haughton returned next. He reached Pier 60 in New York on the afternoon of December 21, one of twenty-five hundred officers and men on board the former White Star liner *Baltic*. Also on board was Capt. Lawrence "Larry" Waterbury, CWS officer, financier, and noted polo player.

Major Haughton was happy to talk about baseball and John Heydler, the newly elected National League president. But he didn't want to talk about the war or his service as a gas officer with the Twenty-Sixth

Division. "Things over there? O, I have nothing to say about that."[7] A baseball fan on the ship had asked about his plans for baseball. "Nothing at all," the major had replied, "at least not until I get a good rest, for I'm dead tired."[8]

The former Harvard football coach spoke two weeks later with James O'Leary of the *Boston Globe*. "I did not meet either Ty Cobb or Christy Mathewson, who were captains in the same service as myself, but I heard good reports of both," he said. Haughton also spoke about the differences between offensive and defensive gas warfare. "Just as soon as a defense against one kind had been organized," he said, "a new kind was introduced so that the same menace in a new form had to be met, which gave those who took the initiative an advantage." The major added:

> I was particularly fortunate when ordered to the front as assistant division gas officer of the 26th Division. In that capacity I was working on the defense end.
>
> Later, when I was ordered to the 5th Army Corps my duties were principally on the offensive, which dealt with the practical use of gas against the Boche, particularly through the medium of artillery.
>
> My assignment to the 26th Division was a very pleasing one to me, for I felt at home with the New Englanders, and because of the showing made by this division, I am proud to be able to say that I was once connected with it.
>
> My experience all-around was also very pleasant, and I would not have missed it for all the money in the world.[9]

Major Haughton didn't return to football at Harvard, joining the banking firm of White, Weld & Company instead. He was also vice president of William Read & Sons, which operated "The Great Outdoors Store" in Boston.[10] Haughton later returned to football in 1923 as head coach at Columbia University in New York City.

Lieutenant George Sisler, Maj. Branch Rickey's baseball protégé, was next out of the army. He had never left the United States. The Browns first baseman trained at Camp Humphreys before receiving a transfer days after the armistice to a gas school at Camp Kendrick, Lakewood, New Jersey.

"My course of army training comprised several weeks' work in the infantry division with a number of weeks additional in the purely chemical warfare department," he wrote. "I received some engineering instruction, and the customary drills which are common to all forms of military training. But my most interesting experiences centered in chemical warfare work."[11]

The Sizzler participated in an athletic meet for officers at Camp Kendrick during early December. "All Sisler did was to make a clean sweep of the four events on the program, the 100-yard dash, the punting of a football for distance, drop-kicking the football for accuracy and distance and throwing a baseball for distance," a wire story said. "Had there been anything else on the program Sisler was ready to do his bit."[12]

The event capped his brief military service. He wired a friend in St. Louis on December 15: "Received discharge from the army. Plans for future very uncertain."[13] Sisler later wrote that he had one regret—"That I didn't get to France."[14]

Major Rickey felt disappointment over missing combat after "a hard six weeks of training" in France. "The chance to shoot gas into these Germans is gone," he wrote, "and our detachment is as a bunt in a 9-to-0 ball game." With little left to accomplish overseas, the Cardinals president was eager to get back to St. Louis despite the many peacetime attractions of France.

"Talking about all the human loveliness over here the most beautiful picture I have seen was when I saw my wife and three kids in a dream," he wrote. "No, I'm not homesick and can stick it out with good spirit and cheer as long as there is any use for me over here, but the first time they call for volunteers to return home I'll be the first one over the top to say 'That's me,' and I am not ashamed to say it because there are two million other Americans over here who feel the same way about it."[15]

Branch sailed from Brest on December 15 on board *George Washington*. The transport reached Hoboken eight days later at 3:30 in the afternoon. The major probably stepped ashore late that day or sometime on Christmas Eve, although a St. Louis newspaper later said it was Christmas Day.

Nobody noticed. As far as sportswriters knew, Branch was still in France. "I succeeded in escaping a battery of newspapermen in New York, and I had hoped to have similar success here," he said after reaching St. Louis on December 30. He added:

> I refused to be interviewed after I had landed for the reason that baseball topics were strange to me, hence I feared I might say the wrong thing. I have had a most wonderful experience since I left St. Louis in October. Right now I am in the best health I ever enjoyed and I only wish I could continue in the work with which I have been connected. France is a wonderful country, and we have been doing a great work over there.[16]

Branch spent time with his family in Lucasville while awaiting his discharge from active duty before returning to the Cardinals. He retained his rank, however, and stayed with the CWS as a reserve officer until 1924. He was only a silhouette in the first memory that his two-and-a-half-year-old daughter formed of him.

"He is standing in the doorway at 5404 Bartmer Ave. in St. Louis," Jane Rickey Jones recalled near the end of her life. "He is in uniform and I remember his legs wrapped in puttees and the sunshine behind him. I was on the staircase and he came to the door. He had just come home from the war."[17]

Professional baseball's only noncommissioned gas soldier, Cpl. Gabby Street, had a long road to recovery. As the fighting continued, a major at an army base hospital in France had asked the old catcher whether he might be interested in taking charge of camp athletics. "Guess you won't want to get back to the front for a while yet," the officer added.

"I'll tell you or General Pershing," Gabby replied, "that once is enough and I've seen all I want to see."[18] He took the coaching job and was still recuperating from his wounds and gassing when the war ended.

Gabby sailed from Bordeaux on December 17 in a casual company of sick and wounded Sammies. Three thousand men filled the transport USS *Aeolus*, the former German liner *Grosser Kurfürst*. Gabby landed at

Newport News, Virginia, on December 30, after a smooth trip across the Atlantic. His next stop was Debarkation Hospital No. 1 in nearby Hampton. A corporal also hospitalized there remembered Gabby well.

"A temporary resident of Ward Twenty-one," the two-striper wrote decades later, "already famous and destined to become more so, was a broad-shouldered, sort of aloof sergeant [*sic*] named Charles E. Street, better known to readers of the sports pages as 'Gabby.' ... The right sleeve of his blouse was decorated near the cuff with a golden 'V.' A guy did not acquire that particular [wound] chevron merely for being a fast talker."[19]

The army then moved Gabby nearer his home, sending the former catcher north to Camp Dix, New Jersey. "Street had been entirely lost sight of until Monday [January 13], when a letter was received from him by Tom Gray, under whom he worked in the old Williamsport Tri-State club before going into the big show," the *Washington Times* reported of the former Senator.[20] Gabby's letter to his old Millionaires teammate read:

Just a few lines to tell you that I am more than glad to get back home. I am not feeling any too good. I have been in the hospital for the last three months. I was gassed on October 14, in the Argonne forest and got a good dose of it. Pretty near got me. Don't know just when I will get discharged out of the army, but hope soon. The doctor took an X-ray picture of my lungs yesterday and if they are all right [I] will get out soon, I think. I will come up to see all the boys when I do.

I went thru every drive the Yanks made and thought I was going to get by without being hurt. Sherman was right when he said war was hell. I sure found it out. I will have a lot to tell you when I see you.[21]

The Alabaman spun a different story for the Volunteers in Nashville, hoping to return to the diamond with them in 1919. "I am just from France, where I have been catching the Huns napping," Gabby wrote to club secretary Chris Haury. "I am in the best of condition and am anxious for the season to open."[22] The gas soldier went home to Williamsport after receiving his honorable discharge on January 30.

"Gabby, who has always been a handsome brute, is pretty well scarred up by the German bullets, gas and shrapnel, but his scars are not very large and are not noticeable except at close range," Memphis sportswriter Bob Pigue wrote. "He says he is 25 pounds under weight, having dropped down while lying in a hospital soaking up medicine and arnica. A few weeks of home cooking and regular home nursing by Gabby's beautiful little wife will soon put the talkative backstop in the original pink of condition and midseason form."[23]

The catcher made the Vols' roster in 1919, at age thirty-six. He got off to a torrid start as fans across the Southern Association celebrated his return. "They pumped gas at him and they bounced shrapnel off his nose but they failed to put him under the shell-torn turf in No-Man's Land. . . . The sensational return to form of Gabby since getting out of the service has been the source of much favorable comment all over the league where Gabby is a popular hero," the *Nashville Banner* proclaimed.[24]

The 1919 season was Gabby's last as a full-time player. His hitting tailed off dramatically as he played in 119 games, and people wondered if he was finished. "It has been known for some time that Connie Mack has desired to have Street go somewhere as a manager so that he could handle Mack's young pitchers," the *Nashville Tennessean* said after the season.[25] That winter the aging backstop accepted a player-manager's position with the Minor League club in Suffolk, Virginia, a source of talent for Mack's Philadelphia Athletics.

"'Gabby' should make the Virginians a good leader, in spite of his fiery temperament," a *Nashville Banner* columnist wrote. "He is getting too old to play, and he carries a stock of baseball knowledge in his ancient dome."[26] Gabby would make excellent use of that knowledge during coming seasons.

Captain Mathewson and Lieutenant Rixey were still overseas as 1919 began. The best account of Matty after the armistice comes from his wife. Jane Mathewson said in a December letter to Cincinnati Reds president Garry Herrmann that she had heard from Matty as recently as November 26. He had recovered from his earlier bout of flu, she said, and added:

He has been stationed at Hendicourt [*sic*], France, ever since hostilities ceased. This is 90 minutes from Metz by motor truck. This is, or was, the front line and was the scene of some heavy fighting.

Captain Mathewson is divisional gas officer of the Twenty-eighth Division, General Hay commanding. This would have meant a big job had the war continued. As it is, he is kept very busy massing the artillery shells loaded with mustard gas, left behind by the Germans; inspecting their abandoned dugouts for gas infernal machines, &c., in order to chalk them "safe," and a hundred other things connected with the gas defense. He found enough mustard gas in his area to kill an army.

The gas office at Hendicourt is in an old French house left standing in spite of shell fire. The owners returned the other day and dug up jewelry and 12,000 francs they had buried before their hasty flight four years before,

Mr. Mathewson does not know when he will be released. In his last letter he said he might be sent into Germany or back to the States. He will let me hear as soon as he knows, and I will communicate with you. His address is the same, care Chief of Chemical Warfare Service, Am. E. F., France.[27]

The captain performed his dangerous duties as conscientiously as ever, and saw the value in doing so. "'Christy' said that he probably saw more of the war than a great many officers who were actually in the fighting," his college alumni magazine noted, "as they were confined to one sector while he as a gas officer covered a great amount of territory."[28] Matty also taught as a gas instructor at the Twenty-Eighth Division's school of tactics. "He is a good one, too, doing excellent work," wrote the lieutenant colonel who served as the school's director.[29]

Matty also found time to tour a city taken from the Germans after the armistice. "The French soldiers capture Metz, the strongest fortress on our front," he noted on a hastily printed postcard. "I saw some homemade Stars and Stripes there. Some of the flags had as many as 8 stars."[30] He added on the back of another: "When I tour Europe I surely want to spend some time in Metz. Four hours gave me just a glimpse."[31]

The Reds grew increasingly anxious over Matty's return. Speculation began in early December that player Heinie Groh, who had filled in for Matty during the last few games of 1918, might again assume the skipper's duties during the coming season. President Herrmann wrote to Jane about Matty before Christmas, "asking her to spur him along: However, it is not a certainty that Matty wants his old job again, as he stated to friends last fall that he had pretty nearly all the baseball he wanted and that in all probability the 1918 season was his last."[32]

Jane Mathewson replied that her husband didn't know when the army would release him. Despite speculation to the contrary, he definitely was trying to return to the Reds, writing to the CWS in mid-December:

1. My business reasons for wishing to return to The United States, is, that I may be there, on or about January 18th, 1919, in order to resume my former occupation of managing a National League professional baseball club.
2. Unless at that time, I give assurance of being able to accept such a position, I could not find such employment during the season of 1919.[33]

Matty later wrote to friends in Factoryville that he probably wouldn't be back in time to pilot the club again in 1919. Herrmann kept wiring, appealing to him to get in touch, but page after page dropped from the calendar with still no direct word. Herrmann had to begin planning for spring training. The *Cincinnati Commercial Tribune* reported on January 25: "'Garry' stated that should the wire from 'Matty' state he could not handle the club for the coming season, or that by the end of three days 'Big Six' had not replied in the affirmative, some one else would be considered for the leadership of the local club."[34]

Herrmann met with Giants coach and former Phillies manager Pat Moran at the end of the month. "The only thing which will stand in the way of Moran's taking the [manager's] position will be an eleventh-hour cablegram from Mathewson that he can be discharged from the service in time to get back to take the Reds on their training trip," the *New York Times* said on January 30. "As no word has been heard from Matty, it is not believed that he will be back in time."[35]

The Reds had hired Moran before they finally heard from Matty during the first week of February. "Herrmann has received a reply to his cablegram to Mathewson asking about the latter's future plans," the *Times* said. "Mathewson's message was brief, merely stating that he would land in America on Feb. 15. No mention was made as to his future plans."[36]

Matty was off by only two days in estimating the date of his return. He reached New York on February 17, on board the troopship ss *Rotterdam*, aware that Moran had taken over as Cincinnati skipper. Speculation immediately swirled that he and Moran essentially would swap jobs—that Matty would sign now as a coach with his old club, the New York Giants, under manager, mentor, and friend John McGraw.

"Of course the thing which interested New Yorkers about Matty wasn't how many German helmets he brought back, but what he was going to do this season," the *New York Times* said. Matty did little to squelch the chatter. "I am under orders to go to Washington immediately, and as I see no further use of instructing any one how to throw gas, I expect to ask for my discharge and get back to civil life." The captain added with good humor, "The only persons I know of in need of gas are the umpires."[37]

Matty said little about his short wartime experience, except to observe that Americans were fortunate to live so far from ravaged Europe. "All that Sherman said about war is true and then some!" he said. "People over here ought to be glad that it was not fought out on this side of the Atlantic."[38]

Despite much hopeful talk at home about baseball becoming popular "over there" during peacetime, Matty doubted the game would ever catch on in Paris. "The French never will take up baseball in a hundred years," Fred Lieb quoted him saying. "A Poilu would rather catch a hand grenade than a hot liner, and he rather would try conclusions with a German 77 than get in front of a hard hit grounder. No, baseball is not a Frenchman's game; I am convinced of that. They say it is too rough, and call it brutal."[39]

Matty left New York for his father-in-law's home in Lewisburg and a reunion with his wife and son. John McGraw announced on March 7 that his former pitching star would rejoin the Giants as pitching coach and assistant manager.

"McGraw will stay at the helm this season and perhaps next," the *New York Times* reported, "but he says that he has almost come to the end of his managerial career after nearly twenty years in the major leagues and is anxious that his successor should be the player who perhaps stands

higher in the estimation of baseball fans than any other man the game
has ever produced."⁴⁰

McGraw's former pitching star never took his eventual elevation to
manager for granted. "I am elated over my return to the Giants," Matty
told the *New York Sun*. "New York has been very good to me and I regard
it as my home town. I also am very pleased to get back with McGraw,
who is without question the greatest manager of baseball." In the same
article, Fred Lieb explained Matty's strange extended silence overseas.

"Oddly enough the failure of the Government to deliver some cablegrams to Capt. Matty in France brings him back to New York," Lieb wrote.
"Herrmann announced yesterday that the directors of the Cincinnati club
voted to reengage Mathewson as manager and that a series of cablegrams
were sent to him in France asking him when he would return. As no word
was received from Mathewson until he landed in New York a fortnight
ago the job was tendered Moran. Mathewson says he did not receive any
of Herrmann's cablegrams."⁴¹

Two days later the sportswriter banged out a few lines about the New
York fans' elation and hopes. "The Giant offices last Saturday were flooded
with letters sent to both Mathewson and the club, congratulating them
on renewal of their former compact," Lieb wrote. "New York never had a
professional athlete of which it thought as much as Mathewson. . . . While
McGraw says he will make Mathewson his successor in a year or two, the
possibilities are largely in favor of the change being made much quicker."⁴²

1st Lt. Eppa Rixey, the first CWS baseballer to reach France, was the last
to get home. He wrote to Philadelphia in late February that he expected to
rejoin the Phillies around the middle of May, after the season had begun.

"In a letter to President Baker the huge hurler said a pleasant time was
being had on the other side, but he was eager and anxious to get back to
the U.S.A. and heave some baseballs instead of practicing with gasless
bombs," Robert Maxwell wrote in the *Public Ledger*. "Loot Rixey is with
the chemical division, and states it is a bum job now they have crabbed
the war. The workless and fightless days are beginning to annoy him and
he longs for action. Our Loot did not say he was in the best shape of his

career and can win the pennant single-handed, but inferred he has been taking good care of himself and might be able to get by."[43]

Eppa wasn't far out on his timeline. He reached Brooklyn from Marseilles on May 19, on board the transport SS *President Wilson*. The army sent him first to Camp Merritt in Bergen, New Jersey, then just as quickly to Camp Kendrick at Lakewood. President Baker had traveled up to New York to greet his pitcher, but couldn't find him. They finally connected by phone and agreed to meet on May 23 at the Baker Bowl. Eppa signed a new contract that day in the president's office, although he missed seeing the game versus the visiting Cubs and the honors the Phillies paid to Pete Alexander on his return to Philadelphia.

"Rixey did not have a chance to see his old friend Alexander get a pounding yesterday as he was closeted with Mr. Baker until the game was nearly over and Alexander had gone to the showers," the *Philadelphia Inquirer* said. "But Rixey was delighted to be back in the 'old town' as he expressed it and as he left the park he said: 'Boys, I will see you all very soon.' . . . Manager [Jack] Coombs made no attempt to conceal his pleasure in seeing Rixey around again. That with the splendid victory over the Cubs made Jawn a very happy boy last night."[44]

The Virginian got his army discharge the following day and headed home to family in Culpeper, expecting to rejoin the club around June 1. An *Inquirer* columnist had a cautionary note for fans, however.

"Rixey looks the picture of health. He is fine and big and has a splendid color," he wrote. "The army life has been of service to him, but whether he can recover all his cunning as a pitcher which he may have lost while serving Uncle Sam remains to be seen. It is evident that Alexander is not the same pitcher he was before he went to France. That trip abroad and the experience the fellows went through seems to have changed them a lot."[45]

It would prove to be a shrewd and timely observation. Eppa nonetheless won his first game back in home flannels, on July 9 in Philadelphia. His 5–4 victory over the Cubs snapped a thirteen-game losing skid for the Phillies and new manager Clifford "Gavvy" Cravath, who had replaced fired Coombs. "Rixey hurled good ball and deserved to win," Robert Maxwell wrote. "He was hit hard, but was steady with men on."[46]

The ex-lieutenant struggled thereafter, pitching for a dreadful, last-place club. He went 6-12 for the season, followed by a dreadful 11-22 record in 1920. The Phillies then traded Eppa to Cincinnati, to pitch there for his old manager, Pat Moran. The refined southpaw would play with the Reds for thirteen seasons.

"Rixey and I were teammates on the old Philly team, he vowed he would retire that fall, as his father wanted him to get into a respectable business and not be thrown in contact with low, uncouth ball players," former hurler Al Demaree wrote in 1933. "He has been 'retiring' ever since."[47] Eppa finally hung up his glove following that season.

The survivors of First Gas Regiment had a hard time getting home. They entrained at Chaumont at 3:20 p.m. on New Year's Eve 1918. After a three-day journey to Brest, the doughboys marched from the railway three miles out of town to Camp Pontanezen. They spent three horrendous weeks at the encampment. The U.S. Army hadn't singled them out for mistreatment there; it treated everyone badly.

The sprawling installation was still unfinished after more than a year of construction. A New Year's Day exposé in the *Washington Post* already had prompted Secretary of War Baker to order an investigation into what the army called a rest camp. George Rothwell Brown, a *Post* correspondent recently back from France, had reported that seventy thousand exhausted and malnourished doughboys were performing backbreaking labor, wallowing in mud, and eating unspeakable food while standing in the rain.

The camp's new commander was Brig. Gen. Smedley Butler, a legendary marine twice awarded the Medal of Honor, his nation's highest decoration for military valor. Butler called Camp Pontanezen "the worst place I have seen anywhere on earth, and I have travelled all over the world."[48] Correspondent Brown's outrage fairly scorched the *Post's* front page, although he directly blamed neither the army nor the marines for the camp's deplorable condition.

"I do not know who is to blame," he wrote, "but I think that the responsibility should not fairly be placed upon the 'A.E.F.' Some day I expect to see it traced straight back to Washington." Brown called the camp a "cesspool" and quoted several soldiers, interviewed separately, who said that what went on there was a crime. "That is precisely what it is, a crime," he wrote, "and the men responsible for it should be dismissed from the service of the government. If I had a brother who was responsible for Pontanezen I would disown him."[49]

The First Gas Regiment had cause for outrage as well. The men were eager to go home after their tremendous exertions at the front, but the army put them to work as stevedores, laborers, and roadbuilders. Under continuous winter rain, they lived for a week in decaying canvas tents, many of which lacked duckboards.

"In the course of ten months at the front," says Chaplain Addison's regimental history, "in every variety of position and circumstance from Ypres to the Swiss border, our men had never had to submit to living conditions worse than those which surrounded them during their first week at Brest. . . . Conditions there were chronic which would not have been permitted by one of our commanders for more than a single day, even under shell-fire."[50]

Sergeant Herbst of Company D later shared an awful account with his hometown newspaper. "He stated that the soldiers at the embarkation camp are obliged to sleep on the ground,—in real mud, with no sign of a bed and but little covering. He said further that the major of his company registered a complaint after several of his men died of pneumonia because of neglect, but that he was threatened with a longer stay in the French seaport unless he kept his mouth shut. He started an investigation, however, when he landed in New York, by going to a New York newspaper office and telling all he knew and produced evidence."[51] Corporal Day of Company E told another paper that "conditions were so bad he felt lucky to get out alive."[52]

Influenza also struck while the regiment waited for a ship home. "I don't think it boosted our mortality any until we got to Brest," a returning private first class told the *Washington Star*. "There A Company lost three men from it—men who had stood all the hard fighting, the marches and been under fire for months at a stretch and gone through unscathed; then to die awaiting ships at Brest. It broke us all up when the parents of one of those boys came to Camp Mills [Long Island] to meet him—came a good many hundred miles, and he wasn't there."[53]

The men finally moved from tents into barracks, and the weather improved a bit. "But the three chief factors of life—deep mud, hard labor, and wild rumors—filled every day. . . . On January 23 we were given a final inspection; the regiment was complimented for its efficient work and cheerful spirit; and the same afternoon orders arrived that we should embark the next morning on H.M.S. Celtic."[54]

The British transport sailed for New York at five o'clock the following afternoon with over thirty-one hundred doughboys on board. The gas soldiers reached America on February 2 after a calm voyage with dry quarters and decent food. New York newspapers gave them the welcome they deserved.

"The First Gas Regiment, also known as the 'gas and flame troops,' whose arduous service and remarkable exploits have not been proclaimed in flaming headlines, got back yesterday from France aboard the White Star liner Celtic after fighting on all sectors many months and becoming the idols of the infantry, whom they saved frequently from great losses by letting loose the terrifying material of their box of chemical magic," the New York Sun said.[55]

Maj. John B. Carlock had brought the regiment home in the absence of Colonel Atkisson, assigned to new duties in France. "The regiment, he said, fought successively on every American front, suffered casualties of half its enlisted strength of 1,500 men and returned with eighty of its members wearing the Croix de Guerre, 30 wearing the distinguished cross and 12 of its officers recommended for distinguished service medals."[56]

The gas troops first stopped at Camp Mills, then continued to Camp Kendrick, New Jersey. Generals Sibert and Fries reviewed the men there, joined by Mrs. Atkisson. The regimental history says of Sibert, "He knew us and our needs; and knowing our record too, he spoke to the officers and men of the fighting arm of his service in words of gratitude that were deeply appreciated, and in words of praise that had surely been earned." Demobilization began immediately. "Slowly the units dwindled, until before the first of March the organization was wholly mustered out, and the First Gas Regiment passed into history."[57]

   The *Portland Oregonian* newspaper later editorialized that Chaplain
Addison's quickly produced regimental history "belongs in the category
of historical accounts that inspire us with confidence in ourselves and
in our future as a nation. . . . It is good to read of the achievements of
individual units, such as the gas and flame division, and the tank service,
and every other branch that called for both bravery and initiative, if for
no other reason than that it helps to get the Brest affair off our minds."[58]

14

Saranac Lake

Christy Mathewson began his coaching duties with the New York Giants at 1919 spring training. He pitched a little while the club was in Florida, and again in chilly Virginia on the way north. "Something caught in my arm, and I have never been able to do anything with it since," he wrote. "It even hurts me to write now. I think I had better learn to stretch an octave on a typewriter."[1]

Neither Matty nor the sportswriters made much fuss about his return once the Major Leagues began a shortened 140-game season in late April. On May 8 he appeared alongside manager John McGraw, second baseman Larry Doyle, and catcher Lew McCarty for a big Liberty Loan rally on Wall Street.

"'Larruping Larry' Doyle, with his trusty willow poised, will take a stand on the Sub-Treasury steps at noon to-day, while Christy Mathewson will try to find the plate from a point at Nassau and Wall Streets," the *New York Tribune* said. "Behind the bat will be Lew McCarty, while John McGraw will call balls and strikes. All the players will be in uniform. Every one in the crowd who catches the ball will enjoy the privilege of buying a Victory Note."[2]

Shortstop Art Fletcher, outfielders George Burns and Benny Kauff, and first baseman Hal Chase appeared as well, along with comedian Louis Mann, stage and film stars Hazel Dawn and Gail Kane, an Italian general, and several other notables. The crowd swelled to twenty-five thousand, a large proportion undoubtedly Giants fans.

The players in their baseball uniforms autographed several baseballs that were auctioned for large sums. The remaining unsigned balls were tossed into the crowd, after which organizers received a stunning offer from industrialist and philanthropist John D. Rockefeller.

"Mr. Rockefeller authorized a representative to announce that if a ball was recovered and Mathewson put his signature on it he would at once take $1,000,000 in Victory notes," said the *Chicago Tribune*, which called it the "world's record price for a baseball."[3] The *New York Tribune* added, "The leaders appealed that some smaller buyer give up his prize and for three minutes there was no response. Finally a young man, standing on the steps of the Morgan Bank, decided that a million for Uncle Sam was worth a personal sacrifice and threw in the ball."[4]

Matty clearly hadn't been forgotten in New York City. After the hurler autographed and delivered the expensive sphere, bankers J. P. Morgan and J. W. Harriman matched Rockefeller's offer. They received balls signed by Fletcher and Doyle. All told, the rally netted $14 million to help America pay for the recent war.

With the season under way, Matty coached a Giants team that included his two troublesome ballplayers from a year earlier, Fred Toney and Hal Chase. Toney had pleaded guilty in January to violating the Mann Act, then was acquitted three days later of conspiracy to evade the military draft. "The fact that the star pitcher is uneducated and unable to read or write is thought to have been largely responsible for his trouble," a sportswriter wrote.[5]

Toney thought about retiring and served four months in jail before returning to the Giants in late May. Matty maintained a coolly professional relationship with him, their names rarely appearing in the same paragraph in the New York sports pages. Matty later sent the pitcher to the mound while filling in for manager McGraw at the end of the season. His ties with Prince Hal, however, were far more fractious and difficult.

Chase had managed to escape the banishment from Organized Baseball that would have followed a conviction on the charges he had tried to throw games. National League president John Heydler heard witnesses and reviewed documents and affidavits during a hearing in late January. Matty hadn't yet returned from France; another key witness, Giants pitcher William "Pol" Perritt, also was unable to testify. The accused, however, stoutly defended himself.

"A frustrated Heydler had no choice but to let Chase off the hook," writes a Chase biographer.[6] In exonerating the first baseman, the league president said in February, "I feel bound to state that both the evidence and the record of the games to which reference was made fully refute this accusation."[7]

Prince Hal had signed with the Giants by the time Matty reached New York. "Mathewson and Chase are supposed to be the worst kind of enemies, both on and off the ballfield," a Cincinnati newspaper said.[8] The former Reds manager adopted the old admonition of "if you can't say something nice . . ." when he stepped ashore from France. "When Matty was informed that Hal Chase had been acquitted of the charges made against him last summer he refused to comment on the case."[9]

Outraged Reds fans, however, loudly expressed their displeasure the first time they saw their old first sacker, during a four-game series with the Giants in mid-June. "Hal Chase will find it hard to forget his bitter reception by the Cincinnati fans," the *Cincinnati Enquirer* said. "They never let up on him, but hissed and booed him with great violence every time he came to the plate. No visiting player was ever given so brutal a reception here."[10]

Matty had little to say to the Giants' first basemen even while standing in the coaching box. Runner Chase was hugging third base at the Polo Grounds during a July game with the Reds when the catcher's errant peg lodged under a tarpaulin.

"Chase lay holding the bag, though he would have had the time to score twice," W. O. McGeehan wrote in the *New York Tribune*. "Mr. Mathewson was coaching at third at the time. It seems that he and Mr. Chase are not on speaking terms; consequently, he could not break the silence by reminding Chase that he should score. When a third party arrived on the scene to transmit Mr. Mathewson's wishes verbally to Mr. Chase it was too late."[11]

The Giants finished the 1919 season in second place in the National League, nine games behind the Reds. Matty often had written for the newspapers and was a natural choice to cover the Chicago-Cincinnati World Series for the *New York Times*.

"Pat Moran deserves all sort of credit," the Reds' former manager wrote after they beat Chicago's Eddie Cicotte in Game 1. "It made me feel a little proud to see the club with which I had been associated making such a good showing. Remember, I have traveled and lived with these men and know them all. The players are showing their gameness in a pinch, as they did several times during the regular season."[12]

Cincinnati won the nine-game series in eight. Some sportswriters suspected Chicago players had intentionally lost the championship, but Matty didn't believe it. "This White Sox team looks like a bad ball club to me," he told Johnny Evers in Chicago.[13]

"The rumors and mutterings about the honesty of these series are ridiculous to me," Matty wrote in the *Times*. "It seems that there are some irrefutable arguments against the possibility of any arrangement being made which would conflict with the natural outcome. . . . Baseball is honest and will stay honest in spite of the abuse it has taken from time to time."[14]

Matty's faith was badly misplaced. Further investigation brought the "Black Sox" scandal, appointment of Judge Kenesaw Mountain Landis as Major League Baseball's first commissioner, a lifetime ban for eight White Sox players, and a permanent stain on the national pastime. But the Christian Gentleman was dealing with a greater, more personal challenge by the time the scandal broke.

Contrary to speculation that he would succeed John McGraw as manager, the rumor in 1920 was that the season would be Matty's last. "Christy Mathewson . . . will write 'Finis' in his baseball book at the close of this season, according to reports," a newspaper in Lewisburg said in late May. "The big pitcher whose name is linked with some of the brightest chapters of baseball during the last decade is to devote his attention to private business next year, his friends say."[15]

The speculation was partly correct. Matty did leave the Giants, but due to illness rather than business. The *New York Times* said on July 4 that he and Jane had left New York City a day earlier, possibly to spend the rest of the summer upstate in the Adirondack Mountains.

"He had decided to take a long vacation for the benefit of his health, which has been none too good lately," the *Times* said. "Bronchial trouble has bothered Matty for the last few days and has kept him away from the Polo Grounds. His physician advised him to go to the mountains to recuperate and the greatest pitcher of his time, if not of all time, decided to follow this advice."[16] The *New York Tribune* added, "Johnny Evers, the little Trojan, will take up the duties of Mathewson in the meantime."[17]

The Associated Press broke the real story before the month was out. In a one-paragraph bulletin datelined Saranac Lake, New York, the AP reported that Matty was "seriously ill with tuberculosis."[18] The shocking news ran on the front pages of the *Brooklyn Eagle*, *Boston Globe*, and other papers with late editions. Fans around the country read further details the following day:

> Christy Mathewson, veteran player, manager and coach, has been at a sanitarium here for the past month undergoing treatment for tuberculosis, it was learned today [July 30].
>
> Mathewson has been confined to his room ever since his arrival, has received no callers and has been undergoing an absolute rest.
>
> It was understood that his condition was not such as to cause any immediate alarm.
>
> The famous pitcher and later manager of the Cincinnati National League Club came here immediately after leaving the New York National team, where he had acted as coach.[19]

Tuberculosis (TB) is an ancient, dangerous disease. "Like all great plagues, tuberculosis has irrevocably changed the fabric of human society," writes health journalist Vidya Krishnan. "The sheer scale of human suffering it has inflicted has inspired great art, literature, poetry, and operatic tragedies."[20] Caused by *Mycobacterium tuberculosis*, a germ that usually spreads through the air, it has clear parallels to the COVID-19 pandemic that swept the world a century after Matty's illness. "Those of us who are TB people look at Covid and say, 'Wow, it's just a sped up version of TB,'" an epidemiologist said in 2021.[21]

"However, not everyone infected with TB bacteria becomes sick," a modern government pamphlet explains. "As a result, two TB-related conditions exist; latent TB infection and TB disease."[22]

People with latent TB don't feel ill, don't exhibit symptoms, aren't infectious, and likely learn they have it because they've taken a skin or blood test. Only about 5–10 percent of people with latent TB ever develop TB disease itself. While still a serious worldwide problem, tuberculosis is very treatable today. But it could be a death sentence during the 1920s.

"Fans of New York in particular and lovers of baseball everywhere will be grieved to learn of the serious illness of Christy Mathewson, so many years the idol of the Polo Grounds," the *New York Tribune* said. Manager McGraw, the paper added, "personally arranged some weeks ago for [Matty's] visit to Saranac Lake to forestall the possibility of an attack by the 'white plague.' It was hoped the congenial airs of that well known health resort would restore him before the end of the summer."[23] Matty confirmed that his friend and mentor had insisted he leave for the mountains after a club doctor discovered TB in his right lung.

Speculation soon arose that Matty's poor health was related to his months with the Chemical Warfare Service in 1918-19. The former captain had spoken little of his time in the army, and the Cobb-Stump account of an accident at Choignes wouldn't see print for more than forty years. The conjecture seemed to stem from the common knowledge that the baseball idol had been a gas officer in France during the war. Matty himself didn't see a connection between his CWS duties and his illness in 1920. Nor would he make such an argument during the difficult years ahead.

"I don't put any faith in the rumors that state I contracted the disease while over in France with the army," Matty said in August at Saranac Lake. "I never was gassed ."[24] But the theory persisted and spread among fans and writers alike. "I asked him about this," a visiting New York state senator wrote in 1922, "and he said that he was the assistant gas officer of the Twenty-eighth Division, but that his health began to fail only when he had been back in this country several months."[25]

"I got a few little sniffs of gas while doing demonstration work in France when I used to go into the gas schools as an officer," Matty said in 1923.[26] He also told another writer that year, "I guess I developed a susceptibility to the disease. Then I got this cold and finally it was diagnosed as T.B."[27] Sportswriter Bozeman Bulger addressed the issue at some length three years later:

Matty, himself, at times believed that his illness was due to exposure to the dampness and chill of a fall and winter in the Vosges region of France. At other times he was convinced that his lungs had been affected by the poison gases of the chemical laboratory in which he worked as a student officer and as an instructor. . . .

A big percentage of the early gas instructors contracted lung diseases from the occasional breathing of the gases that they studied and demonstrated. As Matty did not reach France in time to get in actual battle it is generally believed in the army that he was unconsciously gassed by degrees in trying to perfect his knowledge of these deadly fumes in the instruction camps of the United States as well as in France. He was keenly interested in his work as gas officer as he was in all his undertakings.[28]

Jane Mathewson, however, spoke several times about her husband's exposure to toxic gases. "I think the beginning of it was in France," she said in November 1920. "He had influenza there. Besides, as assistant gas officer to the Twenty-eighth Division, he demonstrated lethal gas shells to students and inhaled much of the gases. When he came back the first hard cold he developed settled into a cough he could not shake off . . . and during that summer he showed a strange lassitude. He had lost the pep that used to be in his baseball work."[29]

The question of whether Matty's exposure to gas had led to his TB gained national importance. Many veterans and their families believed in and feared such a connection. Ex-lieutenant George Sisler, who had chemical and CWS training, wrote of chlorine in March 1919: "Inhaling this gas has a most damaging effect upon the lung tissue even if it does not result in death. It frequently leaves the victim in the first stages of consumption [TB] from which he may ultimately recover provided he was not gassed too severely and has the necessary constitution."[30]

Matty settled into a house at Saranac Lake under a doctor's care and fought to regain his health. "I haven't given it a thought," he said when asked if he planned a return to baseball. "I am concentrating on getting well first and when that time comes I will decide what I'll do."[31] The pitching idol had good spells and bad. "Although he still spends his days reclining in a darkened room, Mathewson is said by his medical adviser, Dr. [E. N.] Packard, to have the balance of chance in his favor," the AP reported in early November 1920.[32]

Ironically, one treatment involved the injection of gas (nitrogen) into his right lung. "The gas causes the lung to collapse," a doctor explained, "thus expelling all air and troublesome secretions, and a rest is given the lung, which is made as immovable as a broken arm in a splint by the action of the gas."[33]

Dr. Packard said shortly before Christmas 1920 that his patient had been in serious condition, but now hoped for a recovery. An upstate newspaper added that Matty's son, Christy Jr., "doesn't like to hear stories that his daddy is not going to get better, and becomes indignant over such reports."[34]

Matty's condition improved somewhat by February 1921. Dr. Packard "now permits him to receive visitors and to indulge in his favorite pastime of checker playing," the *Lewisburg Journal* said. "The next thing in Matty's program is a series of fishing trips this summer."[35] The Giant's coach grew despondent, however, when the club left for spring training without him. "You know this is the first time in 21 years that he has not gone with them," Jane Mathewson said. "He broke down and cried bitterly. I never saw him do that before."[36]

Matty was "in the Adirondacks fighting to keep Death away from the home-plate," a Philadelphia columnist wrote that August. "To him in this hardest battle of his life the best wishes of countless baseball fans go wafted on the wings of affection, admiration and esteem." The scribe added that Big Six's illness, "an attack of the grim white plague, came in the line of patriotic duty."[37]

The narrative that Matty had been stricken with TB because of exposure to gas while serving in France was now firmly embedded in the nation's sports consciousness. It hardly mattered if the former captain gently suggested otherwise. The narrative presented a problem for the U.S. Army. If Matty had been stricken by TB caused by gas, what did that mean for hundreds of thousands of other doughboys who had experienced the same level of exposure or worse?

The Chemical Warfare Service had become a permanent organization within the U.S. Army and was no longer under the Corps of Engineers. Amos Fries was now the CWS chief and once more a brigadier general. But chemical warfare remained controversial, no matter how necessary or important it had become to the United States during the war. Proponents argued that gas was more humane than bullets or high explosives; opponents believed exactly the opposite. An exchange on the editorial pages of the *New York Tribune* reflected the continuing debate.

"The statistics of the World War conclusively prove the humanity of gas as a weapon," a naval expert wrote in September 1921. "Twenty-eight per cent of the casualties and hospital cases in the United States Army were from gas. But of these, only 2 per cent were fatal, and the recovery of patients was complete after a few weeks or months, with no serious after-effects."[38]

The article prompted a swift, furious response by a British major who had lost men during gas warfare. "England and France are seething with men who will never be in good health again, through the forced absorption of this 'humane' weapon of chlorine, which affects the lungs, or phosgene, which affects the heart, or a damnable mixture of both, such as my own unhappy boys."[39]

General Fries soon wrote in reply that the CWS had been studying permanent injuries caused by gas for nearly a year. One observation was particularly relevant to Matty's illness. "Some recent French information is of decided interest along this line," Fries stated, then continued:

They state that certain monkeys were subjected to gassing with various gases for a period of eight months. Certain other monkeys were kept under identical conditions except for gassing and used as a control. The result was absolutely conclusive that there was no increase of tuberculosis or tendency toward tuberculosis from gassing. We do not pretend that there are no cases of permanent injury from gas, but they must be very small in proportion to the whole number gassed. And tuberculosis or an increased tendency to tuberculosis is not a result of gassing.[40]

The CWS chief again mentioned TB in January 1922, repeating that there was no direct evidence linking it to gas exposure. "The records show conclusively that gas does not cause tuberculosis, but careless people go right on repeating the charge, never thinking of the brutal suffering that charge may cause," General Fries insisted. "Over 69,000 American boys now living were gassed in France. Another 500,000 were around gas at one time or another. What dark despair would haunt those men if the charge that gas caused tuberculosis were true?"[41]

The CWS and the army reiterated the point that summer. "Tuberculosis does not develop more frequently in gas victims than in other subjects and those former soldiers who, although enjoying good health at the present time, are laboring under mental worry, fearing symptoms of tuberculosis at any time, have been misled by advisers who, in many cases, have had little experience with warfare gases," the *Washington Star* said. The newspaper quoted a pamphlet prepared by the CWS medical division: "As to the incidence of pulmonary tuberculosis resulting from exposure to gas, it would seem that it is far from convincing that gas played any particular role in this connection and it is doubtful if the incidence of lung tuberculosis among ex-service men is much greater by reason of the part that gas played."[42]

The army continued a strong push to separate tuberculosis from wartime gassing for years afterward. A 1927 study by an army researcher using rabbits found no appreciable link between gassing and tuberculosis. The American Medical Association agreed, saying, "A man is no more liable to tuberculosis as a result of gassing than is a man who has never been gassed."[43]

Maj. Gen. H. L. Gilchrist, who followed General Fries as the CWS chief, referred to Matty's illness in 1931. He minimized any connection to the former captain's duties in France. "The great ball player was said by many to have contracted tuberculosis as the result of being gassed," he said. "We found that Mathewson was in a hospital at Brest suffering with influenza and that he never reached the front. Later we learned that he had been treated at Saranac Lake, N.Y., for tuberculosis before he enlisted. Physicians generally are beginning to accept our conclusion concerning tuberculosis."[44] (The general likely meant the base hospital at Chaumont, rather than Brest, and may have mistaken Branch Rickey's prewar stay at Saranac Lake for Matty's postwar treatment there.)

The Veterans Administration was a predecessor to today's U.S. Department of Veterans Affairs. The agency conducted a joint study with the CWS in 1933, fifteen years after the armistice. Again, no strong link emerged between wartime gassing and tuberculosis.

"The study shows that in some cases this disease has appeared but only in a very few instances can it be attributed directly to the war gas," the *Washington Star* reported. "Gas victims have developed tuberculosis and so have hundreds of others who had no part in the war. In most of the cases where this has appeared it is believed that it was present in a quiescent state before the gassing and merely was reactivated, rather than started, by the experience."[45]

The few modern studies tend to back the government on the effects of gas used during the war. While noting that "information about long-term effects is mainly anecdotal," a 2002 article in the medical journal *The Lancet* cites chronic respiratory disease and cancers of the pharynx, larynx, and lung among British and America veterans gassed during WWI; it makes no mention of TB, however.[46] "The conviction of having been gassed, whether accurate or not, had long term deleterious effects on a person's beliefs about illness and perceptions of health and wellbeing," a 2007 qualitative study adds.[47]

Matty's TB was not likely a result of exposure to toxic gas in France. So, then, where had he contracted the disease?

Matty had seen tuberculosis up close several years before his own illness. His brother Henry had died of TB in July 1917, at age thirty, at the family home in Factoryville. A pitcher like Big Six, "Hank" Mathewson had appeared in three games with the Giants in 1906-7 and played with four teams in the low Minors during 1907 and 1909.

"The deceased had been in poor health for some time, spending much of the past two years in Arizona in hopes of returning his strength, returning home only a couple of weeks ago," said a newspaper in nearby

Scranton, Pennsylvania.[48] Hank left a wife and four young daughters, whom Matty later supported.

Baseball historian, writer, and actor Eddie Frierson speculates that Matty contracted TB about the same time as Hank. Matty complained about pain in his left side while still pitching for the Giants. "It's possible," Frierson writes, "that he'd contracted the disease from his brother Henry and had it since 1914, but the physicians who'd examined him then were looking for muscle strain, not lesions irritating his lung and rubbing the inside of his ribs."[49]

This doesn't mean the Mathewsons were necessarily prone to TB, however. During Matty's illness and treatment, doctors around the country were trying to dispel a common belief that the illness ran within families.

"Tuberculosis is not hereditary," the U.S. Surgeon General wrote in summer 1925. "If you have noticed that consumption seems to run in families that is true largely because of the exposure of the young child to the disease." He added, "A person who has a latent infection may through strain, stress or illness develop active tuberculosis at any period of life."[50] It's noteworthy that researchers in 2019 identified a genetic condition that makes the human immune system susceptible to tuberculosis.[51] It's unknown whether the Mathewson brothers shared this genetic condition or how close their contact was during Henry's illness.

Alternately, Matty might have contracted tuberculosis in Cincinnati while managing the Reds from 1916 through 1918. Although largely successful in combating typhoid fever, the river city had an abysmal record with TB.

"Denver and New Orleans lead the country in their heavy death rate from tuberculosis, Cincinnati remaining third," the *Cincinnati Enquirer* said in February 1915.[52] (Denver ranked highest because many patients sought treatment for TB in Colorado. Consumptive gunfighter John Henry "Doc" Holliday, of O.K. Corral fame, died at Glenwood Spring, Colorado, in 1887.) Despite a slight improvement in death rates, the cities' rankings stood exactly the same in 1919, the year after Matty left Ohio. A total of 756 Cincinnatians died of tuberculosis that year, the fewest since 1910.[53]

It's also conceivable that Matty contracted TB while in the army. "Between July 1, 1917, and April 30, 1919, there were 4,201 cases of tuberculosis of all kinds and 433 deaths reported in the A.E.F.," a journal for military surgeons reported.[54] Overall, army doctors and nurses treated more than twenty-two thousand doughboys for TB, both in the United States and overseas.

"Tuberculosis patients required treatment for longer periods than other sick and wounded," says a WWI medical history, "thus they consumed a disproportionate amount of Medical Department resources."[55] There's simply no way of knowing now whether Captain Mathewson might have contracted TB from a fellow doughboy—on board a crowded troopship, in a barracks, or in a trench during his army service. As Matty fought valiantly to defeat the disease, Dr. Packard spoke hopefully of a path toward recovery.

"Matty has been at death's door three or four times," the physician told umpire and writer Billy Evans in spring 1922. "Twice I have despaired of his recovery." But the baseball idol had since regained his lost weight and was looking well. "In all probability Matty will be able to pay the Polo Grounds a visit some time during the summer for a short stay," Dr. Packard said. "I know that is one ambition he cherishes."[56]

15

....

Cooperstown

P. D. Haughton was the first of baseball's gas and flame men to die during peacetime. The Columbia University football coach succumbed suddenly of a heart attack on October 27, 1924, at age forty-eight.

Columbia held a memorial service in New York to coincide with his funeral in Boston. "A man whose fairness was never questioned, a man whose teams often went down but never went out," said a newspaper in Oklahoma, "Percy D. Haughton well deserves the title that baseball fandom conferred on Christy Mathewson—The Old Master—a master craftsman in one of the greatest games a sport loving world plays today."[1]

Christy Mathewson lived nearly a year longer than P. D. Despite his long fight with tuberculosis, his death, too, was unexpected and shocking. The former Giant had recovered enough by spring 1923 to become president and part owner of the Boston Braves. "It was a challenge Mathewson never should have undertaken," Major League Baseball historian John Thorn writes.[2] The ailing hurler returned to Saranac Lake following a relapse two years later.

On the afternoon of October 7, 1925, Matty listened to Game 1 of the World Series on the radio. Walter Johnson, the Washington Senators' great hurler, went the distance in beating the Pittsburgh Pirates, 4-1. "That is great," Matty said, smiling after the last out. "Good old Walter. He surely deserved it."[3]

Matty died at 10:30 p.m. that night after suffering a hemorrhage, his second in two weeks. Many newspapers and news agencies tied his death to the army. "A hero of the World War as well as of the diamond . . . he died late last night of tuberculosis and pneumonia, the result of being gassed while a captain in the Chemical Warfare Service in France," the Associated Press reported.[4]

"Mathewson really is a casualty of the World War, a subject he was as loathe to talk about as any other man who really carried the scars of conflict," the *New York Post* added. "He was gassed in France, just how never has been publicly related. The germs of the tuberculosis which killed him took life at that time."[5]

Jane Stoughton Mathewson, too, believed that her husband's overseas service had contributed at least indirectly to his fatal illness. She submitted a $10,000 insurance claim to the United States Veterans Bureau soon after his death, stating that he had contracted TB in "Sept 1918 France."[6] She likewise applied for widow's compensation from the Commonwealth of Pennsylvania's Department of Military Affairs, citing Matty's "Pulmonary Tuberculosis contracted in France 1918."[7] Both claims were denied. Pennsylvania reconsidered her application in 1934, only to disapprove it once more. For many fans and writers over the following decades, however, a link between Matty's duties in France and his later death at Saranac Lake was obvious.

Henry LeFort, the former jockey and boxer, died four years after Matty. He was perhaps the First Gas Regiment's last war casualty. Discharged from the army as a private first class, he had returned home to St. Louis and passed through a series of hospitals trying to recover from his wounds and gassing. Along the way LeFort developed great respect for Branch Rickey, whom he may have first met in France.

"Three hundred wounded soldiers at the United States Government Hospital were guests at an interesting talk delivered by Branch Rickey manager of the Cardinals at the Red Cross Hut last night," the *St. Louis Star* said in January 1922. "During the world war, Rickey was a major in the First Gas Regiment of the Chemical Warfare Service. Henry Lefort [*sic*], wounded soldier at the local hospital, who was a member of Rickey's regiment, introduced the leader of the Knot Hole Gang."[8]

LeFort received treatment later that year in Nebraska, where the *Omaha Bee* newspaper remembered him fondly and referred to him by his old sporting pseudonym, Jimmie Stevens. "Jimmie is a familiar figure around the Ak-Sar-Ben race track during the fall festival meeting.... He has been under the care of army physicians since arriving in the 'states' and at the present is quartered at the Bellevue Nebraska Veterans' Institution for Disabled Soldiers. He has been extended an invitation by Secretary Trimble of the Ak-Sar-Ben and last week was renewing old acquaintances among the 'jocks' and race followers."9

The former athlete married one of his nurses in April 1923. Jeannette Fischer LeFort had been wounded during the war, too, in an ambulance crash while serving in France. The couple had twin boys the following February. The *St. Louis Star* shared the new father's dazed amazement after the births.

> LeFort was breathless. He waited, expectant but frightened, for another hour and then he called his old friend, Maj. Branch Rickey.
> "Twin boys," he informed the major over the telephone—"first twins born in St. John's Hospital."
> "What are you going to name them?" Rickey inquired.
> "Names—say, I'm so excited I don't know my own."10

The names the ex-soldier and his wife chose were William Igoe LeFort and Taylor Rickey LeFort, nicknamed Branch. The following year they had a third son, Robert Edgar.

Lefort reunited in 1925 with friend Frank Murray, who likewise had been wounded in France, and with whom he had been hospitalized for seventeen months. "Last month [October], with the announcement of the opening of the Fairmount racetrack at Collinsville, Ill., Le Fort [sic], because of his close association with the racing game and his general knowledge of the requisites of the newspaper men assigned to cover the track, was placed in charge of the Fairmount press box," the *St. Louis Star* said. "His old pal, Murray, was selected by The St. Louis Star to handle the telegraphing instruments at the Fairmount end of their wire and again the pair met."11

By 1929 the LeFort family was living in the St. Louis suburb of Webster Groves. The former gas soldier was "a well-known World War veteran and . . . participated in many meetings and other enterprises in behalf of the wounded men in the Veterans' Hospital here."12 He still suffered terribly from his wounds, however, and grew increasingly despondent.

"Each week an army physician called at the Lefort home, and examined the war veteran's burned throat, while Mrs. Lefort [*sic*], and three little Leforts [*sic*] . . . looked anxiously on," a newspaper said. "Each time the army physician went away shaking his head."[13] The doctor visited for the last time on Sunday afternoon, October 20. LeFort swallowed three grains of bichloride of mercury at nine o'clock that night and died within an hour.

The experts said that gas either killed you right away or you lived. But sometimes it scarred your body and mind so deeply that years later you died by your own hand, despite the love and support of family and friends. A headline in a local German-language newspaper said "Lebensüberdrüssiger Weltkriegsveteran." Translated, it meant "World War Veteran Weary of Life."[14]

Major Rickey spoke before the veteran's flag-draped bier at a military funeral three days later. Branch "recalled that the deceased had received four citations for bravery under fire and that his death was a casualty of the war as certain as that of the man killed in the front line trenches. Le Fort [*sic*] was a sufferer from shell shock and gas ever since he was returned from overseas as an invalid."[15]

Heartbreak for the LeFort family didn't end with Henry's suicide. In January 1945, during World War II, twin son William was killed in action in Belgium, fighting with the 101st "Screaming Eagles" Airborne Division during the Battle of the Bulge. Sergeant LeFort's body was returned to St. Louis in 1948 for burial in the same cemetery as his father. Jeannette LeFort was buried there as well, following her death twenty years later. Each of the three graves is marked by a veteran's headstone.

Branch Rickey went on to change baseball and American society in 1947 by calling up Jackie Robinson, belatedly integrating the Brooklyn Dodgers and Major League Baseball. The former CWS major was inducted into baseball's Hall of Fame in 1967. Former gas officers Christy Mathewson (in the inaugural class of 1936), Ty Cobb (1936), Eppa Rixey (1963), and George Sisler (1939) were already enshrined at Cooperstown. Ned Hanlon, father of Joe, was posthumously inducted in 1996. Matty, Branch, the Georgia Peach, Eppa Jeptha, and the Sizzler each has a medallion affixed beneath his plaque, signifying army service during World War I.

Gabby Street skippered six Minor League clubs over nine seasons beginning in 1920. These were the Suffolk Nuts in the Class B Virginia League;
the Joplin (Missouri) Miners and Muskogee (Oklahoma) Athletics in the
Class C Western Association; and the Augusta (Georgia) Tygers, Columbia (South Carolina) Comers, and Knoxville (Tennessee) Smokies in the
Class B South Atlantic League. And the old catcher found a longtime
home at last in Missouri.

"Gabby was a peppery, devil-may-care sort when he came to Joplin," a
local sportswriter recalled years later. "But it was while he was managing
the Miners, and catching for the club as well, that he met pretty Lucinda
Chandler [Clark], a young woman who was to have a balancing and sal-
utary effect on the remainder of his career."[16]

Both divorced, the couple married and began a family, rearing a son and
a daughter. Gabby gave up hard drinking, contented now with an occasional beer. "From boisterous after-dark gent of other days, Gabby, since
1924, has become exemplar of good conduct," *Sporting News* said later.[17]

The reformed backstop's leadership in the Minor Leagues caught the
attention of an ex-CWS major. "Little did Street, apparently satisfied to
finish his baseball days in the minors, realize his excellent managing at
Joplin attracted the attention of one Branch Rickey, vice-president and
general manager of the Cardinals," the *St. Louis Star-Times* recalled.[18]
Sergeant Street and Major Rickey probably hadn't met in France—Gabby
was wounded while Branch was still recovering from influenza—but they
shared bonds as gas soldiers and baseball professionals, and certainly
had crossed paths while Gabby was managing in the Minors.

"They talked business as well as about their war days in France," an
Associated Press sportswriter later wrote. "The upshot was that Street
stayed on Rickey's little memorandum book and three years later was
offered the job as Cardinal coach."[19]

"Street was considered for several years as a potential member of the
Cardinal organization," the *St. Louis Post-Dispatch* said, offering a slightly
different timeline. "He was recognized as a smart baseball man, but in his
younger days he had one bad habit and [club owner] Sam Breadon and
Branch Rickey wanted to be sure that 'Gabby' was on the water wagon

seriously. When he had stayed on for five years he was accepted and signed as an employe [*sic*] of the Cardinal organization."[20]

The Cards called Gabby back up to the big show as a coach under manager Billy Southworth in 1929. Bill McKechnie replaced Southworth at midseason as the club performed poorly. Following a fourth-place finish, Gabby took the reins in 1930. Now one of the grand old men of baseball, called "Old Sarge" by writers and fans, he led the Cardinals to a 92-62 record and into the World Series, which they lost in six games to Connie Mack's powerful Philadelphia Athletics.

"A man with a record is Sergeant Street, formerly of the Chemical Warfare Service, A.E.F.," John Kieran wrote the following season in the *New York Times*. "He has been to strange places and has seen strange things. . . . He went through the Spanish-American War, the San Francisco earthquake, the Federal League War, the World War and the last world's series."[21] Gabby's Cardinals shone even brighter in 1931, finishing first in the National League at 101-53. They again faced the A's in the World Series.

"I am the happiest man in the world," Old Sarge said when St. Louis won Game 7. "This is the greatest day of my life. I've always wished I could manage a world championship ball club, but I didn't think I could do it at my age [49]."[22]

It was his only World Series. The Cardinals fired Gabby in June 1933. The crosstown Browns hired him as a coach in late 1937, elevated him to manager in 1938, then released him near the end of that season. "On the loose again, Street found another profession calling him."[23] A brewery hired him in 1940 as a commentator for Browns and Cardinals games broadcast on the *Star-Times'* radio network.

Gabby got a new partner after five seasons, first on radio and later on television, "his patient voice fitting perfectly with the rapid and colorful calling of the games by Harry Caray."[24] The popular broadcast duo worked for both clubs before switching solely to the Cardinals in 1947. *Sporting News* publisher J. G. Taylor Spink wrote of the fans who gathered to chat with Gabby at the Sportsman's Park press gate. "He answered all the questions with ease and cordiality. He is a walking encyclopedia on baseball. If he is wrong, no one knows it—and they don't care. They really aren't after information. They merely want to talk to Gabby, get his autograph, go back home and say, 'I talked to Gabby Street today.'"[25]

The Old Sarge died of cancer on February 6, 1951, much mourned in his adopted hometown of Joplin. A St. Louis sports editor remembered him as a "tireless story-teller . . . with his tales of war and romance, baseball and balderdash."[26] Never elected as a player, manager, or sportscaster to the National Baseball Hall of Fame, Gabby was posthumously elected to the state sports halls of fame of Missouri (1966) and Alabama (1983). His old broadcast partner hosted the Missouri induction. "Gabby could talk," Caray said fondly, "because he lived through so much."[27]

Acknowledgments

Thank you to researcher Lori Miller, in St. Louis, and to the librarians and archivists at the Ike Skelton Combined Arms Research Library, Fort Leavenworth, Kansas; U.S. National Archives, College Park, Maryland; Library of Congress, Washington DC; Cincinnati & Hamilton County Public Library; and Worthington (Ohio) Libraries. Thanks as well to screenwriter Kurt Stammberger for sharing his research into the overseas service of Major Rickey and Captains Cobb and Mathewson.

Abbreviations

NARA-165   Records of the War Department General and Special Staffs, Chemical Warfare Service: 1st Gas Regiment (30th Engineers), Records Group 165, National Archives, College Park MD

NARA-PEP   Persons of Exception Prominence collection, U.S. National Archives, St. Louis MO

NBHF   National Baseball Hall of Fame Library, Cooperstown NY

SFGR   Addison, *The Story of the First Gas Regiment*

Notes

1. Nashville

1. "Army and Navy Are Ordered on War Footing," *Nashville Tennessean*, March 26, 1917.
2. "Daguerreotypes Taken of Former Stars of the Diamond," *Sporting News*, November 15, 1934.
3. "No Reason to Be in the Dumps," *Washington Star*, February 9, 1908.
4. "Charlie Street in Huntsville," *Montgomery Advertiser*, December 29, 1909.
5. "1,067 Games in Ten Years," *Chattanooga Times*, March 5, 1913.
6. Johnson and Evans, "Some Experiences of a 'Speed-King.'"
7. Dugan, "Cold Weather Causes Cancelling of Game," *Washington Herald*, March 28, 1917.
8. Dougher, "Johnson Is Due to Twirl Today," *Washington Times*, March 27, 1917.
9. Thompson, "Nashville Games May Take Place," *Washington Star*, March 27, 1917.
10. Pigue, "Senators Play Vols To-morrow," *Nashville Banner*, March 27, 1917.
11. Dougher, "Johnson Is Due."
12. Pigue, The Sportograph, *Nashville Banner*, March 28, 1917.
13. "Dixie League Begins 17th Campaign with Rosy Outlook," *Nashville Tennessean*, April 8, 1917.
14. Horn, "All Vols Save Ernie Herbert Have Now Signed Contracts," *Nashville Tennessean*, April 7, 1917.

2. Gabby

1. Gould, "Gabby Street, Unknown 30 Years Ago, May Prove 'Man of Destiny' for N. L.," *St. Louis Post-Dispatch*, September 14, 1931.
2. "Colorful Career of Gabby Street Closes at 68," *Sporting News*, February 14, 1951.
3. Brundage, "Earthquake Prevented 'Gabby' from Jumping to Outlaw League," *St. Louis Star*, July 16, 1929. Brundage used much of this article again the following year in *Sporting News*.

4. Parrott, "Rickey Road to Fame Paved with Labor, Love, Laughs," *Brooklyn Eagle*, November 1, 1942.

5. "Kel's Conversion," *Sporting Life*, September 3, 1904.

6. "Street Is the Star," *Huntsville Mercury*, June 9, 1906, quoting *Cincinnati Post*, n.d.

7. "Captain Mohler's Ball Tossers Show Up Well in Their Practice Work at Bakersfield," *San Francisco Call*, March 10, 1907.

8. "Hard Work Done by Huntsville Boy in California," *Huntsville Mercury*, January 21, 1908, quoting *Cincinnati Exchange*, n.d.

9. "Seals Have Lots of Third Base Talent," *San Francisco Examiner*, February 5, 1908.

10. Rice, "Nationals Get Sweet Revenge from Wichita," *Washington Times*, April 3, 1908.

11. "Gabby Street Is Signed to Manage St. Paul Ball Club," *Eau Claire Leader*, November 13, 1935.

12. Brundage, "Earthquake Prevented 'Gabby.'"

13. Stockton, "Gabby Street Dead; Managed Both Cardinals and Browns," *St. Louis Post-Dispatch*, February 6, 1951.

14. The World of Sport, *Utica (NY) Globe*, February 13, 1909. Kahoe mistakenly recalled and likely exaggerated Street's performance, as records show no Washington doubleheader in Cleveland in 1908. Sportswriter Tom Rice noted after a late-May series with the Naps, "Charley Street did some high grade catching against Cleveland. Don't let that escape you."—Rice, "Third Win Sheds New Light on Nationals and Falkenberg," *Washington Times*, May 29, 1908.

15. Accounts of the catch varied somewhat over the years. J. G. Taylor Spink, for instance, later wrote that Street caught the thirteenth and final ball. Spink, "Looping the Loops," *Sporting News*, August 20, 1947.

16. "Ball Drops from Sky," *Washington Star*, August 21, 1908. Some old-timers believed Chicago Colts catcher William "Pop" Schriver had accomplished the feat in 1894. Schriver clearly made the attempt, but likely didn't snag any of the dropped balls.

17. "Go Crazy over Catch," *Washington Star*, August 22, 1908.

18. "Street Drops Ball Dropped 500 Feet," *Washington Herald*, August 22, 1908.

19. "Street's Catch of 504-Foot Drop Rare Test of Daring and Skill," *Washington Times*, August 22, 1908.

20. "By Catcher Charles Street," *Washington Herald*, August 22, 1908. Street said decades later that Washington outfielder Bob Granley helped him spot the ball against a "high sky."

21. "Big League Talk," *Washington Times*, August 22, 1908.
22. Johnson and Evans, "Some Experiences of a 'Speed-King.'"
23. "Keeley and Hughes Are Stars of Double Win," *Washington Star*, August 30, 1908.
24. "Colorful Career of Gabby Street."
25. Salsinger, "Ed Ainsmith as an Advertising Asset," *Sporting News*, February 8, 1919.
26. "Would Catch 100 Battles," *Chattanooga Times*, January 31, 1913. Washington traded Street to New York for Knight and a player to be named later.
27. "Again Dons a Uniform," *Utica (NY) Globe*, March 2, 1912.
28. Evans, "Overwork Often Shortens Career of Star Twirlers," *Washington Star*, January 17, 1915.
29. "1,067 Games in Ten Years," *Chattanooga Times*, March 5, 1913.
30. "Diamond Glints," *Chester Times*, April 1, 1912.
31. "Would Catch 100 Battles."
32. Mulligan, "The Names We Forget," *Baseball Magazine*, November 1913.
33. Horn, "Vols Slaughtered by Barons in Opening Game 9 to 1," *Nashville Tennessean*, April 14, 1917.
34. Blinkey Horn, "Today's Engagement with Lookouts Last of Home Stay," *Nashville Tennessean*, June 3, 1917.
35. "Chicks Make Sweep of Series and Capture Fourth Place," *Nashville Tennessean*, September 16, 1917.
36. "Nearly All the Vols Have Left for Their Winter Homes," *Nashville Tennessean*, September 17, 1917.

3. Frightfulness

1. "Form 'Gas and Flame' Unit," *Boston Globe*, October 22, 1917.
2. "Using Gas Bombs," *Keokuk (IA) Daily Gate City*, March 1, 1915.
3. Auld, "Gassed," *Saturday Evening Post*, May 25, 1918.
4. "Gas in Bombs, Too," *New York Sun*, April 26, 1915, reprinting the *Frankfurter Zeitung* via a Reuters correspondent in Amsterdam.
5. Chemical Warfare Service, *The Gas Mask*, 4.
6. Carpenter, "Fighting the Hun Devil with his Own Fire," *Boston Globe*, November 3, 1918.
7. "United States Chemical Warfare Service—I," *Scientific American*, March 29, 1919.
8. Parsons, *The American Engineers in France*, 188.

9. The Germans also used gas on the Eastern Front against Russian troops, who had little or no protection. The British didn't use gas against Turkish troops in their ill-fated Gallipoli campaign, and the Turks had no gas capability.

10. Keegan, *The First World War*, 201.

11. "Hell Fire Battalion Soon Off for Front," *Baltimore Evening Sun*, November 15, 1917.

12. Conant, *The Great Secret*, 11.

13. Roosevelt, "Lest We Forget," May 1919.

14. Kleber and Birdsell, *The Chemical Warfare Service*, 16, 3.

15. Brophy and Miles, *The Chemical Warfare Service*, 2–3.

16. "1,700 Chemists Employed for Gas Service," *Washington Herald*, June 29, 1918.

17. "Van H. Manning Sr., Engineer, Dies at Forest Hills Home," *Brooklyn Eagle*, July 14, 1932.

18. Heller, *Chemical Warfare in World War I*, 37.

19. "U.S. Troops to Use Gas and Flame Tactics," *Washington Times*, September 20, 1917.

20. "U.S. Prepared for Barbarity," *Washington Herald*, September 21, 1917.

21. Clark, "'Hell Fire' Men Are Called For," *Madison (SD) Leader*, December 27, 1917.

22. "Chance to Enlist with Gas and Flame Engineers," *Perth Amboy (NJ) News*, October 24, 1917.

23. Langer, *Gas and Flame in World War I*, xii.

24. "Joins 'Gas and Flame' Men," *Washington Post*, November 7, 1917.

25. "'Gas and Flame' Regiment Draws Few Volunteers," *St. Louis Post-Dispatch*, January 4, 1918.

26. "Crooked Finger Bar to Player; Heinie Groh Out," *Harrisburg Telegraph*, August 8, 1917.

27. "Baseball's War Hero Sobriquet Earned by 'Gabby' Street," *Atlanta Constitution*, April 27, 1919.

28. "'Gabby' Street in Gas and Flame Regiment," *Nashville Banner*, November 15, 1917.

29. Brundage, "Earthquake Prevented 'Gabby.' from Jumping to Outlaw League," *St. Louis Star*, July 16, 1929.

30. "Tagless Dogs Find Quiet Death in Trenches of Gas and Flame Division Out Near Chevy Chase," *Washington Post*, February 24, 1918.

31. "Hell Fire Battalion Soon Off."

32. Horn "Barnhardt Agrees to Terms Offered by Vol Magnates," *Nashville Tennessean*, January 31, 1918.

33. "Baseballs for Hell Fire Men," *Baltimore Sun*, November 9, 1917.
34. "LeFort" is the spelling found in the regimental history and various government documents. Newspaper accounts used that spelling, as well as Lefort and Le Fort.
35. "First Enlistment Here [in] Gas and Flame," *Dodge City Journal*, October 27, 1917.
36. "Henry B. 'Jimmie' Lefort of Journal Staff Leaves To-day for Army Service," *Dodge City Journal*, October 28, 1917.
37. "From Jockey to Ring Battler," *Omaha Bee*, September 17, 1922.
38. "Henry B. 'Jimmie' Lefort."
39. "City News," *Dodge City Journal*, November 8, 1917.
40. "Dogs and Cats Do War Service at American University Camp; Prove Gas and Flame Tests There," *Washington Post*, November 4, 1917.
41. SFGR, 2.
42. "Interesting Letters from Enid Boys with the Colors," *Enid (OK) Eagle*, February 3, 1918.
43. "Tagless Dogs Find Quiet Death."
44. "Local News Briefs," *Washington Post*, August 9, 1918.
45. "City Briefs," *Washington Post*, December 23, 1917.
46. SFGR, 13.
47. "Bremen Soldier Boy Writes Good Long, Letter to His Friends through the Columns," *Lancaster (OH) Eagle*, March 7, 1918.
48. "Gorrow, in Hospital, Tells His Record," *Appleton (WI) Crescent*, December 24, 1918.
49. Langer, *Gas and Flame in World War I*, xxii.
50. Killam, "W. H. Killam Writes Herald Letter from Camp," *Modesto Herald*, January 6, 1918.
51. Then and Now, *American Legion Monthly* 4, no. 3 (March 1928): 39.
52. "Walter Johnson Given Big Cut in Salary for Season," *Washington Herald*, January 13, 1918. The reporter mistakenly spelled the catcher's name "Streets," corrected here.
53. Gould, "The 'Old Sarge' Returns," n. p., February 1938, Charles Evard Street file, NBHF.
54. Horn, "'Gabby' He Was as Vol, Now Sergt. Street, 30th Engineers," *Nashville Tennessean*, February 15, 1918.
55. "'Gabby' Street Writes Letter from Ft. Myer," *Nashville Tennessean*, February 27, 1918. Clark Griffith's hugely successful Ball and Bat Fund provided free baseball equipment for troops both at home and overseas. "Sammies" was another popular name for doughboys.

4. Winter

1. "Rucker Pitched; That Is Enough," *Philadelphia Inquirer*, June 22, 1912.
2. Menke, "Carrigan Not Discouraged Yet," *Lima (OH) News*, October 9, 1915. The same nickname had been applied earlier to Washington Senators pitcher Frederick 'Cy' Falkenberg.
3. Dryden, "A Tall Mr. Rixey Tames Cubs While Phils Banish Lavender; Dooin Accused of Trickery," *Chicago Examiner*, July 20, 1912.
4. Lieb, "Rixey Dies Month after Election to Shrine," *Sporting News*, March 16, 1963.
5. Sanborn, "College Hurler Blanks Cubs, 4–0," *Chicago Tribune*, July 20, 1912.
6. Fullerton, "Phillies Rely on Alexander to Pitch the Team to Victory," *El Paso Herald*, October 6, 1915.
7. Grayson, "Hurler Rixey Never Did Overcome Stage Fright," *Fresno Bee*, July 3, 1943.
8. "News of the Old Dominion," *Alexandria (VA) Gazette*, August 2, 1912.
9. Eppa Rixey Jr., registration card, May 26, 1917, U.S. National Archives, https://www.ancestry.com.
10. Brundidge, "Eppa Rixey, Beginning 17th Year in Big League Bally Still Pitching Ace," *St. Louis Star*, May 16, 1929.
11. "Phillies Startle the Baseball World by Selling Alexander and Killefer to the Chicago Cubs," *Philadelphia Inquirer*, December 12, 1917.
12. Robert, "Eppa Rixey, Big Leaguer," *Elmira (NY) Star-Gazette*, September 11, 1952.
13. "Rixey Joins Uncle Sam," *Baltimore Sun*, December 17, 1917.
14. Maxwell, "From the Diamond to the Army to the Mines Looks Like an Eppa Rixey Double Play," *Philadelphia Public Ledger*, May 22, 1919.
15. "Branch Rickey to Succeed Lloyd Rickart as Secretary of Browns; Roger in Town," *St. Louis Star*, November 14, 1912.
16. Holland, "Mr. Rickey and the Game."
17. "Browns Will Lose Big Asset if Rickey Hops to Cardinals," *St. Louis Star*, March 20, 1917.
18. "Marvin Goodwin Wires Confirmation of Rumor He Has Become Aviator," *St. Louis Post-Dispatch*, December 2, 1917.
19. Lloyd, "Pitcher Goodwin Is First Card to Join Uncle Sam's Forces," *St. Louis Star*, December 1, 1917.
20. Lloyd, "Will Talk Trade for Any Player but Hornsby, Says Rickey," *St. Louis Star*, December 4, 1917.

21. Davis, Sport Salad, *St. Louis Post-Dispatch*, December 4, 1917.
22. Davis, Sport Salad, *St. Louis Post-Dispatch*, December 18, 1917.
23. "Jack Miller Enlists in U.S. Marine Corps," *St. Louis Star*, December 17, 1917.
24. "Mrs. Miller 'Doing Her Bit,'" *St. Louis Star*, December 27, 1917.
25. Lloyd, "Cardinals Could Make Good Use of Herzog at Second," *St. Louis Star*, December 19, 1917.
26. Davis, Sport Salad, *St. Louis Post-Dispatch*, January 3, 1918.
27. "Diamond Dust," *Wilkes-Barre (PA) Record*, January 12, 1918.
28. Interesting Sport Paragraphs, *Washburn (WI) Times*, April 25, 1918.
29. "Army Sanitary Corps Created," *Engineering News-Record*, August 30, 1917.
30. "Rixey on Way to Do U. S. Sanitary Work," *Evansville (IN) Journal-News*, February 1, 1918.
31. "Work of Changing Prairie into Camp for 30,000 Troops Starts West of City," *Fort Worth Star-Telegram*, July 26, 1917.
32. "Red Cross Money Aids 350,000 Men in the Southwest," *Attica (KS) Independent*, March 7, 1918.
33. "Famous Twirler of Phillies Sent Here for 'Gas' Courses," *Fort Worth Star-Telegram*, February 1, 1918.
34. Utect, "Preparing Texas and Oklahoma Brain and Brawn for Mortal Combat with the Hun," *Fort Worth Star-Telegram*, January 27, 1918.
35. "Philly Star Rixey, Now Lieutenant, Is Sent to California," *Fort Worth Star-Telegram*, February 21, 1918.
36. Page, *Our 110 Days' Fighting*, 161.
37. "Soldiers Like Tent Life in Snappy Air of New Camp Fremont," *San Francisco Examiner*, January 6, 1918.
38. Elder, "Fremont Team Is Looking for Troubles," *San Francisco Call*, February 6, 1918.
39. "Life of Christy Mathewson, Baseball's Immortal," *Pittsburgh Post*, February 18, 1926. Part of a lengthy series, the syndicated article carries no byline; a subhead states: "As told by Bozeman Bulger through courtesy of Mrs. Mathewson." Some newspapers running the series credit only Bulger, while others cite both him and Jane Mathewson.
40. Thorn, "The Very Respectable Adventures of Gentleman Matty and Dime-Novel Frank," Narratively, February 18, 2015, https://narratively.com/the-very-respectable-adventures-of-gentleman-matty-and-dime-novel-frank.
41. "Ohio Soldiers," *Cincinnati Enquirer*, January 3, 1918.
42. "Christy Mathewson Dies Unexpectedly," *New York Times*, October 8, 1925.

43. Ryder, "Soldiers May See Reds Train," *Cincinnati Enquirer*, January 6, 1918.

44. "'Regular Fellow' Verdict on 'Matty,'" *Montgomery Advertiser*, January 10, 1918.

45. "Matty Busy While at Camp Sheridan," *Montgomery Advertiser*, January 8, 1918.

46. "Ohio Soldiers Brave Chill Winds and Carry on Across Sheridan's Icy Drill Fields," *Montgomery Advertiser*, January 15, 1918.

47. "Matty Gets Free Training for Reds," *New York Times*, February 25, 1918.

48. "Mathewson an Example of Reward that Sometimes Comes to Clean-Cut Athlete," *Buffalo (NY) Commercial*, February 27, 1918.

49. "Reds Officially Welcomed to City at 'Hut' Luncheon," *Montgomery Advertiser*, March 13, 1918.

50. Hall, "Cincinnati Reds and U. of A. Clash on Soldiers' Field Today," *Montgomery Advertiser*, March 16, 1918.

51. Ryder, "Real Team Against the Redlegs," *Cincinnati Enquirer*, March 18, 1918.

52. "Notes of the Game," *Cincinnati Enquirer*, March 25, 1918.

53. "Military Funeral Was Held for Ralph Sharman," *Portsmouth (OH) Times*, May 29, 1918.

5. Good Scout

1. "'Matty' Proves Popular Pilot," *Scranton (PA) Republican*, June 15, 1918. New York columnist Dan Daniels, in contrast, later paraphrased a Cincinnati sportswriter's take on the 1918 season: "He says that Matty, who is not a good mixer, did not assume a friendly attitude toward the other writers and that they felt peeved thereover."— Daniels, High Lights and Shadows in All Spheres of Sport, *New York Sun*, March 10, 1919.

2. "Soldiers in France Calling for Matty," *New York Times*, April 25, 1918.

3. "Matty Has Not Made Up His Mind," *Cincinnati Enquirer*, April 26, 1918.

4. "Matty May Go to France—High Honor, Says Herrmann," *Pittsburgh Gazette Times*, April 26, 1918.

5. "Notes of the Game," *Cincinnati Enquirer*, April 27, 1918.

6. "Red Officials Want to Retain Big Six," *Pittsburgh Gazette Times*, April 27, 1918.

7. "John Ward May Accompany Matty," *New York Sun*, April 28, 1918.

8. "Notes of the Game," *Cincinnati Enquirer*, April 28, 1918.

9. "Matty to Stay with Reds," *New York Times*, April 29, 1918.

10. "Notes of the Game," *Cincinnati Enquirer*, April 29, 1918.

11. Knox, Over the Top in Sport, *New York Telegram*, April 29, 1918.

12. "Trenches Want Mathewson," *Harrisburg (PA) Telegraph*, April 30, 1918.
13. "Mathewson Never Said He Will Not Go Abroad," *New York Post*, May 4, 1918.
14. Wray, "Wray's Column," *St. Louis Post-Dispatch*, May 6, 1918.
15. "Still Seek Matty for Duty in France," *New York Times*, May 1, 1918.
16. "Still Seek Matty."
17. "What 'Matty' Says," *Cincinnati Commercial Tribune*, May 1, 1918.
18. "Matty May Accept Call 'Over There,'" *New York Sun*, May 2, 1918.
19. "Notes of the Game," *Cincinnati Enquirer*, May 2, 1918.
20. "Matty to Find Out What Duties Are before Going Over," *Cincinnati Commercial Tribune*, May 2, 1918.
21. Phelon, "Asks What Soldiers Want of Him in France," *Sporting News*, May 2, 1918.
22. "Matty's Indefinite Call," editorial, *Sporting News*, May 2, 1918.
23. "Notes of the Game," *Cincinnati Enquirer*, May 3, 1918.
24. "Matty Has Not Refused," *New York Times*, May 5, 1918.
25. Fullerton, "Cubs' Sensational Work Due to their Pitchers," *New York World*, May 6, 1918.
26. "Come On, Matty," *Stars and Stripes*, May 10, 1918.
27. "Matty's Call Is Cancelled," *Sporting News*, July 4, 1918.
28 Thomas Rice (as "Rice"), "All Set for World's Series, but How about Labor Day?," *Brooklyn Eagle*, August 24, 1918.
29. Ryder, "New Men to Bolster Red Staff," *Cincinnati Enquirer*, June 26, 1918.
30. Thompson, "Burke Is Puzzled by Tales that Baseball Is Tottering," *Washington Star*, July 9, 1918.
31. "Evers Prefers Going to France before Baseball," *Syracuse (NY) Journal*, June 6, 1918.

6. CWS

1. Clark, "As Chemical Warfare Chieftain," *Chemical Warfare Bulletin*, July 1941.
2. Fries, *History of the Chemical Warfare*, 43.
3. "Annual Report [of] Director of Chemical Warfare Service for Fiscal Year Ending June 30, 1919," *House Documents, 66th Congress, 2d Session, vol. 17*, 188.
4. "War Organization Specializes on Gas," *Lincoln (NE) State Journal*, July 3, 1918.
5. "Dick Livasy Gets Wound Stripe," *Maryville (MO) Democrat-Forum*, September 13, 1918.

6. "Letters from France," *Carbondale (PA) Leader*, October 9, 1918.

7. "New Chemical Insignia," *Stars and Stripes*, October 25, 1918.

8. "'Our Boys Just Burnt the Boche to Ashes,' Writes Honolulu Lad; Gas and Flamers 'Gives Huns Hell,'" *Honolulu Star-Bulletin*, October 18, 1918.

9. "Army and Navy News," *Washington Star*, July 28, 1918.

10. "Genius Wanted for Flame Corps," *Cleveland Plain Dealer*, July 19, 1918.

11. Farrow, *Gas Warfare*, 17.

12. U.S. Army War College, *Memorandum on Gas Poisoning in Warfare with Notes on Its Pathology and Treatment*, 15.

13. Fries and West, *Chemical Warfare*, 150.

14. "Mustard Gas," *Gas Defender*, August 1, 1918.

15. "The Use of Gas in Warfare and What the United States is Doing Both in the Offensive and Defensive," *Official U. S. Bulletin*, September 21, 1918. The *Bulletin* was a daily publication of the Committee on Public Information.

16. "Gas Regiment Back with Fine Record," *New York Sun*, February 3, 1919.

17. Hildebrand, "A Year in France with the Chemical Warfare Service," 131.

18. Langer and MacMullin, *With "E" of the First Gas*, 15.

19. Moore, "Gassing the Gassers," *American Legion Weekly*, October 27, 1922.

20. Kieran, "Sports of the World," *New York Times*, March 22, 1933.

21. Mousby, "Demonstrating Gas Warfare in Europe," *Chemical Warfare*, May 15, 1923.

22. "Glass Is Scarce at Verdun," *Sioux City (IA) Journal*, December 20, 1918.

23. "U.S. Gas Units Outhurled the Enemy 5 to 1," *New York Tribune*, February 3, 1919.

24. "Hanover Soldier Caught Between U.S. and Hun Fire," *Hanover (PA) Evening Sun*, September 11, 1918.

25. SFGR, 86.

26. "Gives Thrilling Description of Battles," *Fort Wayne News and Sentinel*, September 12, 1918.

27. "Flower Pots Like Bombs," *Salem Oregon Statesman*, November 1, 1918.

28. "With the First Gas Regiment," *University of Pennsylvania Gazette*, February 28, 1919.

29. "Protection from Poison Gases Used by Germans in France," *Washington Star*, March 3, 1918.

30. "The Use of Gas in Warfare."

31. Axelrod, *Selling the Great War*, x. Creel disputed the propaganda label. "Our work is educational and informative, for we have such confidence in our case that we feel that no more than a fair presentation of the facts

is needed to win the war."—"America's Danger at Hand, Says Beck," *New York Times*, April 5, 1918.

32. "His Land Life-Preserver," *Welding Engineer*, October 1918.

33. "It Sure Is a Great Game," *Maryville (MO) Democrat-Forum*, August 20, 1918.

34. "Once Worthless Things that Have Suddenly Become of Value," *Popular Science Monthly*, December 1918.

35. "Save Pits to Save Our Boys," *Columbia Missourian*, September 11, 1918.

36. D. M. Reed Company advertisement, *Bridgeport (CT) Times*, September 9, 1918.

37. Burgess-Nash Company advertisement, *Omaha Bee*, September 8, 1918.

38. "Young Are Asked to Gather Nuts," *Washington Star*, November 4, 1918.

39. "Gas Mask Day Observed Tomorrow," *Annapolis Gazette*, November 8, 1918.

7. France

1. NARA-165, Exhibit H, "Papers Concerning First Gas Regiment (30th Engineers)," History (Data), Box 302.

2. "Former Canton Boy Is Proud of Gas Outfit," *Canton (NY) Commercial Advertiser*, September 24, 1918.

3. SFGR, 18–19.

4. "Three Kingman Boys Meet on Board U.S. Transport," *Kingman (KS) Leader-Courier*, March 15, 1918.

5. "Sammies Tackle Speaking French," *Rushville (IN) Republican*, April 23, 1918.

6. "From Will Speiglemire," *Kingman Leader-Courier*, April 19, 1918.

7. "Cycle Club Boys Hear from Bunnell," *Carbondale (PA) Leader*, May 1, 1918.

8. "Gabby Street Is in France and Wild for Tobacco," *Nashville Tennessean*, April 16, 1918.

9. "Frankie Cox Is Now in France," *Albany (NY) Argus*, April 28, 1918.

10. "Dr. Keizer on British Front," *Marshfield and North Bend (OR) Coos Bay Times*, March 23, 1918. Captain Keizer later would be reported killed in action when his signature on a casualty form was mistakenly added to his list of the dead.

11. "Patriotism above Politics in East Writes W. H. Killam," *Modesto Herald*, April 18, 1918.

12. SFGR 32.

13. "Interesting Letters from Enid Boys with the Colors," *Enid (OK) Eagle*, June 9, 1918.

14. "From Our Exchanges," *Sidney (NE) Telegraph*, March 21, 1919, quoting *Des Moines (IA) Register*, n.d.

15. SFGR, 58.

16. "News about the Soldier Boys," *Weeping Water (NE) Republican*, December 26, 1918.
17. "War Department Deserts Chemical Warfare Service," *Chemical and Metallurgical Engineering*, October 1, 1919.
18. Albert, "Chaumont Center of Wars," *Spokane Spokesman-Review*, April 19, 1919.
19. Mousby, "Demonstrating Gas Warfare," *Chemical Warfare*, May 15, 1923.
20. Langer and MacMullin, *With "E" of the First Gas*, 33.
21. Spencer, "A History of Pittsburg and Western Pennsylvania Troops in the War," *Pittsburgh Press*, July 20, 1919.
22. Hildebrand, "A Year in France," 138.
23. *Loyola College Annual*, 68–70.
24. Fries, *History of the Chemical Warfare*, 60b–c.
25. SFGR, 54.
26. SFGR, 55–56.
27. "To Be Hanlon Park," *Baltimore Sun*, January 7, 1920. Twohig misspelled "Panuska," corrected here.
28. Phipps, "Letter from Some of the Boys in France," *Columbia Alumni News* 10, no. 11 (December 20, 1918), 388.
29. "Honors Lieut. Hanlon," *Baltimore Sun*, October 3, 1918.
30. SFGR, 67.
31. "Combatant Gas Troops Had Leading Part in U.S. Victory," *Brooklyn Eagle*, May 18, 1919.

8. Summer

1. "Bits of Shrapnel," *Augusta (GA) Herald*, Camp Hancock *Trench and Camp* edition, November 7, 1917.
2. "Ty Cobb Had His First Drill Lesson," *Houston Post*, March 29, 1917.
3. "Cobb Likely to Enlist," *New Britain (CT) Herald*, January 8, 1918.
4. "Cobb Denies Marine Yarn," *Detroit Free Press*, January 9, 1918.
5. "Ty Cobb Classified for the Next Draft," *Augusta (GA) Herald*, January 19, 1918.
6. "Cobb Re-classified; Goes in Class Two," *Augusta (GA) Herald*, January 23, 1918.
7. "Sporting Comment," *Stars and Stripes*, June 14, 1918.
8. "Ty Cobb Will Quit at Season's End to Enlist," *Washington Times*, July 13, 1918.
9. "Haughton Trained at First Plattsburg Camp," *Boston Globe*, July 27, 1918.

10. "Haughton to Coach Harvard," *Boston Post*, April 11, 1916. The headline refers to a time when Haughton's continuation as coach had been uncertain.
11. Friedman, *The Coach Who Strangled the Bulldog*, 9.
12. Farley, "Percy Duncan Haughton," 469.
13. "Percy Haughton Buys Braves," *Boston Globe*, January 8, 1916.
14. Rice, The Sportlight, *New York Tribune*, January 15, 1916.
15. Flatley, "Haughton in Right with Scribes," *Pittsburgh Press*, January 22, 1916.
16. Webb Jr., "Harvard Football Started Off Well," *Boston Globe*, September 26, 1917.
17. "Sportsman," Live Tips and Topics, *Boston Globe*, October 13, 1917.
18. "Ready for Plattsburg," *Boston Transcript*, August 9, 1915.
19. "Percy D. Haughton, Famous Football Coach, Now a 'Rookie' at Plattsburg," *Muncie (IN) Press*, August 17, 1915.
20. "Baseball Again Is Booming Preparedness," *Washington Herald*, February 24, 1917.
21. "Science of Football and War Have Same Object, Says Coach Haughton," *Buffalo (NY) Courier*, December 9, 1917.
22. Rice, The Sportlight, *New York Tribune*, November 11, 1916. Rice used the British spelling of "defence."
23. Farley, "Percy Duncan Haughton," 468.
24. It's unclear whether the anecdote refers to Harvard's victory in 1908 or 1915. Carlisle beat the Crimson in 1911. Jim Thorpe played for Carlisle in 1908 and 1911.
25. Wray, "Wray's Column," *St. Louis Post-Dispatch*, April 7, 1919.
26. "Major Percy Haughton Resigns from Braves," *New York Tribune*, July 30, 1918.
27. "National in Favor of Starting Sept. 2," *Philadelphia Public Ledger*, August 3, 1918.
28. Arms, "Chemical Warfare Service Should Appeal to Fandom," *New York Tribune*, September 8, 1918.
29. Fries, *History of the Chemical Warfare*, 44.
30. "Matty Plans for War Work Overseas," *New Britain (CT) Herald*, August 10, 1918.
31. Mann, *Branch Rickey*, 95.
32. Lowenfish, *Branch Rickey*, 103.
33. Lloyd, "Cards Tackle Braves in a 3-Game Series," *St. Louis Star*, August 16, 1918.

34. "Rickey Wants to Engage in War Work in France," *St. Louis Globe-Democrat*, August 17, 1918.

35. "Branch Rickey Going to France either on Y.M.C.A. or War Work," *St. Louis Post-Dispatch*, August 17, 1918.

36. Mann, *Branch Rickey*, 96. Mann wasn't specific about what commission Haughton meant. A scientific journal during the war offered a contrary perspective on Canadian approaches to gas warfare: "We only wish to note, in passing, that the Canadian authorities have failed so far to recognize chemical talent as worthy of a uniform, either in any of our local ball players or among our chemists."—"Recognition 'Here and There,'" *Canadian Chemical Journal* 2, no. 9 (September 1918): 243.

37. Gould, "Rickey Applies His Psychology to Study of Baseball Slumps," *St. Louis Star*, February 17, 1919.

38. NARA-PEP, Branch Rickey file: Ty Cobb, Willard Hotel, Washington DC, letter to director of Chemical Warfare Service, Washington DC, August 13, 1918.

39. "Branch Rickey Is Major in Army's Chemical Section," *St. Louis Post-Dispatch*, August 24, 1918.

40. Lloyd, "Call for Foreign Service Awaited by Major Rickey," *St. Louis Star*, August 24, 1918.

41. "Ty Cobb Passes Test for Army," *Augusta (GA) Herald*, August 17, 1918.

42. Jackson, "War May Aid Detroit Club, Pointing It to New Policy," *Detroit Free Press*, August 19, 1918.

43. Jackson, "Cobb, Only Officer from Tigers, Now May Laugh at Lieut. Tuthill," *Detroit Free Press*, August 29, 1918.

44. "Lambert Tells Sprightly Stories of Field Service," *St. Louis Post-Dispatch*, November 19, 1917.

45. "Four St. Louisans Helped Move 6500 Men," *St. Louis Post-Dispatch*, November 18, 1917.

46. "Marion Lambert Is Pupil at School of Machine Gun Fire," *St. Louis Globe-Democrat*, February 28, 1918.

47. The *St. Louis Post-Dispatch* later offered a contradictory history. Lambert, it said, "went to Princeton last January and studied five months in the United States School of Aeronautics, at the conclusion of which he went to France, where he was commissioned First Lieutenant in the gas regiment, to which he was attached the first part of October."—"L. J. Lambert Tells of First U.S. Gas Unit in France," *St. Louis Post-Dispatch*, February 19, 1919.

48. Albert Lambert, president of the family company, commanded a balloon school in Texas during the war. A great proponent of aviation, he supported Charles Lindbergh's historic flight across the Atlantic Ocean to Paris in 1927. The St. Louis airport, originally called Lambert Field, bore his name.

49. Harper, "Ex-Aide Describes Colorful Career of Hornbostel," *Pittsburgh Sun-Telegraph*, August 16, 1954.

50. "United States Chamber of Commerce—Greetings," *Proceedings of the Annual Meeting of the American Life Convention*, 1931.

51. Arms, "Chemical Warfare Service Should Appeal."

9. Final Innings

1. "All-Navy Team Beats All-Army in Great Game," *Oakland Tribune*, July 30, 1918. Luckless throughout his career, Chappell died of pneumonia resulting from influenza at Letterman Hospital on November 8, three days before the war's end.

2. "Rixey, Fremont's Star Pitcher, Is Leaving, Report," *San Jose Mercury Herald*, August 1, 1918.

3. Crowell and Wilson, *Road to France*, 99–100.

4. "Statement of Lieut. Col. Amos Fries," 288.

5. Ryder, "Oldfield Has Nothing on Matty," *Cincinnati Enquirer*, August 28, 1918. The *Enquirer* identified the officer only as "Colonel Shivers," a name that doesn't appear on various CWS rosters.

6. "Hiding behind Skirts," letter to the editor, signed A Traveler, *Cincinnati Enquirer*, September 2, 1918.

7. "Says 'Pull' Made Many U.S. Officers," *New York Sun*, October 10, 1919.

8. "No Bomb-Proof Jobs for Cobb and Matty," *Boston Globe*, September 9, 1918.

9. "The Use of Gas in Warfare and What the United States is Doing Both in the Offensive and Defensive," *Official U. S. Bulletin*, September 21, 1918.

10. Clark, "Army of Baseball Players and Fans," *Carbondale (PA) Leader*, March 28, 1919.

11. "War Department Deserts Chemical Warfare Service," *Chemical and Metallurgical Engineering*, October 1, 1919. Fries had reverted to postwar rank of lieutenant colonel.

12. Sheridan, "Slacker May Cheapen After-War Baseball Popularity," *Ogden (UT) Standard*, August 10, 1918.

13. "Notes of the Game," *Cincinnati Enquirer*, August 10, 1918.

14. "Notes of the Game," *Cincinnati Enquirer*, August 16, 1918.

15. "Notes of the Game," *Cincinnati Enquirer*, August 11, 1918.

16. Letter, Maj. Charles Richardson, Chemical Warfare Service, Washington, DC, to Christopher Mathewson, c/o Cincinnati Base Ball Club, August 19, 1918. Christopher Mathewson file, NBHF.

17. "Matty and Rickey May Form Battery in Overseas Game," *St. Louis Star*, August 27, 1918.

18. "Mathewson Quits Position as Manager of Redlegs to Assume Duties as Captain," *St. Louis Star*, August 27, 1918.

19. Ryder, "Oldfield Has Nothing on Matty." Pittsburgh is nearer to 300 miles from Cincinnati, and halfway to Factoryville.

20. "Double Header Briefs," *Cincinnati Enquirer*, August 29, 1918.

21. "Christy Mathewson Here," *Lewisburg (PA) Journal*, September 6, 1918.

22. "Christie' Mathewson Visits Gas Mask Plant," *New York Daily Star*, September 9, 1918.

23. "Ames and Perritt Pitch in First Game," *St. Louis Post-Dispatch*, August 26, 1918.

24. "Rickey Expects to Manage Cards on Return to Game," *St. Louis Post-Dispatch*, September 6, 1918.

25. "Rickey Quits City; To Report for Duty with Army Sept. 15," *St. Louis Star*, September 10, 1918.

26. "Peaceful Sisler Is No Pretty Picture," *Sporting News*, October 3, 1918.

27. "Major Rickey Here; On Way to France," *Portsmouth (OH) Daily News*, September 13, 1918.

28. "Peaceful Sisler Is No Pretty Picture."

29. Lieb, "Yanks and Tigers Each Win Game," *New York Sun*, August 25, 1918.

30. "Cobb Exit Is Made in Blaze of Glory," *New York Times*, August 25, 1918.

31. Holland, "Cobb and Sisler Pitch as Farewell Stunt to Major League Ball in St. Louis," *St. Louis Globe-Democrat*, September 2, 1918.

32. Davis, Sport Salad, *St. Louis Post-Dispatch*, September 2, 1918.

33. "Captain Ty Cobb at Augusta Home," *Augusta (GA) Herald*, September 9, 1918.

34. Jackson, "Can a Star Ball Player Come Back after Year Out? Cobb, Away Now after Second Best Season, May Answer," *Detroit Free Press*, September 22, 1918.

35. "Captain Ty Cobb Off for Service," *Augusta (GA) Herald*, September 30, 1918.

36. Davis, Sport Salad, *St. Louis Post-Dispatch*, August 29, 1918.

37. Inspired by army records presented on a 2003 episode of the television program *Antiques Roadshow*, a 2021 historical novel places Cobb, Rickey,

Mathewson, and several other Hall of Fame players in a secret U.S. Army unit, with the Chemical Warfare Service as their cover story. The premise is entertaining but not credible. Every man was demonstrably elsewhere on dates listed in the documents.

10. Shipping Out

1. "Matty Sees Future in Army," *Sporting News*, September 26, 1918. The uncredited writer author might have been Ernest J. Lanigan, who wrote the article that preceded it.
2. Bulger, "Life of Christy Mathewson, Baseball's Immortal," *Pittsburgh Post*, February 16, 1926.
3. "Sidney Nurse Home from Trouble Zone," *Dayton Daily News*, June 15, 1919.
4. *Report of the Surgeon General U.S. Army*, 2,100.
5. Great Britain Ministry of Health, *Report on the Pandemic of Influenza*, 285.
6. "Matty in French Hospital Pokes Fun at Boss Ebbets," *Brooklyn Eagle*, October 22, 1918. The byline was "By a Former Brooklyn Sporting Writer Now Overseas." Christie served at the hospital and later wrote a byline piece for the *Eagle* on President Wilson's postwar visit to Chaumont.
7. "News of Matty," *Cincinnati Commercial Tribune*, October 29, 1918,
8. "St. Louis Soccer League Forced to Suspend Schedule," *Sporting News*, October 17, 1918.
9. Lowenfish, *Branch Rickey*, 104.
10. Crowell and Wilson. *The Road to France*, II, 442.
11. *Report of the Surgeon General U. S. Army*, 2,035.
12. Lowenfish, *Branch Rickey*, 104.
13. "Rickey in France, Recovering from Pneumonia Attack," *St. Louis Star*, November 8, 1918. *Sporting News*, also published in St. Louis, incorrectly reported that Rickey had been treated "in a hospital in England," rather than in an English hospital. "Celebration Ought to Convince 'Em All," *Sporting News*, November 4, 1918.
14. "Maj. Rickey Now in Training School," *St. Louis Post-Dispatch*, November 8, 1918.
15. "News of Alexandria," *Washington Post*, September 23, 1918.
16. "Ty Cobb to Camp," *Alexandria (VA) Gazette*, September 23, 1918.
17. Dougher, Looking 'Em Over, *Washington Times*, October 8, 1918.
18. Maxwell, "With Throwing Arm Gone from Salutin,' Ty Ready for Action," *Philadelphia Public Ledger*, October 5, 1918.
19. Gravy, Sportography, *El Paso Herald*, October 17, 1918.
20. "Letters to the Editor," *Philadelphia Daily News*, February 12, 1962.

21. "Waterloo's Own Ambulance Company to Have First Reunion Since War," *Waterloo (IA) Courier*, November 7, 1930. U.S. Army Transport Service documents show that troops boarded *Baltic* on October 12, sailed on the 13th, and touched at Liverpool October 24.
22. "Steel League after St. Louis Players," *Philadelphia Public Ledger*, August 17, 1918. The paper misstates the names of Allen Sothoron and Charles Kelchner.
23. "Commission for Sisler," *Boston Globe*, September 13, 1918.
24. "Caught on the Fly," *Sporting News*, August 29, 1918.
25. Huhn, *The Sizzler*, 32.
26. "Ebbets First to Bar 'Evaders;' Griner, Ship League, Off His List," *Detroit Free Press*, September 13, 1918.
27. "St. Louis Almost off Baseball Map," *Sporting News*, September 26, 1918.
28. "Peaceful Sisler Is No Pretty Picture," *Sporting News*, October 3, 1918.
29. "The Manager Always Supplies the Uniform," *New York Tribune*, October 10, 1918.
30. Dougher, "Looking 'Em Over."
31. Lloyd, "Sisler Takes Up Intensive Study of Gas Fighting," *St. Louis Star*, October 14, 1918.
32. Dougher, Looking 'Em Over.
33. Sisler, "Why I Enlisted in the Army."

11. Autumn

1. "George E. Herbst Gets Baptism of Artillery Fire," *Hanover (PA) Evening Sun*, August 8, 1918.
2. NARA-165, "Miscellaneous G-3 Memos," n.d., Box 303.
3. "Irl Rogers Gets Eyes Ful of Mustard Gas," *Modesto Herald*, August 9, 1918.
4. "A Herald Boy Makes the Supreme Sacrifice," *Modesto Herald*, October 31, 1918.
5. SFGR, 32.
6. Braucher, "Gabby Knows How to 'Four Flame' on the Boys—He Learned in France," *Indianapolis Times*, September 29, 1930.
7. "Many Yankee Nines Batting 'Em Around," *Stars and Stripes*, May 17, 1918.
8. Historically, U.S. Army regiments had no Company Q, to avoid any possible confusion with Company G in handwritten orders. In the regular army, Company Q sometimes referred to guardhouse prisoners.
9. Dougher, Looking 'Em Over, *Washington Times*, February 12, 1919.
10. Kieran, Sports of the World, March 22, 1933.
11. Carter, *St. Mihiel*, 7.

12. SFGR, 115.

13. NARA-165, "War Diary of Thirtieth Engineers," n.d., Box 307.

14. SFGR, 123.

15. "Shrapnel Passed So Close, Thot [*sic*] He Was Hit," *Salem (OR) Capital Journal*, March 11, 1919.

16. Pershing, *My Experiences*, 294.

17. SFGR, 138.

18. Capt. Sidney Moore in Ford, *A History of Jefferson City*, 228. The ellipses are Moore's.

19. Brundage, "Gabby Street, a Fighter All of His Life, Spurns Title of Miracle Man, but Career Shows He Deserves It," *Sporting News*, October 2, 1930.

20. Edwards, *From Doniphan to Verdun*, 58.

21. Brundage, "Gabby Street, a Fighter." In 1947, following World War II, the regiment's Company A made Street its honorary first sergeant.

22. Cline, *The Story of the Sixteenth Infantry in France*, 51.

23. U.S. Army, Chemical Warfare Service, *History of Chemical Warfare Service*, III.5.17. This volume is the official regimental history, distinct from the unofficial history written by Chaplain Addison.

24. Kieran, Sports of the World, March 22, 1933.

25. Pigue, "Gabby Street Comes Back with Gas and Wound Scars," *Memphis News Scimitar*, February 13, 1919.

26. Eaton, "Dave Robertson May Join Griffmen," *Sporting News*, February 13, 1919.

27. Loesch, Inside Stuff, *Little Rock Arkansas Gazette*, February 19, 1919.

28. NARA-165, "Report of Operations by First Gas Regiment during Month of October, 1918," operations report, October 1918, Box 307.

29. Gillespie, "Life-Long Friends Are Reunited at Fairmount Race Track After Series of Fateful Experiences," *St. Louis Star*, November 2, 1925.

30. "Stork Bombards War Hero and His Wife with Twins," *St. Louis Star*, February 22, 1924.

31. "With Our Soldiers," *Coffeyville (KS) Journal*, November 12, 1918.

32. Clark, "Army of Baseball Players."

33. Clark, "Army of Baseball Players."

12. Choignes

1. "The Three Musketeers of Baseball," *St. Louis Star*, January 26, 1921.

2. "Maj. Rickey Now in Training School," *St. Louis Post-Dispatch*, November 8, 1918.

3. "Captain Cobb, U. S. A., Arrives Safe in France," *Detroit Free Press*, October 29, 1918.

4. Fries and West, *Chemical Warfare*, 88.

5. "Protection from Poison Gases Used by Germans in France," *Washington Star*, March 3, 1918.

6. Fries, *History of the Chemical Warfare*, 45.

7. Bulger, "Life of Christy Mathewson, Baseball's Immortal," *Pittsburgh Post*, February 20, 1926.

8. "Then and Now," *American Legion Monthly*, March 1928.

9. Spencer, "A History of Pittsburg and Western Pennsylvania Troops in the War," *Pittsburgh Press*, July 20, 1919.

10. Cobb and Stump, *My Life in Baseball*, 190–91.

11. "War Letters to The Eagle from Brooklyn Boys Overseas," *Brooklyn Eagle*, June 16, 1918.

12. "Former Herald Employe [sic] Writes from France," *Modesto Herald*, March 22, 1918.

13. "Wilmington Soldier in France Gets His Tobacco through Journal's Fund," *Wilmington (DE) Journal*, June 26, 1918.

14. "Aviators' Depot Is a Busy Place at Camp Taylor," *Paducah (KY) Sun*, January 10, 1918.

15. "Dr. Voorhees' Life Will Be Saved," *Hartford Courant*, June 25, 1918. The clergyman, Rev. Dr. John Brownlee Voorhees, later suffered a shattered leg when his YMCA hut was struck during a German shelling.

16. Eddy, *With Our Soldiers in France*, 49.

17. "War Letters to The Eagle from Brooklyn Boys Overseas," credited to George V. Christie, *Brooklyn Eagle*, August 1, 1918.

18. "Spies Work at Camp Cody," *Cook (NE) Courier*, reprinted in *Nebraska City Nebraska Press*, April 23, 1918.

19. "Haverhill Man Had Many Unfortunate Experiences," *Boston Globe*, August 12, 1918.

20. "Close Call from Shell," quoting Capt. Louis E. Goodrich, *Baltimore Sun*, October 21, 1918.

21. Roberts, "Ty Cobb Did Not Commit Murder," 28.

22. Leerhsen, *Ty Cobb: A Terrible Beauty*, 386–87.

23. Alexander, *Ty Cobb*, 237.

24. Rickey with Riger, "Mathewson, McGraw Pals," *Philadelphia Inquirer*, January 26, 1966. Excerpt from Rickey and Riger, *The American Diamond*, 19.

25. Farrell, "Clubs' Departures Sadden Mathewson," *Pittsburgh Press*, February 21, 1921.

26. "'Matty' Back in the Game as Bravest of the Braves," *Baltimore Sun*, April 15, 1923.

27. Winship, "Maj Haughton Back, Approves Heydler," *Boston Globe*, December 22, 1918.

28. "Matty May Not Return to Reds," *New York Times*, January 10, 1919.

29. "Matty Returns to America as Gas Goes Out of Use with the Signing of the Armistice," *New York Herald*, February 18, 1919.

30. "Mathewson Returns to United States," *Geneva (NY) Daily Times*, March 17, 1919.

13. Homecomings

1. "Same Old Johnny Evers Home from France," *Albany (NY) Journal*, December 17, 1918.

2. Bullion, "Ty Cobb Returns to Native Heath Alive and Well," *Detroit Free Press*, December 17, 1918. Somewhat contradicting this timeline, Ty said later that he "was to have been sent to the front on November 14th," but the war ended beforehand. "Captain 'Ty' Cobb Returns to Augusta," *Augusta (GA) Chronicle*, December 21, 1918.

3. "Gen. Barnett, Capt. Ty Cobb Notables Aboard Leviathan," *Brooklyn Eagle*, December 16, 1918.

4. "8,870 War Heroes Here on Leviathan; Many Wear Medals," *New York Sun*, December 17, 1918.

5. "Cobb to Quit Baseball," *New York Times*, December 17, 1918.

6. Bullion, "Ty Cobb Returns."

7. Winship, "Haughton Back, Approves Heydler," *Boston Globe*, December 22, 1918.

8. Sportsman, Live Tips and Topics, *Boston Globe*, December 26, 1918.

9. O'Leary, "Wouldn't Have Missed War for Anything, Says Haughton," *Boston Globe*, January 5, 1919.

10. "Read," advertisement, *Boston Globe*, April 10, 1919.

11. Sisler, "Why I Enlisted in the Army."

12. "Sisler Captures All the Trophies," *El Paso Herald*, December 5, 1918.

13. "Sisler Receives Army Discharge; Hornsby Is Here," *St. Louis Post-Dispatch*, December 16, 1918.

14. Sisler, "Why I Enlisted in the Army."

15. "Branch Rickey Sore Because He Had No Time at Bat in War," *Cincinnati Commercial Tribune*, December 13, 1918.

16. "Maj. Branch Rickey Arrives in St. Louis on Furlough," *St. Louis Post-Dispatch*, December 30, 1918.

17. Fleisher, "A look at Branch Rickey, 'Through a Daughter's Eyes,'" *Elmira (NY) Star-Gazette*, February 15, 2004.

18. "New Joplin Boss Was Wounded in Action in France," *Joplin (MO) Globe*, March 26, 1922.

19. Jackson, *Fall Out to the Right of the Road!*, 455–56.

20. "Street Suffering from Gas Attack," *Washington Times*, January 16, 1919.

21. "Charley Street, Badly Gassed, In Hospital at Camp Dix," *Williamsport (PA) Gazette and Bulletin*, January 14, 1919.

22. "'Gabby' All Set for League Ball; Back from War," *Nashville Tennessean*, January 13, 1919.

23. Pigue, "Gabby Street Comes Back with Gas and Wound Scars," *Memphis News Scimitar*, February 13, 1919.

24. "'Heinies' Couldn't Stop Gabby. Neither Can the Dixie Hurlers," *Nashville Banner*, May 11, 1919.

25. "Gabby Street May Not Come Back," *Nashville Tennessean*, October 1, 1919.

26. Ray, Looking Over the Dope, *Nashville Banner*, December 28, 1919.

27. "Gas House Is Matty's Hang Out," *Cincinnati Enquirer*, December 28, 1918. The village Jane Mathewson calls Hendicourt apparently is Heudicourt-sous-les-Côtes, located thirty miles southwest of Metz.

28. "'French Poor Ball Players' Says Matty," *Bucknell University Bucknellian*, February 25, 1919.

29. "Col. Thompson Determined to Stick to End," *Pittsburgh Press*, January 5, 1919.

30. Untitled, unmailed postcard, Heudicourt, France, November 25, 1918, Christopher Mathewson file, NBHF.

31. "Metz. Deutsches Tor," unmailed postcard, November 24, 1918, Christopher Mathewson file, NBHF.

32. Frank Lane, "'Reds Are Not on Market,' Says President Herrmann," *Cincinnati Commercial Tribune*, December 17, 1918.

33. Letter, Capt. Christopher Mathewson to Chief of Chemical Warfare Service, Second Army, A. E. F., re: Reply to telegram, no. 1164, Deputy Chief, C.W.S., A.E.F., dated December 17, 1918, Christopher Mathewson file, NBHF.

34. "Mathewson Given the S.O.S.," *Cincinnati Commercial Tribune*, January 25, 1919.

35. "Pat Moran Will Direct Fortunes of Cincinnati Reds," *New York Times*, January 30, 1919.

36. "Matty Back on Feb. 15," *New York Times*, February 6, 1919.

37. "Christy Mathewson May Return to Scene of Former Triumphs as Assistant to McGraw," *New York Times*, February 18, 1919.

38. "Matty Returns to America as Gas Goes Out of Use with the Signing of the Armistice," *New York Herald*, February 18, 1919.

39. Lieb, "Stories of French Taking to Baseball Knocked into Cocked Hat by Capt. Mathewson on Return from Overseas," *New York Sun*, February 18, 1919.

40. "Matty to Be Next Leader of Giants," *New York Times*, March 8, 1919.

41. Lieb, "Mathewson Again Becomes a Giant," *New York Sun*, March 8, 1919.

42. Lieb, "Eight Yanks Are on Holdout List," *New York Sun*, March 10, 1919.

43. Maxwell, "Jack Coombs Hopes to Have Eppa Rixey on Mound This Year," *Philadelphia Public Ledger*, March 8, 1919.

44. "Eppa Rixey Signs Phillies' Contract," *Philadelphia Inquirer*, May 24, 1919. Alexander took the loss in the Phillies' 7–2 victory over the Cubs.

45. The Old Sport's Musings, *Philadelphia Inquirer*, May 26, 1919.

46. Maxwell, "Tex Richard Stung on the Big Fight; Made but $100,000," *Philadelphia Public Ledger*, July 10, 1919.

47. Demaree, "Eppa Finds Retiring a Hard Proposition," *Waterloo (IA) Courier*, May 24, 1933.

48. "'Worst Place on Earth,' Gen. Butler Calls Camp at Brest He Commands," *Washington Post*, January 1, 1919.

49. Brown, "70,00 Yanks at Brest Toil in Mud While Waiting at Rest Camp," *Washington Post*, January 1, 1919.

50. SFGR, 195.

51. "Sergeant Herbst Commends Y.M.C.A. for Its War Work," *Lancaster (PA) New Era*, February 17, 1919.

52. "Shrapnel Passed So Close, Thot [*sic*] He Was Hit," *Salem (OR) Capital Journal*, March 11, 1919.

53. "Washington Boy in Gas and Flame Division," *Washington Star*, March 16, 1919.

54. SFGR, 197–98. The transport ship, a White Star liner in peacetime, was previously designated RMS *Celtic*.

55. "Gas Regiment Back with Fine Record," *New York Sun*, February 3, 1919.

56. "How We Worked the Gas," *Poughkeepsie Eagle-News*, February 3, 1919.

57. SFGR, 199.

58. "Fighting with Gas," editorial, *Portland Oregonian*, September 6, 1919.

14. Saranac Lake

1. Mathewson, "Mathewson Deduces from World's Series that National League Outclasses Its Rival," *New York Times*, October 12, 1919.

2. "Doyle, McGraw and Matty to Aid in Big Loan To-day," *New York Tribune*, May 8, 1919.

3. "Rockefeller Pays $1,000,000 for Ball at Rally for Loan," *Chicago Tribune*, May 9, 1919.

4. "Baseballs at Loan Rally Bring $1,000,000 Each," *New York Tribune*, May 9, 1919.

5. Ray, "'I Am Lacking in Brains,' Says Pitcher Fred Toney," *Pittsburgh Press*, April 10, 1919.

6. Kohout, "Hal Chase."

7. Macbeth, "Hal Chase Exonerated by John A. Heydler on Charge of 'Throwing' Games," *New York Tribune*, February 6, 1919.

8. "Big Six Might Be Next Leader of Gotham Nine," *Cincinnati Commercial Tribune*, February 1, 1919.

9. "Baseball Is Too Brutal for French," *Philadelphia Inquirer*, February 18, 1919.

10. "Notes of the Game," *Cincinnati Enquirer*, June 14, 1919.

11. McGeehan, "McGraw's Star Triumphs in Duel of Southpaws," *New York Tribune*, July 24, 1919.

12. Mathewson, "'Hitting Power of the Reds Will Carry Team to Victory'— Matty," *New York Times*, October 2, 1919.

13. Mathewson, "Mathewson Deduces."

14. Mathewson, "Baseball Is Not Crooked in Spite of Big Bets on Games, Declares Christy Mathewson," *New York Times*, October 16, 1919.

15. The Gossiper, *Lewisburg (PA) Journal*, May 28, 1920.

16. "Matty Leaves Giants," *New York Times*, July 4, 1920.

17. "Mathewson Ill; Goes to Adirondacks for a Long Rest," *New York Tribune*, July 4, 1920.

18. "Christy Mathewson Seriously Ill with Tuberculosis," *Boston Evening Globe*, July 30, 1920.

19. "Christy Mathewson, Famous Ball Player, Seriously Ill with Tuberculosis," *Richmond (VA) Times-Dispatch*, July 31, 1920.

20. Krishnan, *Phantom Plague*, 3.

21. Mandavilli, "Tuberculosis, like Covid, Spreads by Breathing, Scientists Report," *New York Times*, October 19, 2021.

22. "TB Elimination: The Difference Between Latent TB Infection and TB Disease," Centers for Disease Control and Prevention, accessed December 30, 2021, https://www.cdc.gov/tb/publications/factsheets/general/ltbiandActivetb.pdf.

23. "Matty, the idol of All Fandom, Seriously Ill of Tuberculosis," *New York Tribune*, July 31, 1920.

24. Shannon, "Mathewson in Fight for Life," *Boston Post*, August 8, 1920.

25. Davenport, "Christy Mathewson," *Outlook*, August 30, 1922.

26. Williams, "The Comeback of Christy Mathewson," *Albuquerque Journal*, December 2, 1923.

27. "'Matty' Back in the Game as Bravest of the Braves," *Baltimore Sun*, April 15, 1923.

28. Bulger, "Life of Christy Mathewson," February 20, 1926.

29. "Pitcher 'Matty' Getting Better, Wife Declares," *Cincinnati Commercial Tribune*, November 11, 1920.

30. Sisler, "Why I Enlisted in the Army."

31. "Christy Mathewson Visits Friends in the Town of His Boyhood Days," *Cincinnati Commercial Tribune*, August 11, 1920.

32. "Mathewson Recovering from Tuberculosis Siege," *Richmond (IN) Palladium and Sun-Telegram*, November 9, 1920.

33. "Dr. Gath Tells How Mathewson Is Being Cured," *Cincinnati Commercial Tribune*, November 12, 1920.

34. "Here's the Real Truth about Christ Mathewson," *Syracuse (NY) Journal*, December 21, 1920.

35. "'Big Six' Improving," *Lewisburg (PA) Journal*, February 4, 1921.

36. Farrell, "Clubs' Departures Sadden Mathewson," *Pittsburgh Press*, February 21, 1921.

37. The Old Sport's Musings, *Philadelphia Inquirer*, August 15, 1921.

38. "Poison Gas in Naval Warfare," article signed "Quarterdeck," editorial page, *New York Tribune*, September 25, 1921.

39. de Bles, "Poison Gas Warfare," letter to the editor, *New York Tribune*, September 27, 1921.

40. Fries, "Gas as a War Element," letter to the editor, *New York Tribune*, September 30, 1921.

41. "Poison Gas Most Humane Weapon, Says Gen. Fries," *Washington Herald*, January 17, 1922.

42. "Mistake to Regard Tuberculosis Common Result of Warfare Gases," *Washington Star*, July 4, 1922, quoting army publication "The After-Effects of Gas Poisoning."

43. "War Gases and Tuberculosis," *Journal of the American Medical Association* 89 (July 16, 1927): 206. Quoted in Byerly, *Good Tuberculosis Men*, 147.

44. "Chemicals Most Humane Weapon," *Cincinnati Enquirer*, February 6, 1931.

45. Henry, "Fear of War Gas Dispelled," *Washington Star*, July 20, 1933.

46. Volans and Karalliedde. "Long-Term Effects of Chemical Weapons," *Lancet*, December 2002, https://doi.org/10.1016/S0140-6736(02)11813-7.

47. Jones, Palmer, and Wessely, "Enduring Beliefs about Effects of Gassing in War: Qualitative Study," *BMJ* 2007; 335: 1,313, accessed December 29, 2021, https://www.bmj.com/content/335/7633/1313.
48. "Obituary," *Harrisburg (PA) Times*, July 2, 1917.
49. Frierson, "Christy Mathewson."
50. Cumming, "Your Health," *New Britain (CT) Herald*, August 25, 1925.
51. "Researchers Find Genetic Link to Tuberculosis," Rockefeller University Science News in Brief, May 8, 2019, https://www.rockefeller.edu/news/25808-researchers-find-genetic-link-tuberculosis/.
52. "Lowest Death Rate," *Cincinnati Enquirer*, February 4, 1915.
53. "Dr. Gath Tells How Mathewson Is Being Cured," *Cincinnati Commercial Tribune*, November 12, 1920.
54. Emerson, "Survey of Communicable Diseases in the A.E.F.," 412.
55. Byerly, *"Good Tuberculosis Men"* 122.
56. Evans, "Baseball Idol Getting Well," *Ogden (UT) Standard-Examiner*, April 8, 1922.

15. Cooperstown

1. "Percy D. Haughton," editorial, *Sapulpa (OK) Herald*, editorial, November 8, 1924.
2. Thorn, "The Very Respectable Adventures of Gentleman Matty and Dime-Novel Frank," Narratively, February 18, 2015, https://narratively.com/the-very-respectable-adventures-of-gentleman-matty-and-dime-novel-frank.
3. Mill, "Mathewson Hero in Death as on Diamond and in War Zone," *Syracuse (NY) Herald*, October 8, 1925.
4. "Christy Mathewson Dead, Mourned by Base Balldom: Pittsburgh under Handicap," *Washington Star*, October 8, 1925.
5. "Entire World of Sport Joins Baseball Folk in Eulogy of Christy Mathewson," *New York Evening Post*, October 8, 1925.
6. NARA-PEP, Christopher Mathewson file: Jane S. Mathewson, Application of Widow, United States Veterans Bureau, November 3, 1925.
7. Jane Stoughton Mathewson, Pennsylvania Veteran's Compensation application 285661, October 31, 1934, https://search.ancestry.com/.
8. "Rickey Address 300 Wounded War Vets at Government Hospital," *St. Louis Star*, January 18, 1922.
9. "From Jockey to Ring Battler," *Omaha (NE) Bee*, September 17, 1922.
10. "Stork Bombards War Hero."
11. Gillespie, "Life-Long Friends Are Reunited at Fairmount Race Track after Series of Fateful Experiences," *St. Louis Star*, November 2, 1925.

12. "Three Little Babe Ruth's [*sic*]," *St. Louis Star*, March 12, 1929.

13. "Eleven Years Later," *Murphysboro (IL) Independent*, October 22, 1929.

14. "Lebensüberdrüssiger Weltkriegsveteran," *St. Louis Westliche Post*, October 21, 1929.

15. "Funeral Service Held for World War Hero," *St. Louis Globe-Democrat*, October 24, 1929.

16. Stubblefield, "Joplin Mourns Sterling Citizen Street," *Sporting News*, February 14, 1951.

17. "Daguerreotypes Taken of Former Stars of the Diamond," *Sporting News*, November 15, 1934.

18. "Gabby's' Still the Main Street in St. Louis," *St. Louis Star-Times*, August 5, 1941.

19. Gould, "Rickey Encouraged Street to Seek Position as Minor Leader after World War," *St. Louis Post-Dispatch*, September 23, 1931.

20 Stockton, "Street, New Cardinal Pilot, Is a Popular, Plain Man and A Fountain of Wit and Wisdom," *St. Louis Post-Dispatch*, November 1, 1929.

21. Kieran, Sports of the Times, *New York Times*, August 18, 1931.

22. Dunkley, "Bedlam in Clubhouse after Triumph; Baseball's Biggest Men Join in Celebration," *St. Louis Post-Dispatch*, October 11, 1931.

23. "'Gabby's' Still the Main Street."

24. "'Gabby' Street in Windsor," *Clinton (MO) Henry County Democrat*, January 8, 1948.

25. Spink, "Looping the Loops," *Sporting News*, August 20, 1947.

26. Stockton, "Gabby Street Dead; Managed Both Cardinals and Browns," *St. Louis Post-Dispatch*, February 6, 1951.

27. "Charles Evard 'Gabby' Street," Missouri Sports Hall of Fame, accessed January 2, 2022, http://mosportshalloffame.com/inductees/charles-evard -gabby-street.

Bibliography

"Adapting Pits to the Mask." *Gas Defender*, October 1, 1918.

Addison, James Thayer. *The Story of the First Gas Regiment*. Boston: Houghton Mifflin, 1919.

Alexander, Charles C. *Ty Cobb*. New York: Oxford University Press, 1984.

American Battle Monuments Commission. *American Armies and Battlefields in Europe: A History, Guide, and Reference Book*. Washington DC: Center of Military History, United States Army, 2018 [reprint]. https://history.army.mil.

Arnold, Catherine. *Pandemic 1918: Eyewitness Accounts from the Greatest Medical Holocaust in Modern History*. New York: St. Martin's Griffin, 2018.

"Athletes Make Good Officers." *Gas Defender*, October 1, 1918.

Auld, S. J. M. *Gas and Flame in Modern Warfare*. New York: George H. Doran, 1918.

———. "Gassed," *Saturday Evening Post*, May 25, 1918.

Axelrod, Alan. *Selling the Great War: The Making of American Propaganda*. New York: Palgrave Macmillan, 2009.

"Baseball in the Military: America's Pastime Goes to War." *Stars and Stripes*, 2008.

Baskerville, Charles. "'Gas' in this War: The Vast Development of a New Military Weapon." *American Review of Review* 58, no 3 (September 1918): 273–80.

Beamish, Richard J., and Francis A. March. *America's Part in the World War: A History of the Full Greatness of Our Country's Achievements*. Philadelphia: John C. Winston, 1919.

Bell, Lindsay John. "Reconstructing Baseball's Image: Landis, Cobb, and the Baseball Hero Ethos, 1917–1947." PhD. diss., Iowa State University, 2020. https://lib.dr.iastate.edu/etd/18066.

Benwell, Harry A. *History of the Yankee Division*. Boston: Cornhill, 1919.

Brophy, Leo P., and Wyndham D. Miles. *The Chemical Warfare Service: From Laboratory to Field*. Washington DC: Center of Military History, United States Army, 1988.

Byerly, Carol R. *"Good Tuberculosis Men": The Army Medical Department's Struggle with Tuberculosis*. Fort Sam Houston TX: Office of the Surgeon General, 2013.

Carey, Charles. "Walter Johnson." SABR BioProject. sabr.org/bioproject.

Carter, Daniel A. *St. Mihiel: 12–16 September 1918*. Washington DC: Center of Military History, 2018.

Cary, Lusican. "Mathewson's Biggest Victory." *Good Housekeeping* (August 1923): 48, 174–76.

Ceresi, Frank. "Chemical Warfare Service: World War I's House of Horrors." In *When Baseball Went to War*, edited by Todd Anton and Bill Nowlin 32–36. Chicago: Triumph Books, 2008.

Chambrun, Jacques Aldebert de Pineton, comte de, and Charles Marenches. *The American Army in the European Conflict*. New York: Macmillan, 1919.

Charles Evard Street file, National Baseball Hall of Fame Library, Cooperstown NY.

Chemical Warfare Service. *The Gas Mask: An Illustrated Digest of the History and Development of the Military Gas Mask*. Washington DC: War Department, November 1942.

"Chemical Warfare Service: It's History and Personnel." *Chemical Engineer* 26, no. 10 (September 1918): 379–84.

Christopher Mathewson file, National Baseball Hall of Fame Library, Cooperstown NY.

Clark, Edward B. "As Chemical Warfare Chieftain." *Chemical Warfare Bulletin* 27, no. 3 (July 1941): 83–89.

Class of 1889, Harvard College, Thirtieth Anniversary 1889–1919, Eighth Report of the Class Secretary. Cambridge MA: Harvard College, 1919.

Cline, Thomas S. *The Story of the Sixteenth Infantry in France*. Montabaur-Frankfurt, Germany: Martin-Flock, 1919.

Cobb, Ty with Al Stump, *My Life in Baseball: The True Record*. Garden City NY: Doubleday, 1961.

Coleman, Kim. *A History of Chemical Warfare*. Houndmills UK: Palgrave Macmillan, 2005.

Conant, Jennet. *The Great Secret: The Classified World War II Disaster that Launched the War on Cancer*. New York: W. W. Norton: 2020.

Cords, Annette. "Camp Fremont: Trench Warfare in Menlo Park." *Interaction Point* 3, no. 1 (January 1992): 5.

Creel, George. *How We Advertised America: The First Telling of the Amazing Story of the Committee on Public Information that Carried the Gospel of Americanism to Every Corner of the Globe*. Harper & Brothers, 1920.

———. *The War, the World, and Wilson*. New York: Harper & Brothers, 1920.

Crowell, Benedict. *America's Munitions, 1917–1918*. Washington DC: Government Printing Office, 1919.

Crowell, Benedict, and Robert Forrest Wilson. *The Road to France: I & II. The Transportation of Troops and Military Supplies, 1917–1918*. New Haven: Yale University, 1921.

Dalessandro, Robert, John Wessels, et al. *World War I Battlefield Companion*. Arlington VA: American Battle Monuments Commission, 2018. https://www.abmc.gov.

Deane, Bill. *Baseball Myths: Debating, Debunking, and Disproving Tales from the Diamond*. Lanham MD: Scarecrow Press, 2012.

Dock, Lavinia L., Sarah Elizabeth Pickett, et al. *History of American Red Cross Nursing*. New York: Macmillan Co., 1922.

Driver, David. "Eppa Rixey." *The National Pastime* 15 (1995): 85–87.

Eddy, Sherwood. *With Our Soldiers in France*. New York: Association Press, 1917.

Edwards, Evan Alexander. *From Doniphan to Verdun: The Official History of the 140th Infantry*. Lawrence KS: World Company, 1920.

Emerson, Haven. "Survey of Communicable Diseases in the A. E. F.," *Military Surgeon* 49, no. 4 (October 1921): 389–420.

Emery, Theo. *Hellfire Boys: The Birth of the U.S. Chemical Warfare Service and the Race for the World's Deadliest Weapons*. New York: Little, Brown and Company, 2017.

Farley, J. W. "Percy Duncan Haughton," *The Harvard Graduates' Magazine* 33 (1924–1925): 464–71.

Farrow, Edward S. *Gas Warfare*. New York: E. P. Dutton, 1920.

Faulkner, Richard S. *Meuse—Argonne: 26 September–11 November 1918*. Washington DC: Center of Military History, 2018.

Finkel, Jan. "Eppa Rixey." SABR BioProject, sabr.org/bioproject.

Fitzgerald, Gerard J. "Chemical Warfare and Medical Response During World War I." *American Journal of Public Health* 98, no. 4 (April 2008): 611–25.

Fleitz, David L. *Ghosts in the Gallery at Cooperstown: Sixteen Little-Known Members of the Hall of Fame*. Jefferson NC: McFarland, 2004.

Ford, James Everett. *A History of Jefferson City, Missouri's State Capital, and of Cole County*. Jefferson City MO: New Day Press, 1938.

Freemantle, Michael. *Gas! Gas! Quick, Boys!: How Chemistry Changed the First World War*. Stroud, Gloucestershire: History Press, 2013.

Friedman, Dick. *The Coach Who Strangled the Bulldog: How Harvard's Percy Haughton Beat Yale and Reinvented Football*. Lanham MD: Rowman & Littlefield, 2018.

Frierson, Eddie. "Christy Mathewson." SABR BioProject. sabr.org/bioproject.

Fries, Amos A. "Chemical Warfare." *Journal of Industrial and Engineering Chemistry* 12, no. 5 (May 1, 1920): 423–29.

Fries, Amos A. "Gas in Attack." *National Service* 5, no. 6 (June 1919): 327–36.
———. "Gas in Attack." *National Service* 6, no. 1 (July 1919): 7–12.
———. "Gas in Defense." *National Service* 7, no. 1 (January 1920): 17–21.
———. *History of the Chemical Warfare Service in France*. Washington DC: War Department, Chemical Warfare Service, 1919.
Fries, Amos A., and Clarence J. West. *Chemical Warfare*. New York: McGraw-Hill, 1921.
Gilchrist, H. L. *A Comparative Study of World War Casualties from Gas and Other Weapons*. Washington DC: Government Printing Office, 1928.
Ginsburg, Daniel. "Ty Cobb." SABR BioProject. sabr.org/bioproject.
Gordon, Martin K., et al. "A Brief History of the American University Experimental Station and U.S. Navy Bomb Disposal School, American University." Washington DC: Office of History, U.S. Army Corps of Engineers, June 1994.
Great Britain Ministry of Health. *Report on the Pandemic of Influenza, 1918–19*. London: H. M. Stationery Office, 1920.
Gurtowski, Richard. "Remembering Baseball Hall of Famers Who Served in the Chemical Corps." *Army Chemical Review* (July–December 2005): 52–54.
Hanlon Park: Landmark Designation Report. Baltimore MD: Commission for Historical and Architectural Preservation, 2018.
Hartley, Michael. *Christy Mathewson: A Biography*. Jefferson NC: McFarland: 2004.
Hayes, Bertram. *Hull Down: Reminiscences of Wind-Jammers, Troops and Travellers*. New York: Macmillan, 1925.
Heller, Charles E. *Chemical Warfare in World War I: The American Experience, 1917–1918 (Leavenworth Papers 10)*. Fort Leavenworth KS: Combat Studies Institute, 1984.
Hildebrand, J. H. "A Year in France with the Chemical Warfare Service." *University of California Chronicle* 21, no. 2 (April 1919): 129–38.
Hillier, Alfred J. "Albert Johnson, Congressman." *Pacific Northwest Quarterly* 36, no. 3 (July 1945): 193–211.
Holland, Gerald. "Mr. Rickey and the Game." *Sports Illustrated*, March 7, 1955
House Documents, 66th Congress, 2d Session, vol. 17, December 1, 1919–June 5, 1920. Washington: Government Printing Office, 1920.
Hoyt, Charles B. *Heroes of the Argonne: An Authentic History of the Thirty-Fifth Division*. Kansas City MO: Franklin Hudson, 1919.
Huhn, Rick. *The Sizzler: George Sisler, Baseball's Forgotten Great*. Columbia: University of Missouri Press, 2013.

Jackson, Edgar B. *Fall Out to the Right of the Road!* Verona VA: McClure Press, 1973.

Johnson, Walter, as told to Billy Evans. "Some Experiences of a 'Speed-King' or, My Life-Story." *St. Nicholas Illustrated Magazine*, October 1914.

Keegan, John. *The First World War*. New York: Vintage Books, 2000.

Kleber, Brooks E., and Dale Birdsell. *The Chemical Warfare Service: Chemicals in Combat*. Washington DC: Office of the Chief of Military History, U.S. Army, 1966.

Kohout, Martin. "Hal Chase." SABR BioProject. sabr.org/bioproject.

Koontz, A. R. "War Gasses and Tuberculosis: An Experimental Study." *Archives of Internal Medicine* 39, no. 6 (June 1927): 833–64.

Krishnan, Vidya. *Phantom Plague: How Tuberculosis Shaped History*. New York: PublicAffairs, 2022.

Lamberty, Bill. "George Sisler." SABR BioProject. sabr.org/bioproject.

Lane, F. C. "Baseball's Bit in the World War." *Baseball Magazine*, March 1918.

Langer, William L. *Gas and Flame in World War I*. New York: Alfred A. Knopf, 1965.

Langer, William L., and Robert B. MacMullin. *With "E" of the First Gas*. Brooklyn NY: Holton Printing, 1919.

Leerhsen, Charles. *Ty Cobb: A Terrible Beauty*. New York: Simon and Schuster, 2015.

Lefebure, Victor. *The Riddle of the Rhine: Chemical Strategy in Peace and War*. New York: Chemical Foundation, 1923.

Lieb, Fred. *Baseball as I Have Known It*. Lincoln NE: University of Nebraska Press, 1996.

Lowenfish, Lee. *Branch Rickey: Baseball's Ferocious Gentleman*. Lincoln NE: University of Nebraska Press, 2007.

Loyola College Annual. Baltimore MD: Loyola College, 1918.

Lynch, Mike. "Fred Toney." SABR BioProject. sabr.org/bioproject.

Mann, Arthur William. *Branch Rickey: American in Action*. Boston: Houghton Mifflin, 1957.

Markham, E. M. "Past, Present and Future of Fort Humphreys." *Military Engineer* 21, no. 116 (March–April 1929): 125–28.

McCue, Andy. "Branch Rickey." SABR BioProject. sabr.org/bioproject.

McGraw, John J. *My Thirty Years in Baseball*. New York: Boni and Liveright, 1923.

Mead, Frederick S., ed. *Harvard's Military Record in the World War*. Boston: Harvard Alumni Association, 1921.

Moore, William E. "Gassing the Gassers." *American Legion Weekly*, October 27, 1922.

Murray, John F. "Tuberculosis and World War I." *American Journal of Respiratory and Critical Care Medicine* 192, no. 4 (August 15, 2015): 411–14.

Page, Arthur W. *Our 110 Days' Fighting.* Garden City NY: Doubleday, Page, 1920.

Parsons, William Barclay. *The American Engineers in France.* New York: D. Appleton, 1920.

Paxson, Frederic L., Edward S. Corwin, and Samuel B. Harding, eds. *War Cyclopedia: A Handbook for Ready Reference on the Great War.* Washington DC: Government Printing Office, 1918

Pennsylvania in the World War: An Illustrated History of the Twenty-Eighth Division. Pittsburgh: States Publication Society, 1921.

Pershing, John J. *My Experiences in the World War.* 2 vols. New York: Frederick A. Stokes, 1931.

Pettit, Dorothy Ann. "A Cruel Wind: America Experiences Pandemic Influenza, 1918–1920, A Social History." PhD diss., University of New Hampshire, 1976. https://scholars.unh.edu/dissertation/1145.

Piazzi, Mike. "Hank Mathewson." SABR BioProject. sabr.org/bioproject.

Report of the Surgeon General U. S. Army to the Secretary of War 1919, vol. 2. Washington DC: Government Printing Office, 1919.

Rickey, Branch, and Robert Riger. *The American Diamond: A Documentary of the Game of Baseball.* New York: Simon and Schuster, 1965.

Riegelman, Harold. "A Chemical Officer at the Front." *Chemical Warfare Bulletin* 23, nos. 3 and 4 (July and October 1937): 106–16, 151–63.

Roberts, Doug. "Ty Cobb Did Not Commit Murder." *National Pastime* 16 (1996): 25–28.

Roosevelt, Archibald. "Lest We Forget" (two parts). *Everybody's Magazine,* May and June, 1919.

Sisler, George. "Why I Enlisted in the Army," *Baseball Magazine,* March 1919.

Smart, Jeffrey A. "History of Chemical and Biological Warfare: An American Perspective." In *Medical Aspects of Chemical and Biological Warfare,* edited by Frederick R. Sidell, et al., 9–86. Washington DC: Office of the Surgeon General, 1997. https://www.globalsecurity.org/wmd/library/report/1997/cwbw/Ch2.pdf.

"Statement of Lieut. Col. Amos Fries." *Army Appropriation Bill: Hearings Before the Subcommittee of the Committee on Military Affairs, United States Senate.* Washington DC: Government Printing Office, 1919.

Stieglitz, Julius. "The New Chemical Warfare" *Yale Review* 7, no 3 (April 1918): 493–511.

Thomas, Henry W. *Walter Johnson: Baseball's Big Train.* Lincoln NE: University of Nebraska Press, 1995.

United States Army in the World War, 1917–1919: Meuse-Argonne Operations of the American Expeditionary Forces. Washington DC: Historical Division, Department of the Army, 1948.

United States Army in the World War, 1917–1919: Reports of Commander-in-Chief, A. E. F., Staff Sections and Services. Washington DC: Historical Division, Department of the Army, 1948.

"United States Chemical Warfare Service," parts 1 and 2, *Scientific American,* March 29 and April 12, 1919.

U.S. Army, Chemical Warfare Service. *History of Chemical Warfare Service, American Expeditionary Forces, First Gas Regiment.* n.p.: First Gas Regiment, 1919.

U.S. Army, Corps of Engineers. *The Offensive in Gas Warfare Cloud and Projector Attacks.* Washington DC: Government Printing Office, 1918.

The U.S. Army in the World War I Era. Washington DC: Center of Military History, 2017.

U.S. Army War College. *Gas Warfare,* parts 1–3. Washington DC: Government Printing Office, 1918.

——. *Memorandum on Gas Poisoning in Warfare with Notes on Its Pathology and Treatment.* Washington DC: Government Printing Office, 1917.

Volans, Glyn N., and Lakshman Karalliedde. "Long-Term Effects of Chemical Weapons." *Lancet,* Supplement 360 (December 2002): 35–36.

Walters, Douglas B. "The WWI Chemical Warfare Service and . . . Baseball?" *Journal of Chemical Health & Safety* 22, no. 1 (January–February 2015): 2–4.

Wancho, Joseph. "Gabby Street." SABR BioProject. sabr.org/bioproject.

——. "It Weighed 300 Pounds and Traveled 95 MPH." *Inside Game* 15, no. 4 (September 2015): 1–6.

Ward, Robert deC. "Weather Controls Over the Fighting during the Spring of 1918." *Scientific Monthly* 7, no. 1 (July 1918): 24–33.

Wilcox, Barbara. "'Fremont, the Flirt': Unearthing Stanford's World War I Battleground." *Sandstone & Tile* 37, no. 2 (Spring–Summer 2013): 3–15.

Williams, Helena Lorenz. "The Come-Back of Christy Mathewson." *Survey* 51, no. 5 (December 1, 1923): 248–51.

Yockelson, Mitchell. *Forty-Seven Days: How Pershing's Warriors Came of Age to Defeat the German Army in World War I.* New York: NAL Caliber, 2016.

Index

Addison, James Thayer, 68, 143, 145
Adirondack Mountains, 149. *See also* Saranac Lake NY
AEF. *See* American Expeditionary Forces (AEF)
Aeolus, 134
Agamemnon, 63, 64
Ainsmith, Eddie, 10
Ak-Sar-Ben race track, 160, 161
Alabama: army camp in, 41; Gabby Street's employment in, 11; Gabby Street's family in, 5; records on Gabby Street, 118; Reds in, 43; sports hall of fame in, 165
Albany NY, 87
Alexander, Charles, 127
Alexander, Grover Cleveland "Pete": army's draft of, 33; honoring of, 141; with Phillies, 31–32, 34; pitching records of, 93; success of, 40
All-Army baseball team, 89
Allies, 15, 17
All-Navy baseball team, 89
ambulance companies, 106
ambulances, 86–87
America, 64
American Ambulance Field Service, 86
American Association, 37

American Expeditionary Forces (AEF): appeal to Christy Mathewson, 45, 48, 51; chemical warfare responsibilities of, 54; gas officers with, 92; gas regiments of, 63; headquarters of, 67; tuberculosis cases in, 158
American League, 2, 34, 35, 73, 100, 108
American Medical Association, 155
American University, 21–22, 24
American University Experimental Station, 24
American University Training Camp, 25, 26
animal experiments, 24–25
Antiques Roadshow, 187n37
Antivivisection Society, 25
architects, 87
Argonne Forest, 119
armistice, 62, 63, 90, 128–29
Arms, Louis Lee, 81, 85, 87, 88
Army and Navy League, 107
Associated Press: on Christy Mathewson, 48, 150, 153, 159; on failure of pit and shell collection campaign, 62; on Gabby Street's enlistment and training, 21; on Rickey-Street association, 163; on Ty Cobb, 85

Atkisson, E. J., 24, 113, 144
Atlanta Constitution, 21
Atlantic Ocean, 104
Augusta (Georgia) Tygers, 163
Augusta GA, 73, 74, 85, 99, 131
Augusta Herald, 74, 99
Ayer MA, 78

Baccarat, France, 113
Baker, Frank "Home Run," 107
Baker, Newton, 26, 55, 111, 142
Baker, William, 32 140, 141
Bakersfield CA, 6
Baltic, 106, 131, 188n21
Baltimore MD, 22, 23, 71, 107
Baltimore Orioles, 22
Baltimore Sun, 17, 22, 23
Barrett, Charley, 97
baseball: in France, 113–14, 139; industrial leagues for, 107; integration of, 162; P. D. Haughton's postwar plans in, 132; popularity in military, 40, 42, 43, 45, 47, 75, 89, 133; Ty Cobb's departure from, 131
baseball games, fixing of, 93–94, 147–49
Baseball Magazine, 11
Bat and Ball Fund, 28, 175n55
Battle of Arras, 58
Battle of Loos, 17
Battle of the Bulge, 162
Belgium, 4, 15, 162
Belleau Wood, 69, 114
Bellevue Nebraska Veterans' Institution for Disabled Soldiers, 161
Bergen NJ, 141
Bethlehem Steel League, 107–9
bichloride mercury, 162

Birmingham Barons, 11
"Black Sox" scandal, 149
Blackwell, Harry, 86
Boise ID, 34
Bordeaux, France, 134
Boston Beaneaters, 6
Boston Braves: administration of, 76, 77; Christy Mathewson with, 159; in military, 89, 114; ownership of, 77; Percy Haughton's resignation from, 81; Reds vs., 95; war's effect on, 78
Boston Globe, 76, 77, 126, 128, 150
Boston MA, 159
Boston Post, 77
Boston Red Sox, 32, 103
Boy Scouts, 61
Breadon, Sam, 163
Brest, France: Branch Rickey's departure from, 133; Christy Mathewson in, 155, 156; gas regiment in, 26, 64, 142, 143, 145; U.S. troop transports in, 90, 130
British Expeditionary Force (BEF), 17
Brooklyn Dodgers, 103, 162
Brooklyn Eagle, 5, 18, 52, 102, 130, 150, 187n6
Brooklyn NY, 84, 141
Brooklyn Superbas (Dodgers), 22
Brown, George Rothwell, 142–43
Buffalo NY, 20
Bulger, Bozeman, 41, 123, 151–52, 177n39
Bunnell, Henry C. "Bun," 55, 65
Bureau of Mines, 18, 24, 25, 54
Burns, George, 146
Busch, Adolphus A., III, 86
Butler, Smedley, 142
Butterworth, Frank, 79

Buzancey, 121

Camp, Walter, 83
Camp A. A. Humphreys. *See* Camp
    Humphreys VA
Camp American University, 27. *See
    also* American University
Camp Belvoir VA, 23
Camp Bowie TX, 38–39
Camp Cody NM, 126
Camp Devens, 78
Camp Dix NJ, 135
Campfire Girls, 61
Camp Fremont CA, 39–40, 89, 90
Camp Hancock, 73
Camp Humphreys VA, 23, 88, 105–6,
    110, 132
Camp Kendrick NJ, 133, 141, 144
Camp Leach, 24
Camp Merritt, 141
Camp Mills, 143, 144
Camp Pontanezen, 142–44
Camp Sheridan, 41–44, 45, 51
Camp Zachary Taylor KY, 125
Canada, 84, 119, 184n36
Cantillon, Joseph "Pongo Joe," 7
Cantwell, Mike, 75
Caray, Harry, 164, 165
carbon, 61
Carlisle Indian Industrial School, 80–
    81, 183n24
Carlock, John S., 58, 59, 144
Carter, E. C., 45, 50
Celtic, 144
Central League, 5
Chappell, Larry, 89, 185n1
charcoal, 61
Chase, Hal, 93–94, 147
Château-Thierry, 66, 69, 114, 119

Chattanooga Lookouts, 11
Chattanooga TN, 10, 13
Chaumont, 67, 71, 102, 114, 142, 156,
    187n6
checkers, 41–42
chemical warfare: advances in, 17,
    60; Allies' use of, 17; army per-
    sonnel for, 38; defense against,
    16–18, 38; deployment of, 15–16;
    experimentation with, 24–25;
    organization of U.S. departments
    for, 54; public attitudes toward,
    19, 154; U.S. development of, 18.
    See also gas warfare
Chemical Warfare Service (CWS):
    anonymity of, 56, 66; Branch
    Rickey's postwar position in,
    134; chemists in, 89; first combat
    death in, 71; headquarters of,
    98; health problems associated
    with, 151–56, 159; historical novel
    about, 187n37; insignia of, 55–56;
    leadership of, 54, 55; organization
    of, 55–56; Percy Haughton's com-
    mission in, 76; Percy Haughton's
    suitability for, 79–80, 81; as per-
    manent organization, 154; public
    attitudes toward athletes in, 90–
    92, 93; qualities of recruits for, 82,
    88, 90–91; recruitment for, 56,
    81–83, 87, 108, 109; sports figures
    in, 22–24, 81–86, 88, 90–92, 123.
    See also Thirtieth Engineers/First
    Gas Regiment
chemists: athletes as, 8, 31, 33, 111;
    British, 16; Bureau of Mines, 18,
    24, 25; in CWS, 89, 90–91; U.S.
    recruitment of, 19, 55, 56
Cheppy, 117

Chicago Colts, 172n16

Chicago Cubs, 32, 33, 95, 103, 141. *See also* Chicago Nationals

Chicago Examiner, 30

Chicago IL, 50

Chicago Nationals, 50. *See also* Chicago Cubs

Chicago Tribune, 30, 147

Chicago White Sox, 50, 89, 99, 102, 148–49

chlorine, 15, 57, 124, 152, 154

Choigznes, 67, 71, 107, 122, 124, 127, 151

Christie, George V., 102–3, 187n13

Cicotte, Eddie, 148

Cincinnati Commercial Tribune, 49, 50, 138

Cincinnati Enquirer: on athletes' commissions, 185n5; on Christy Mathewson, 41, 46, 47, 48, 50, 51, 52, 95; on game fixing, 94; on Hal Chase, 148; on illness in city, 157; on Reds vs. soldiers game, 43

Cincinnati OH, 157

Cincinnati Reds: army recruits from, 21; Branch Rickey with, 34; Christy Mathewson with, 45, 46, 48, 49–50, 82, 137–38, 140; Eppa Rixey with, 142; fans of, 148; Gabby Street with, 5, 6; management of, 40, 137–39; 1918 season of, 93–95, 103; training camp of, 42–43; uniforms of, 44; in World Series (1919), 148–49

Cincinnati Times-Star, 30

Clark, Edward B., 19, 54, 87–88, 92, 120–21

Clarke, Jay, 74, 75

Cleveland Indians, 98

Cleveland Naps, 8, 172n14

Cleveland Plain Dealer, 56

Cobb (film), 126

Cobb, Charlie Lombard, 100

Cobb, Paul, 74–75

Cobb, Tyrus Raymond: biographers of, 126–27; career of, 73; commission of, 91; Gabby Street compared with, 3; gas accident of, 126, 127, 128, 151; in Hall of Fame, 162; in historical novel, 187n37; joining of military, 74–75; military training of, 105–6, 122, 123, 124, 130; 1918 season of, 98–100; P. D. Haughton and, 132; postwar plans of, 99, 100, 131; recommendation of Branch Rickey, 85; recruitment for CWS, 85; reputation of, 93; return to U.S., 130–31, 191n2

Cobb: A Biography (Stump), 126

Collinsville IL, 161

Colorado, 157

Columbia (South Carolina) Comers, 163

Columbia University, 22, 71, 132, 159

Comiskey, Charles, 50

Commonwealth of Pennsylvania Department of Military Affairs, 160

Company Q. *See* U.S. First Replacement Company

Conant, Jennet, 17

Coombs, Jack, 141

Cooperstown NY. *See* National Baseball Hall of Fame

Cornell University, 76

COVID-19, 150

Cravath, Clifford "Gavvy," 141

Creel, George, 60, 181n31

Creel Committee. *See* U.S. Commit-
        tee on Public Information
Criger, Lou, 10
Croix de Guerre, 69, 144
Cuba, 5
CWS. *See* Chemical Warfare Service
        (CWS)
cylinders, 58, 59

Daniels, Dan, 178n1
Davis, Lynn C., 36, 37, 99, 100
Dawn, Hazel, 146
Day, Robin, 115–16, 143
Dayton OH, 108
Dean, Dizzy, 122
Debarkation Hospital No. 1, 135
Demaree, Al, 142
Denver CO, 157
Detroit Free Press: on athlete-officers,
        122; on George Sisler, 109, 110; on
        Ty Cobb, 74, 85, 99, 130, 131
Detroit MI, 110, 127
Detroit Tigers, 9, 43, 73, 85, 98–99
De Witt, William, 97
dichloroethyl sulfide. *See* mustard gas
Dickman, Joseph T., 120, 121
Dodge City Journal, 23, 24
Dougher, Louis A., 2, 110, 114
Doyle, Larry, 146, 147
draft, military: baseball trades and,
        32; eligibility for, 12, 75; Eppa
        Rixey's eligibility and registra-
        tion for, 31, 33; evasion of, 93, 147;
        exemptions from, 107; George
        Sisler's registration for, 111; Ty
        Cobb's status in, 74, 85
Dryden, Charley, 30

Eastern Front, 174n9

Ebbets Field, 103
Elberfeld, Norman "Kid," 10, 11
Ellam, Roy, 3, 65
ethyl bromoacetates grenades, 14–15
Evans, Billy, 10, 158
Evers, Johnny, 53, 130, 149, 150
Exchange Hotel, 43

Factoryville PA, 95, 96, 138, 156
Fairmount racetrack, 161
Falkenberg, Frederick "Cy," 176n2
Federal League, 11, 164
First Alabama Volunteer Infantry, 5
First Hague Peace Conference
        (1899), 15, 16
Fischer, William F., 71
Fisher, George J., 47, 48, 49–50, 51, 52
flamethrowers, 14
Fletcher, Art, 146, 147
football, 76–78, 79–80, 81, 132, 133
Fort Belvoir VA. *See* Camp Hum-
        phreys VA
Fort Myer VA, 27–28, 63
Fort Slocum NY, 21, 27
Fort Worth Star-Telegram, 38, 39
Foster, Eddie, 107
France: allies of, 4; ambulances in
        86; ballplayers, in 91–92, 103,
        124; baseball in, 113–14, 139;
        Branch Rickey's departure
        from, 133–34; Branch Rickey's
        deployment to, 96–97, 103–4;
        Branch Rickey's intention to go
        to, 83–84; chemical warfare of,
        14–15, 16, 17; Christy Mathew-
        son in, 136; Christy Mathewson
        invited to, 45, 48, 53; Christy
        Mathewson's deployment to, 96;
        Col. Atkisson's postwar work in,

144; cooperation with American forces, 66, 69; CWS in, 54, 55; CWS personnel to, 56, 57, 101–2; Edward Clark in, 88; Eighth Division to, 90; Gabby Street in, 134; gas regiment deployed to, 26–27, 63–64; gas training casualties in, 126, 127, 128; gas training in, 67, 105; Grantland Rice in, 79; Henry LeFort in, 119; hospitalization of wounded in, 161; illnesses contracted in, 151–52, 153, 159, 160; Joe Hanlon's experience in, 68; Knights of Columbus in, 130; major battles in, 116; marines deployed to, 75; recruiting staff from, 82; Rickey-Street association in, 163; transport routes to, 102; troop losses due to gas, 154; Ty Cobb's departure for, 99–100, 106; value of gas regiment officers in, 69; warnings of gas attacks in, 123; YMCA in, 45, 47, 50, 51, 52

Frankfurter Zeitung, 15–16

Friedman, Dick, 77

Frierson, Eddie, 157

Fries, Amos A.: and ballplayers in CWS, 90; as CWS chief, 154, 155; on demand of gas regiment's skills, 69; on demands of CWS personnel, 92; experience of, 54–55; on mustard gas, 57; on officers' qualities, 123; on officers' training, 122; rank of, 179n2, 186n11; recruiting efforts of, 82; review of troops, 144; on work of First Gas Regiment, 66–67

fruit pits, 61–62

Fullerton, Hugh, 51

Gallipoli campaign, 174n9

gas chambers, 124–26

Gas Defense Plant, 61

Gas Defense Service, 25

gases: effects of, 57, 60, 62, 127, 151, 152, 153, 154, 155, 156, 159, 162; exposure to in training, 125–27; knowledge about, 92; masks for, 125; types of, 57; used by Gabby Street, 114; weapons for firing, 58

Gas Mask Day, 62

gas masks: British use of, 16; design of, 60–62, 124–25; effectiveness of, 57, 60; fitting of, 106; importance of, 123; production of, 96; proper use of, 92; training with, 17, 18, 124, 125, 126; wearing of, 86, 112–13

gas officers: backgrounds of, 90; in baseball Hall of Fame, 162; commendation of, 144; duties of, 55, 92, 93, 132, 137, 151–52; qualities of, 123; recruiting of, 108; return to U.S., 130–31

gas regiments, 63. *See also* Thirtieth Engineers/First Gas Regiment

Gas Service with the American Expeditionary Forces, 54

gas warfare: casualties in 119, 162; early uses of, 15, 174n9; importance of, 112; in Meuse-Argonne, 116; offensive vs. defensive, 132; public attitudes toward, 92, 154; public knowledge about, 86; regiment devoted to, 14; at St. Mihiel, 115; strategies of, 123; training in, 27, 64, 67, 105, 106,

107, 110, 113, 122–28, 133, 137, 152;
    wounds sustained in, 118. *See also*
    chemical warfare
George Washington, 90, 133
Georgia, 74
Germany: chemical warfare against,
    14, 15, 114–16; chemical warfare
    by, 15–16, 17, 112, 174n9; gas
    supplies and equipment of, 55,
    57, 137; pit and shell collection
    in, 61; ships confiscated from,
    64; signing of armistice, 128–29;
    sinking of *Lusitania*, 4; strafing of
    troops, 118; U.S. Army occupation
    in, 130; U.S. gas men near lines
    of, 59; at Vauquois Hill, 117
Gilchrist, H. L., 155
Gleason, William "Kid," 22
Glenwood Springs CO, 157
Golden Gate Hotel, 6
Goodwin, Marvin, 35–37
Gould, James M., 28
Gowdy, Hank, 114, 118
Granley, Bob, 173n20
Gray, Tom, 135
Great Britain: allies of, 4; chaplains
    from, 68; chemical warfare
    against, 15, 57; chemical warfare
    by, 15, 16, 17, 174n9; cooperation
    with American forces, 65, 66, 70;
    gas deployment weapons of, 58;
    gas masks from, 60; gas training
    from, 27, 64, 65; hospitals of, 104,
    187n13; soldiers of, 14; transports
    to, 102; troopships of, 102, 106;
    war-related illness in, 154, 156
Griffith, Clark, 10, 28, 107, 175n55
Groh, Henry, "Heinie," 21, 137
Grosser Kurfürst. See *Aeolus*

Guilefuss, Harry H., 71

Hague Convention. *See* First Hague
    Peace Conference (1899)
Hampton VA, 135
Hanlon, Edward "Ned," 22, 23, 70–71,
    162
Hanlon, Joseph T. "Joe": combat
    experience of, 69, 70–72; corre-
    spondence of, 67–69; death of,
    71–72, 119; with Thirtieth Engi-
    neers, 22; work life of, 23
Hanlon Field, 126, 128, 130
Harriman, J. W., 147
Harrisburg Telegraph, 48
Harvard Club, 82
Harvard University, 76–81
Haughton, Percy D.: background of,
    76; commission of, 89, 91; death
    of, 159; duties in CWS, 123; in
    France, 90, 101; at front, 105; at
    Harvard, 76–81, 183n10; mili-
    tary training of, 78–79; postwar
    occupation of, 132; recruitment
    efforts of, 84–85; reputation of,
    92; return to U.S., 128, 130, 131;
    "System" of, 79–80
Haury, Christian, 28, 135
Hay, General, 137
Hedges, Robert, 34–35
Hedin, Naboth, 52
Helfaut, France, 27
Hendicourt, France. *See*
    Heudicourt-sous-les-Côtes
Hendricks, John C. "Jack," 37, 95, 96,
    97
Henry Holt & Company, 82
Herbst, George E., 59, 112, 143
Hermitage Hotel, 2, 3

Herrmann, Garry, 47, 50, 94, 136, 138–39, 140
Heudicourt-sous-les-Côtes, 136, 137, 192n27
Heydler, John, 131, 147–48
Hill 253, 116
Hirst, Mabel Grace, 6
Hoboken NJ, 26, 63, 90, 103, 130, 133
Hog Island shipyard, 109, 110
Holliday, John Henry "Doc," 157
Hopkinsville Browns, 5
Horn, Claude "Blinkey," 4, 11, 22, 28
Hornbostel, Henry F., 87, 123
Hornsby, Rogers, 96
horses, 60
Houston Post, 73
Huggins, Miller, 37
Huhn, Rick, 108
Humes, France, 64, 113
Huntsville, AL, 5, 7, 13

Idaho, 34
Indianapolis Indians, 37
infantry, 115, 117, 133, 144
influenza: Christy Mathewson with, 130, 136, 152, 155; deaths from, 113, 185n1; effect on troops, 90; among returning troops, 143; on troopships, 102, 103, 104, 106
Ingersoll-Rand, 23
International League, 11

Jackson, Joe, 3
Jackson, Joe S., 85, 99
Jennings, Hughie, 22
Johnson, Walter: background of, 2; Gabby Street and, 3, 65; pitching performance of, 8, 9, 10; success of, 40; in World Series (1925), 159

Jones, Jane Rickey. *See* Rickey, Jane Moulton
Joplin (Missouri) Miners, 163
Joplin MO, 163, 165
Judge Advocate General's Department, 91

Kahoe, Mike, 7–8, 9, 172n14
Kane, Gail, 146
Kansas, 116
Kauff, Benny, 146
Kauffman, Dick, 13
Keegan, John, 17
Keizer, Phil J., 60, 65, 181n10
Kelchner, Charles, 107–8, 188n22
Kelley, Joe, 5
Kentucky—Illinois—Tennessee League, 5
Kieran, John, 114, 164
Killam, Walter, 27, 65, 112, 123
Killefer, William "Reindeer Bill," 32, 33, 34
Kitty League, 5
Knight, Jack, 10, 173n26
Knights of Columbus, 42, 53, 97, 130
Knox, P. T., 48
Knoxville (Tennessee) Smokies, 163
Krishnan, Vidya, 150

Lakewood NJ, 41, 133
Lambert, Albert, 185n48
Lambert, Albert Bond, 87
Lambert, Gerard B., 87
Lambert, J. D. Wooster, 87
Lambert, Marion L. J., 86–87, 185n47
Lambert Field, 185n48
Lambert Pharmacal Company, 86
The Lancet, 156
Landis, Kenesaw Mountain, 149

Langer, William L., 20, 27, 58, 67

Langres, France, 64

Lanigan, Ernest J., 187n1

Leary, Leo, 78

Lebanon PA, 107, 108, 109

Leerhsen, Charles, 127

LeFort, Henry B., 23–24, 119, 120,
    160–62

LeFort, Jeannette Fischer, 161, 162

LeFort, Robert Edgar, 161

LeFort, Taylor Rickey, 161

LeFort, William Igoe, 161

Lemme, 116

Lens, 119

Les Islettes, 116

Letterman Hospital, 89, 185n1

Leviathan, 120, 130–31

Lewisburg Journal, 153

Lewisburg PA, 96, 139

Lieb, Fred, 30, 98, 139, 140

Lindbergh, Charles, 185n48

Little Rock Arkansas Gazette, 118–19

Livens, William H., 58

Livens projectors, 58, 69

Liverpool, England, 102, 106, 188n21

Loesch, Henry, 118–19

Long Island City NY, 61, 106

Lorraine, 130

Lorraine sector, 113

Lowenfish, Lee, 83, 104

Loyola College, 22, 68

Lucasville OH, 97, 104, 134

Lusitania, 4

Mack, Connie, 43, 136, 164

Maine, 27

Major Leagues: commissioners of,
    149; critique of, 93; draft-eligible
    players in, 12; Gabby Street's

departure from, 11; integration
of, 162; players from in war work,
107; shortened season of, 146; Ty
Cobb's entry into, 73; war's effect
on, 74

Mann, Arthur William, 84, 184n36

Mann, Louis, 146

Mann Act, 93, 147

Manning, Van H., 18, 24

Marks, Benny, 119

Marne offensive, 67

Marne River, 64, 67

Marseilles, France, 141

Mason, Hiram W., 96, 104

Mathewson, Christy "Matty," "Big
    Six": career of, 40; checker play-
    ing of, 41–42, 153; commission
    of, 91, 94; contributions to war
    effort, 47, 48, 51; death of, 159;
    departure from baseball, 149;
    departure from Cincinnati, 95–
    96; deployment of, 106; enlist-
    ment of, 82; to front, 128–29; gas
    accident of, 126, 127, 128, 130; as
    Giants manager, 140; Hal Chase
    and, 93, 94, 147, 148; in Hall of
    Fame, 162; in historical novel,
    187n37; hospitalization of, 105;
    illness of, 102–3, 130, 149–50,
    152–53, 156–57, 158; nicknames
    of, 41; 1918 season of, 93–94; P.
    D. Haughton and, 132; pitching
    of, 94–95; popularity of, 40–45,
    48, 49, 50, 123, 140, 147, 153;
    postwar activities of, 101, 136–39,
    146; reputation of, 45, 92, 178n1;
    return to U.S., 130, 139; training
    of, 122, 123, 124; travel to France,
    101–2; at Wall Street rally, 146,

147; on World Series (1919), 148–49; YMCA and, 41–43, 45–53

Mathewson, Christy, Jr., 96, 100, 153

Mathewson, Henry, 156–57

Mathewson, Jane Stoughton: in Adirondack Mountains, 149; on husband's illness and death, 103, 152, 153, 160; on husband's postwar activities, 136–37, 138; husband's war service and, 100; newspaper series and, 177n39; in Pennsylvania, 96

Maxwell, Robert W., 34, 105, 140, 141

McCarty, Lew, 146

McCormick, Harry "Moose," 11

McGeehan, W. O., 148

McGraw, John, 22, 40, 139–40, 146, 147, 151

McGuire School of Chemical Research, 86

McIntosh, Carl, 113, 125

McKechnie, Bill, 164

McNamee, J. T., 70

Memphis Chicks, 12

Memphis News Scimitar, 118

Menlo Park CA, 39, 40

Metz, France, 136, 137

Meuse-Argonne, 116–17, 120

Mexico, 24

Miller, Jack "Dots," 36, 37, 75

Miller, Pearl, 36

Minor Leagues, 12, 43, 75, 136, 156, 163

Missouri, 116, 163, 165

Modesto (California) Herald, 27, 65, 112, 113, 125

Montgomery AL, 41, 42–43, 44

Moran, Pat, 31, 37, 138, 139, 140, 142, 148

Morgan, J. P., 147

mortars. See Stokes mortars

Mount Vernon, 105

Mount Vernon, 64

munitions plants, 83

Murray, Frank, 119, 161

Muskogee (Oklahoma) Athletics, 163

mustard gas: Christy Mathewson's work with, 137; effects of, 57, 118–19, 126; training with, 124, 125; used by Gabby Street., 114; victims of, 112–13

My Life in Baseball (Cobb), 124, 127, 128

Napoleon, 64

Nashville Banner, 3, 136

Nashville Tennessean, 4, 13, 136

Nashville TN, 93

Nashville Volunteers: in army, 28; effect of war on, 4; Gabby Street's correspondence with, 65; Gabby Street's return to, 135, 136; Gabby Street with, 11, 22; losses of, 11–13; players on, 1

National Baseball Hall of Fame, 9, 33, 162, 165

National League: Boston Braves' record in, 78; Boston team in, 76, 77; Cardinals' standing in, 96, 164; Christy Mathewson's invitation to France and, 49; first basemen in, 93; game fixing in, 94, 147–48; leadership of, 131; pennants won by, 22; pitching records in, 93; players and teams in, 5; presidents' meeting of, 81; trades within, 32

National Security League, 83

National War Work Council, 46, 51

Navin, Frank, 130

Nebraska, 160, 161

New Orleans LA, 157

New York Central Railroad, 11

New York City: Christy Mathewson's popularity in, 147; Christy Mathewson's return to, 139; CWS recruitment in, 81–83; gas mask factory in, 96; gas regiment's return to, 144; newspapers in, 143, 144; P. D. Haughton memorial in, 159; troops' return to, 131; Ty Cobb in, 105, 106

New York Giants: Christy Mathewson with, 40, 45, 138, 139, 146–49; Fred Toney with, 93; game fixing and, 94; Hal Chase with, 147–48; Hank Mathewson with, 156; management of, 22, 139–40; 1918 season of, 95; Reds vs., 82; spring training of, 153; world tour of, 102

New York Highlanders, 10, 11, 34, 173n26. *See also* New York Yankees

New York Post, 160

New York Sun, 50, 98, 140, 144

New York Telegram, 48

New York Times: on Christy Mathewson, 42, 45, 128, 149; on Gabby Street, 114; on John McGraw, 139–40; on Reds management, 138–39; on Ty Cobb, 98; on World Series (1919), 148

New York Tribune: on autographed baseball, 147; on chemical warfare debate, 154; on Christy Mathewson, 148, 150, 151; on

CWS recruiting, 81; on George Sisler, 109; on Percy Haughton, 77; on Wall Street rally, 146

Newberry PA, 11

Newport News VA, 135

New York Yankees, 11, 37, 98, 107

Norfolk VA, 33

nurses, 101, 102

Oakland CA, 87

Oakland Oaks, 89

Oakland Tribune, 89

Office of Strategic Services, 20

Official U.S. Bulletin, 180n15

Ohio, 63, 97

Ohio National Guard, 41–44

Ohio State University, 34

Ohio Wesleyan University, 34

Oklahoma, 38

O'Leary, James, 132

Olympic, 102–3

Omaha Bee, 23, 160

Pacific Coast League, 6, 89

Packard, E. N., 153, 158

Palace De Grace, 119

Panuska, George T., 71

Paris, 119, 130

Parris Island SC, 74

PCL. *See* Pacific Coast League

Peach Stone Committees, 62

Pennock, Herb, 32–33

Pennsylvania, 41, 48, 95, 96, 103, 128, 160

Perritt, William "Pol," 147

Pershing, John J., 54, 106, 116, 120

Phelon, Bill, 30

Philadelphia Athletics, 32–33, 43, 136, 164

Philadelphia Inquirer, 32, 141

Philadelphia PA, 109

Philadelphia Phillies: Eppa Rixey
  with, 30, 31–32, 140, 141–42; loss
  of players to war, 37; Pete Alexander honored by, 141; pitching
  records of, 93; trades of, 32–33

Philadelphia Public Ledger, 34, 105–6,
  107, 140

phosgene, 57, 114, 117, 154

Pigue, Bob, 3, 118, 135–36

Pittsburgh PA, 46, 47, 87

Pittsburgh Pirates, 108, 159

Pittsburgh Press, 123

Plattsburg Movement, 78

Plattsburg NY, 78–79

pneumonia, 102, 104–5, 143, 159,
  185n1

Polar Bear Expedition, 90

politicians, 88

Polo Grounds, 158

Popular Science Monthly, 61

Portland Oregonian, 145

Portsmouth OH, 97

Potomac River, 27, 105

President Grant, 26, 66, 103–4

President Wilson, 141

Princeton NJ, 87

projectors, 58, 59, 69, 115, 116

Providence Grays, 11

Red Cross, 36, 38, 61

Red Cross Hut, 160

Redland Field, 95

Registration Day, 12

Rice, Grantland, 77, 79–80

Rice, Thomas, 7, 52, 172n14

Richardson, Charles E., 81, 82, 94

Richmond VA, 33, 86

Rickey, Jane Moulton, 83, 100,
  104, 134

Rickey, Mabel, 100

Rickey, Wesley Branch: career of, 5–6,
  34; commission of, 91; departure for France, 96–97, 103–4,
  106; Gabby Street and, 163; on
  gas training accident, 127, 128;
  at Henry LeFort's funeral, 162;
  Henry LeFort's respect for, 160,
  161; in historical novel, 187n37;
  illness of, 104–5, 156, 187n13;
  integration of baseball, 162; loss
  of players to war, 36, 37; military
  service of, 83; recruiting efforts
  of, 84–85, 108, 109, 111; reputation of, 92; return to U.S., 130,
  133–34; training of, 122, 123

Rixey, Eppa "Jeptha," Jr: background
  of, 31; ballplaying in military, 89;
  baseball career of, 30, 31–33; commission of, 37–39; deployment of,
  106; in France, 101; at front, 120–
  21; in Hall of Fame, 162; military
  orders of, 89–90; nicknames of,
  30, 176n2; postwar activities of,
  140–42; return to U.S., 140, 141

Roberts, Doug, 127

Robinson, Jackie, 162

Robinson, Wilbert, 22

Rockefeller, John D., 146–47

Rogers, Irl, 112–13

Roosevelt, Archibald, 17

Roosevelt, Theodore, 17, 19, 78

Rotterdam, 139

Royal Field Artillery, 70

Russia, 174n9

Russwood Park, 12

Ruth, Babe, 3

Ryder, Jack, 52

Saint-Nazaire, France, 104
Salem Capital Journal, 115–16
Sanborn, I. E., 30
San Francisco CA, 6, 89, 164
San Francisco Examiner, 7, 40
San Francisco Seals, 6–7, 89
sanitary trains, 39, 89
Santa Fe division. *See* U.S. Thirty-
    Fifth Division
Saranac Lake NY, 34, 150, 155, 156, 159
School of Machine Gun Fire, 87
Schriver, William "Pop," 172n16
Schwarzenburg, prince of, 67
Scientific American, 16
Seattle, 64
Sebring, Jimmy, 6
Seward AK, 20
Sharman, Ralph, 43, 44
Shaw, Jim, 107
shells, gas, 58, 59
shells, seed and nut, 61–62
Sheridan, J. B., 93
Sherman, James, 10
Sherman, William Tecumseh, 135, 139
shipyards, employment at, 109–10
Shivers, Colonel, 185n5
Shreveport LA, 42
Siberia, 90
Sibert, William L., 54, 55, 57, 60,
    91, 144
Sisler, George, 98–99, 107–11, 132–33,
    152, 162
Sloane, William, 46, 51
smoke barrages, 116
Society for the Prevention of Cruelty
    to Animals, 25
Soissons-Rheims, 70

Soldiers and Sailors Memorial Hall
    (Pittsburgh), 87
Sothoron, Allen, 107, 108, 188n22
Souilly, 116, 120
Southampton, England, 102
South Atlantic League, 163
South Dakota, 91
Southern Association, 2, 4, 11, 136
South Kentucky College, 5
Southworth, Billy, 164
Spanish-American War, 5, 164
Spink, J. G. Taylor, 164, 172n15
The Sporting Life, 6
Sporting News: on Branch Rickey, 97,
    98, 187n13; on Christy Mathew-
    son, 50, 101, 187n1; on Gabby
    Street, 1, 9, 10, 118, 163, 164; on
    George Sisler, 109; on "Pop"
    Kelchner, 108
Sportsman's Park, 164
Stars and Stripes, 51, 55–56, 113
Stevens, Jimmie. *See* LeFort, Henry B.
St. John's Hospital, 161
St. Louis Browns: Bethlehem Steel
    League and, 107, 108; Branch
    Rickey with 34–35; Gabby Street
    with, 164; George Sisler with,
    108, 111; scouts for, 108; Tigers
    vs., 98–99
St. Louis Cardinals: Branch Rickey
    with, 35, 83, 96–97; Gabby Street
    with, 163–64; leadership of,
    96–97; players in military, 35–37;
    Reds vs., 95; scouts for, 108; in
    World Series, 164
St. Louis Globe-Democrat, 83, 87, 99
St. Louis MO: airport in, 185n48;
    Branch Rickey's return to, 133,
    134; Henry LeFort in, 160, 162;

infantrymen from, 117; social elite in, 86; war news in, 104

St. Louis Post-Dispatch, 49, 84, 85, 96, 104, 163, 185n47

St. Louis Star: on athlete-officers, 122; on Branch Rickey, 35, 97, 160; Branch Rickey's letter in, 104; on Branch Rickey's wartime service, 83; on George Sisler, 110; on Henry LeFort, 119, 161; on Jack Miller's enlistment, 36, 37; on Reds vs. Cardinals, 94, 95

St. Louis Star-Times, 163, 164

St. Mihiel, 114–16

Stokes mortars, 58–59, 70

Stovall, George, 35

Street, Charles Evard "Gabby": background of, 1–2, 5; ballplaying in army, 22; baseball career of, 5–6; as broadcaster, 164; with Cardinals, 163–64; catching of Johnson pitches, 9–10; catching stunts of, 8–9, 172nn15–16, 173n20; as coach, 134; correspondence of, 65; death of, 165; deployment to France, 63; discharge from army, 135; draft ineligibility of, 12; effect of war on, 4; enlistment of, 13, 21; friendship with Walter Johnson, 2–3; illness and injuries of, 9, 10, 11, 12, 21, 118–19, 134; marriage and family of, 6, 163; in Meuse-Argonne offensive, 116, 117; nicknames of, 7, 11; offseason jobs of, 11; as player-manager, 136; popularity of, 164–65; postwar activities of, 135, 136, 163; rank of, 113, 114; with Reds, 34; return to U.S., 134–35; with Senators, 7–8,

10–11, 173n26; as soldier, 27–28; on sounds of gas attacks, 58

Street, Lucinda Chandler (Clark), 163

Stump, Al, 124, 126–27, 151

Suffolk Nuts, 163

Suffolk VA, 136

Suize River, 67

sulfur dioxide, 15

Sulphur Dell, 11

Sundays, 5, 34, 97

Surgeon General's Department, 25

Taft, William Howard, 10

tear gas, 114

Tener, John K., 49

Terre Haute Hottentots, 5

Texas, 38, 87, 185n48

Texas League, 5

thermite, 59, 115, 116

Thirtieth Engineers/First Gas Regiment: animal experiments by, 24–25; athletes in, 22–24; casualties of, 119, 160; chaplain for, 68; combat experience of, 69, 70; demobilization of, 144; deployment of, 26, 28; function of, 14; headquarters in France, 67; at Meuse-Argonne, 116, 117; nickname for, 24; postwar work of, 143; recruitment of, 19–21; redesignation of, 55; return to U.S., 142, 144; at St. Mihiel, 114–16; success of, 112, 119–20, 144; training of, 21–22, 122; transport of, 104. *See also* U.S. First Gas Regiment

Thompson, Denman, 2, 53

Thorn, John, 41, 159

Thornton, Cornelia Elizabeth, 102

Thorpe, Jim, 183n24

Titanic, 102

tobacco, 65

Toney, Fred, 93, 147

Toul sector, 69

Tours, France, 104

trench warfare, 59

Triangle Factory League, 108

Trimble, Secretary, 161

Tri-State League, 6

True, 126, 127

tuberculosis: contraction of 156–58, 160; description of, 150–51; gas exposure and, 152, 153, 154, 155, 156, 159, 160; treatment of, 153, 158

Tumulty, Joseph P., 76

Turkish troops, 174n9

Twohig, John J., 70–71

typhoid fever, 157

United Press, 127

United States: entry into war, 4, 17, 18; gas officers' return to, 130; quality of gas masks from, 60

United States Veterans Bureau, 160

University of Michigan, 34, 108, 111

University of Virginia, 30, 33

U.S. Eighth Division, 39, 89, 90

U.S. Eighty-Second Division, 115

U.S. Eighty-Sixth Division, 101

U.S. Fifth Corps, 128, 132

U.S. First Army, 114, 116

U.S. First Corps, 120

U.S. First Division, 117, 118

U.S. First Gas Regiment: area of operation, 59; deployment of, 63, 66; descriptions of operations of, 59–60; insignia of, 56; Thirtieth Engineers as, 55; training of, 64,
65, 67. *See also* Chemical Warfare Service (cws); Thirtieth Engineers/First Gas Regiment

U.S. First Replacement Company, 113

U.S. Second Division, 114

U.S. Sixteenth Infantry Regiment, 117–18

U.S. Twenty-Sixth Division, 128, 131–32

U.S. Twenty-Eighth Division, 128, 137, 151

U.S. Thirty-Fourth Division, 106

U.S. Thirty-Fifth Division, 116, 117

U.S. Forty-Second Division, 114, 118

U.S. Seventy-Sixth Division, 78

U.S. Ninetieth Division, 115

U.S. 101st Airborne Division, 162

U.S. 138th Infantry Regiment, 117

U.S. 140th Infantry Regiment, 117

U.S. 165th Infantry Regiment, 70, 118

U.S. Army: athletes in, 32, 33, 75, 83, 90–92; ballplaying in, 23; Branch Rickey's postwar rank in, 134; chemical warfare defense of, 17–18; chemical warfare organization within, 54, 55; and Christy Mathewson's death, 159; Company Q in, 189n8; in cws, 55; Eppa Rixey's commission in, 37–38; Gabby Street's attitude toward, 28; Gabby Street's enlistment in, 13, 21; and gas-related health problems, 153–56; gas training in, 105; George Sisler's commission in, 109, 110, 111; historical novel about, 187n37; intentional exposure to gases by, 125; medical care provided by, 160; occupation of Germany, 130;

Percy Haughton's connections in, 78; ranks in, 88; recruiting by, 14, 20, 87; restriction of transport passengers, 106; on success of chemical warfare, 16; training at Plattsburg, 78–79; training of ballplayers, 73; training of Thirty-Seventh Division, 41; treatment of soldiers, 142, 143; tuberculosis cases in, 157–58; uniforms of, 109–10

U.S. Army Corps of Engineers, 54, 66, 154

U.S. Army Medical Department, 38, 158

U.S. Army Medical Reserve Corps, 38

U.S. Army Nurse Corps, 101

U.S. Army Ordnance Department, 54, 56

U.S. Army Quartermaster Corps, 91

U.S. Army Sanitary Corps, 37–38, 39

U.S. Army Signal Corps, 54, 113, 119

U.S. Army Transport Service, 188n21

U.S. Committee on Public Information, 60, 180n15

U.S. Department of the Interior, 18

U.S. Department of Veterans Affairs. See Veterans Administration

U.S. government: on chemical warfare development, 18–19; chemists in, 55; Christy Mathewson's invitation to France and, 48–49; failure to deliver cablegrams, 140; on influenza deaths, 104; procurement of carbon, 61–62; studies on gas-related illness, 156

U.S. Marine Corps: athletes in, 74–75, 83; at Belleau Wood, 69; at Château-Thierry, 114; command

of army camp, 142; gas training of, 125–26; Jack Miller in, 36; Ty Cobb's consideration of, 74

U.S. Navy, 33, 75, 83, 88, 104

U.S. Navy Ordnance Department, 8

U.S. Surgeon General, 157

Vaterland. See Lorraine

Vauquois Hill, 117

Verdun, 86, 114, 116, 119

Veterans Administration, 156

Victory notes, 146–47

Villa, Francisco, 17, 24

Villers-sur-Fère, 70

Virginia, 31, 105, 141

Virginia-Carolina Chemical Company, 33

Virginia League, 163

Vladivostok, Russia, 90

Voorhees, John Brownlee, 125, 190n15

Vosges region, 152

Wagner, Honus, 50

Wall Street, 146–47

Ward, John Montgomery, 47

War Department: chemical warfare knowledge of, 18; deployment of Thirtieth Engineers and, 26; organization of chemical warfare agencies, 54; personnel in, 19, 24; records on gas and flame battalion, 22; recruiting by, 33, 75; Ty Cobb recommended to, 85

Warner, Glenn S. "Pop," 76

Warner, Jack, 7, 9

War Saving Stamps, 98

Washington, George, 105

Washington DC: Branch Rickey in, 97, 98; CWS recruits in, 84–85;

enlistees in, 20; gas and flame battalion in, 22; gas and flame training in, 21; George Sisler in, 110; marine baseball team in, 75; Thirtieth Engineers' camp near, 27; Thirtieth Engineers' deployment from, 26; Ty Cobb in, 75–76

Washington Herald, 2, 8, 19, 28

Washington Monument, 8, 172nn15–16, 173n20

Washington Post, 21–22, 25, 26, 105, 142

Washington Senators: in All-Star game, 107; cuts from, 10; Detroit Tigers vs. 85; Frederick Falkenberg with, 176n2; Gabby Street with, 7, 9, 10–11, 173n26; in Nashville, 3; players on, 1, 2, 7, 9; Walter Johnson with, 9; in World Series (1925), 159

Washington Star: on balls dropped from monument, 8; on Christy Mathewson, 53; on CWS, 56; on Gabby Street, 2, 9; on gas-related illness, 155, 156; on returning troops, 143

Washington Times, 2, 8, 19, 76, 113–14, 135

Waterbury, Lawrence "Larry," 88, 131

Waterloo IA, 106

Waxahachie TX, 73

Webster Groves MO, 161

Weeghman, Charles, 50

Western Association, 163

West Point, 54, 84, 87

White House, 76

White Slave Traffic Act. *See* Mann Act

Wilhelm II, Kaiser, 14

Williams, Alva "Rip," 173n26

Williamsport Millionaires, 6, 135

Williamsport PA, 6, 13, 135

Wilson, Woodrow, 1, 187n6

women, 61–62

Wood, Leonard, 78

work, war-related, 107, 111

"work or fight" order, 75

World Series: 1914, 77; 1915, 32; 1918, 103; 1919, 148–49; 1925, 159; 1930, 164

World War I: baseball affected by, 33, 35–37, 74, 75, 83; baseball Hall of Fame inductees in, 162; casualties of, 160; chemical warfare of U.S. in, 18; financing of, 147; football affected by, 78; gas-related illness during, 156; sanitary trains in, 39; tuberculosis treatment in, 158

World War II, 16, 18, 20, 162

Wray, John, 49, 81

Yale University, 77, 78, 79, 83

YMCA: Branch Rickey and, 84, 85; at Camp Hancock 73; Christy Mathewson and, 41–43, 45–53, 101; clergyman with, 125; shelling of, 190n15

Young, Cy, 10, 40

Young Men's Christian Association. *See* YMCA

Ypres, Belgium, 15, 143